PAT BROWN, MBA

Financial Literacy For First Responders (Firefighters, Police, Paramedics)

"Smart Money Moves for Those Who Serve First and Sacrifice Most"

ABRAM · 47 · BROWN

First published by AbramBrown47 2025

First edition

ISBN: 978-1-967737-36-9

This book was professionally typeset on Reedsy.
Find out more at reedsy.com

Contents

Preface

Why I Wrote This Book—and Who I Wrote It For

Before anything else, let me say this from the heart:

Thank you.

Thank you to every firefighter who runs into danger when others are running out.

Thank you to every police officer who kisses their family goodbye not knowing what the shift might bring.

Thank you to every paramedic who steadies chaos with calm hands and a clear mind.

Thank you to the dispatchers behind the scenes, the corrections officers holding the line, the volunteers, the rookies, the veterans, and every first responder who shows up when the world is falling apart.

You don't hear "thank you" enough—not for the hours, the stress, the trauma, the patience, the judgment calls, or the courage it takes to do this job day in and day out.

And that's why I wrote this book.

This Book is Personal to Me

I don't wear a badge. I don't ride the truck. But I come from your world.

I've got friends who are first responders.

I've got family who has worn the uniform.

I've sat at dinner tables with people who've seen things they'll never forget and carry weight most civilians don't understand.

I've watched people I care about face danger, exhaustion, public scrutiny, and paperwork—often all in the same week.

And I've also watched many of them struggle with the same financial challenges over and over again:

– Not knowing what to do with their pension.

– Trying to make sense of overtime taxes.

– Living paycheck to paycheck despite good salaries.

– Facing injury or burnout with no backup plan.

– Retiring after 25 years of service and realizing they don't feel financially safe.

That didn't sit right with me.

So I decided to do something about it.

You Deserve Better Than "Figure It Out"

This country trains you to respond to emergencies.

But nobody trains you to build wealth.

They don't teach you how your pension really works.

They don't explain the difference between a 457(b) and a Roth IRA.

They don't walk you through how to protect your family if the unthinkable happens.

They don't tell you that trauma can cloud your money decisions—or that overtime income can sabotage your tax bracket if you're not careful.

Instead, you're told: "Just do the job. The money will work itself out."

But you and I both know that's not true.

Financial security doesn't happen by accident. It happens by design.

And too often, first responders are left to figure it out on their own—with no clear plan, no mentorship, and no one explaining what it means to retire with *confidence* instead of just *relief.*

That's Where This Book Comes In

This book is your blueprint.

It's your shift partner in the world of money.

It's the financial planning guide written in your language—for your life.

Each chapter is grounded in reality, built for busy lives, and written with respect. It's not theory. It's not fluff. It's not a lecture.

It's practical.

It's digestible.

It's focused on helping you protect what matters most: your peace of mind, your future, and your family.

I'll walk you through how to use your benefits wisely.

How to think about retirement from day one.

How to avoid common traps around taxes, credit, insurance, and legacy.

And how to make financial decisions that reflect the courage and care you bring to the job every single day.

From My Family to Yours—Thank You

I see the sacrifice you make.

I see the long nights, the missed holidays, the emotional armor you carry.

And I see how easy it is to put off your own planning while taking care of everyone else.

That stops now.

This book is here to remind you:

You've earned the right to retire well.

You've earned the right to build wealth.

You've earned the right to feel confident, protected, and proud—not just in uniform, but in your finances.

Let this book be your financial fire extinguisher, first aid kit, and backup radio all in one.

Whether you're a rookie just out of the academy, a veteran thinking about the finish line, or somewhere in between—this book is for you.

You've spent your career helping others.

Now it's time to help yourself—and the people you love.

You've already proven you're brave.

Now let's make sure you're *prepared.*

Let's make your financial plan just as strong as your service.

You've had everyone's back.

This book is here to have yours.

How to Use This Book

No Fluff. No Jargon. Just Real-World Tools That Work Like You Do.

This isn't a college textbook. It's not a retirement manual collecting dust on a shelf. And it's definitely not a lecture from someone who's never worked a 24, chased a suspect, or seen a family on their worst day.

This book is built like your shift gear—sturdy, reliable, and ready to work. Every page is meant to serve you: the firefighter, the police officer, the paramedic, the dispatcher, the corrections officer, the responder who signed up to protect others... but who also deserves to protect their future.

Here's how to get the most out of it.

Read It Like You'd Train a Rookie

Start at the beginning or jump to what matters most. You won't break anything by skipping around.

Think of this book as your personal "financial operations manual." Some chapters build foundational knowledge. Others are situation-specific, like:

- What to do if you're injured on the job
- How to prep your money when retirement is five years out
- What to ask when hiring a financial advisor
- How to explain money to your kids (even if no one ever taught you)

If a topic is calling your name, go there. The structure is clear, the tone is respectful, and the goal is to meet you where you are—not where someone *thinks* you should be.

Don't Expect Financial Theory—Expect Financial Clarity

You've dealt with enough red tape. You don't need complicated charts, jargon, or generic tips that don't apply to a first responder's reality.

Instead, this book breaks things down with:

- Plain-language explanations
- Real-world examples
- "You've probably lived this" scenarios
- Straightforward action steps you can take right now

You don't have to be a math whiz, an investment pro, or a spreadsheet expert. You just have to care enough to read—and act. You've already proven you have discipline. Now we'll help you aim it in the right financial direction.

Use It With Your Partner, Crew, Union, or Advisor

You don't have to do this alone. This book is meant to start conversations—with your spouse, your team, your union rep, or your financial advisor. Use it to ask better questions. Use it to advocate for yourself.

Examples:

- Bring the retirement chapters to your benefits meeting.
- Talk through the family protection sections with your spouse.
- Review the insurance guidance with your local union.
- Use the tax planning and investment chapters as prep for your advisor.

And if you don't have an advisor yet? We'll help you choose one the right way—with no pressure and no B.S.

Revisit It as Your Career Evolves

First responders live in stages—rookie, mid-career, senior, retired. Your money should evolve with each one. This book is designed to grow with you.

- Just started? Focus on budgeting, credit, and understanding your paycheck.
- Ten years in? Start optimizing your pension, saving with intention, and planning for kids or homeownership.
- Close to retirement? Dive deep into healthcare costs, asset protection, and legacy planning.
- Already retired? Use the income distribution and lifestyle chapters to make your money last and give back on your terms.

Wherever you are, this book shows up for you. No judgment. Just smart, calm, clear guidance.

Use It as a Mindset Shift—Not Just a Money Manual

Yes, this book is about financial planning. But really? It's about peace of mind. About reclaiming your time, your energy, and your future from the stress that money problems can bring.

You've faced trauma, chaos, risk, and sacrifice. You've made it through calls that would shatter most people.

Now it's time to focus on *you*—to build wealth with intention, retire with dignity, and pass on something better to the people you love.

That starts with knowledge.

And knowledge starts right here.

A Final Note Before You Dive In

You didn't take this job because it was easy.

You took it because you care.

So let's apply that same care and courage to your finances.

Open the next chapter.

Highlight what hits home.

Reread the tough parts.

Talk about it with your spouse or crew.

Take one step at a time.

And never forget:

You've already done the hard part—showing up for everyone else.

Now let's show up for *you.*

You've got this.

And this book's got you.

Let's begin.

About the Author

Patrick Brown, MBA is a financial educator, wealth advisor, and longtime advocate for public servants navigating money, service, and legacy. With over two decades of experience in financial planning and health insurance, Patrick has worked closely with families across America—including many in uniform—helping them turn chaotic paychecks and uncertain futures into calm, confident financial plans.

But this isn't just business for him. It's personal.

Patrick is the son of a mother who believed in service above self, the brother of a police officer, the cousin of a firefighter, and a lifelong friend to paramedics, dispatchers, and veterans who carry more than their share of the world's weight. He's seen up close the strain—and the sacrifice—that come with answering the call. And he's made it his mission to help first responders build the kind of financial strength that honors the work they do and protects the families they love.

A former Division I football captain at the University of Kansas, Patrick also played in the CFL before entering the financial field. That background taught him discipline, resilience, and what it means to show up every day even when you're exhausted. It's the same mindset he brings to financial literacy—especially for those who never had a seat at the table.

Today, Patrick is the founder of multiple financial literacy platforms, including ones dedicated to student-athletes, doctors, lawyers, educators, and most recently—first responders. He also serves as a hospital board trustee, a Rotary board member, and a frequent speaker in faith-based and community spaces, especially those historically underserved by the financial industry.

He believes financial literacy isn't a luxury. It's survival.

And first responders deserve to retire in peace—not in pieces.

Patrick lives in Kansas with his wife Cassandra. He writes like he talks—direct, honest, and rooted in lived experience. And he's never forgotten where he came from… or who he's writing for.

Why This Book Matters

This book isn't about stocks, budgets, or retirement accounts—

It's about peace of mind.

It's about the firefighter who straps on 80 pounds of gear to run into burning buildings but still lies awake at night wondering if his family could afford the mortgage if something happened to him.

It's about the police officer who works overtime every week, not because they want to—but because they're afraid their pension won't cover college tuition or medical bills down the road.

It's about the paramedic who saves lives for a living, but isn't sure how to build financial safety for their own.

It's about the dispatcher, the corrections officer, the EMT, the rookie, the 25-year veteran—anyone who answers the call while carrying the weight of financial uncertainty in their back pocket.

Why does this book matter?

Because first responders are the backbone of our communities—and too often, they've been overlooked in conversations about wealth, planning, and financial freedom. You've been told to serve, to sacrifice, to suck it up. But you haven't been given the tools to retire with dignity, protect your family with confidence, or build wealth that outlasts the badge.

This book exists to change that narrative.

It's not a lecture. It's not a sales pitch. It's a toolbox, a flashlight, a firehouse kitchen table conversation between equals. It was written with deep respect for your profession and a clear understanding that your life doesn't follow a tidy 9-to-5 script. Shift work, trauma, overtime, side gigs, burnout, pride—it's all part of your financial reality. And this book was built for that reality.

You won't find gimmicks here. Just straight talk. Real strategies.

And most importantly—hope.

Because financial peace is possible, even for those who've been running toward danger their whole life.

You've spent your career protecting others.

This book is about finally protecting yourself.

And that's why it matters.

Welcome to Financial Literacy for First Responders

You've spent years mastering crisis response, lifesaving protocols, teamwork, communication, and showing up in moments when most people would rather run the other way.

You know how to stay calm when a house is on fire.

You know how to lead when adrenaline is pumping and outcomes hang by a thread.

You know what it means to be the one that people call—on their worst day.

But here's what doesn't get talked about in briefing rooms, academy training, or union meetings:

Too many first responders are financially unprepared.

Not because you're careless.

Not because you're bad with money.

But because no one ever showed you how this stuff works.

You didn't learn investing in the fire academy.

They didn't teach retirement planning during defensive tactics training.

There's no "Wealth 101" elective for paramedics on your continuing education hours.

And yet—how you handle your money will shape your entire life.

Whether you can retire with dignity, support your family during a crisis, go part-time without panic, or walk away from the job one day feeling ready—not rattled.

This book was written for you.

Not to judge. Not to overwhelm.

But to fill the gap—so you stop flying blind when it comes to your money.

What Do We Mean by Financial Literacy?

Financial literacy doesn't mean becoming a Wall Street expert.

It doesn't mean reading tax code or buying meme stocks.

It means knowing how to:

- Read your pay stub and understand your withholdings
- Distinguish between a pension, a 457(b), and a Roth IRA
- Budget in a way that reflects *your* values—not someone else's lifestyle
- Build an emergency fund that makes you less dependent on overtime
- Know when to say "yes" to opportunities—and when to walk away
- Protect your family if something happens to you on the job
- Make decisions with logic and clarity—not shame, fear, or fatigue

That's financial literacy.

Why First Responders Are Especially Vulnerable

You may be trained for everything else life throws your way—but the financial system wasn't built with your schedule, trauma, or compensation model in mind. That's why so many first responders feel like they're "behind," even when they've been doing everything right.

Here's what we see again and again:

1. **Overtime = Exhaustion, Not Strategy**

Many responders use OT to "solve" every problem—pay off debt, cover emergencies, make up for low base pay. But that's unsustainable. Your body and mind weren't built to work 60+ hours forever.

2. **Pension Confusion**

Pensions can give a false sense of security. If you don't know how yours works—or what it doesn't cover—you might be shocked at how far short it falls.

3. **Delayed Planning Due to Trauma or Fatigue**

You're wired to put others first. But financial planning requires turning the mirror on yourself—and that's hard when you're already mentally drained.

4. **Identity Overload**

Being a first responder isn't just a job. It's a calling. Which makes it easy to tie your identity so tightly to the badge that you forget to plan for what comes *after* the uniform.

5. **Fragmented Benefits**

You've got union perks, retirement options, shift differentials, hazard pay, death benefits, and insurance layers—but no one ever sits down to show you how it all fits together.

Real-Life Financial Gaps

- The firefighter who retired with a strong pension—but didn't realize his spouse wouldn't get survivor benefits unless he selected a reduced payout
- The police officer who worked 20 years, never maxed her retirement plan, and now wonders if she has to take a side job in retirement
- The paramedic who got hurt off-duty and didn't have disability coverage beyond sick leave
- The corrections officer who bought a house based on OT income—only to lose it when budgets changed
- The dispatcher who paid into Social Security *and* their pension—but doesn't know how they interact

These aren't hypothetical stories. They're real.

And this book was written so yours doesn't become one of them.

Why This Stuff Isn't Taught (And Why That's Not Your Fault)

The system assumes you'll "figure it out."

It gives you a pension packet and a deferred comp brochure—and hopes you're not too tired to read them. But this information is often vague, outdated, or one-size-fits-some.

You wouldn't throw someone into a burning building with a pamphlet and good luck wishes.

You deserve better than that when it comes to your money.

What Happens When First Responders Get Financially Clear

You take back control of your life.

You start building—not just surviving.

You set boundaries with OT.

You invest with purpose.

You prepare your family for anything.

You create an exit strategy—not just a "hope I make it to 25 years" plan.

What This Book Will Help You Do

- Break down your pension and understand your options
- Decode your benefits and spot the gaps
- Build a real-world budget around shift work
- Balance OT income with actual life planning
- Set up retirement accounts even if you're starting late
- Choose the right kind of insurance for your job and family
- Understand what's taxable, what's protected, and what's risky
- Ask your HR or union rep the *right* questions
- Avoid scams, overpriced products, or well-meaning bad advice
- Plan for life *after* the badge—with confidence, not fear

Closing the Gap—One First Responder at a Time

I didn't write this book to impress anyone with financial jargon.

I wrote it because I know—and love—people who wear the uniform.

I have friends who are firefighters. Family members who are police officers. Clients who are paramedics, dispatchers, and corrections officers. I've sat across the table from people who save lives for a living—but feel completely lost when it comes to their own financial future.

That's not right. That's not fair. And that's not your fault.

You've handled more in a single shift than some people do in a lifetime.

You've earned the right to retire with dignity, provide for your family, and live in peace.

This book won't do the work for you—but it *will* walk with you.

Page by page. Chapter by chapter. Building clarity, confidence, and control.

Let's get to work.

You've already run toward danger.

Now it's time to run toward wealth.

Part I: Rookie Years – Laying the Financial Foundation (Years 0–5)

The rookie years are filled with adrenaline, pride, and pressure—and for most first responders, it's the first time they're earning a full-time paycheck with benefits. But with that new income comes responsibility. This section lays the groundwork for a financially secure career by helping new firefighters, police officers, and paramedics build smart habits from day one.

You'll learn how to read your paycheck, manage taxes and union dues, and set up the right bank accounts to keep your money organized. You'll understand the critical importance of building credit early and responsibly—especially in a profession where your background, character, and financial stability are often scrutinized.

This section also breaks down your department's benefits—health insurance, disability coverage, pensions, and life insurance—in plain English. You'll see why ignoring these details can cost you and your family down the line, and how to take full advantage of what your agency offers.

We'll walk through real-life scenarios, like whether you should buy or lease your first vehicle, rent or buy a home, or take on extra shifts to get ahead. You'll learn how to create a budget that fits the unique rhythm of shift work and variable income, and you'll begin to build your emergency fund—your personal financial turnout gear.

Finally, Part I sets the tone for your entire career. It's not about getting rich fast—it's about creating **systems that protect your peace of mind** and give you **options down the road**. Because the best first responders don't just train for the next call—they prepare for the long haul.

Chapter 1: Welcome to the Job – What They Didn't Teach You at the Academy About Money

So you graduated from the academy. You've got the uniform, the badge, the schedule, and maybe even a little swagger in your step. You've learned how to clear a building, run an arrest scenario, apply a tourniquet, or break down a door.

But you probably weren't taught how to read your first paycheck.

You weren't taught how your pension works—or doesn't.

You weren't told how fast your new income can disappear if you don't have a plan.

And you sure as hell weren't handed a manual on how to balance a career that asks you to risk your life with a life that still needs rent, groceries, insurance, and peace of mind.

This chapter is your unofficial welcome packet—the one the department didn't give you, but the one every first responder deserves.

This Chapter Is for You If:

- You're looking at your first real salary and wondering where it all goes.
- You've heard of a Roth IRA but have no idea how it works.
- You're trying to figure out what to do with your department benefits.
- You're committed to this job—but want to make sure your money is working just as hard as you are.

Whether you're 24 or 44, a rookie firefighter, a probationary police officer, or an EMT on your second job—you'll find something in this chapter that makes you stop, think, and take action.

What They Don't Teach You at the Academy

The academy teaches you how to survive the job. But it doesn't teach you how to survive life on the job.

And money? That's rarely touched—if at all.

No one broke down how:

- Overtime can wreck your tax bracket
- You need to think about retirement *now*, not 25 years from now
- Your benefits can be your best friend—or your blind spot
- Working more doesn't always mean you're keeping more

This chapter is the truth serum. It's the calm voice in the chaos saying: "Slow down. Let's get your financial house in order now, so it doesn't collapse later."

Your First Paycheck: Why It Feels Smaller Than You Expected

You trained for months. You earned your badge. You passed your boards, your PT tests, your background check.

Then you got your first paycheck—and it felt... underwhelming.

Let's break it down.

Your base salary is only part of the story. Once the deductions hit—taxes, union dues, health insurance, retirement contributions, Social Security (if applicable), and more—what you *take home* might feel like a gut punch.

That's normal. But it doesn't have to be discouraging.

Here's the key: learn how to live on your **net income**, not your **gross salary**.

Set your budget up around what actually hits your bank account. That's your reality. Everything else is paperwork.

Benefits Are Your Hidden Paycheck—But You Have to Read the Fine Print

Most rookies skip the HR packet. Don't be like most rookies.

Your department likely offers:

- Health insurance (but what's the deductible?)
- Life insurance (basic policy may not be enough)
- Short- and long-term disability
- Retirement contributions (457(b), pension, or both)
- Legal protection or union resources
- Employee assistance programs (mental health, counseling)

You must understand this stuff **early**. Because here's what no one tells you:

If something happens to you—on or off duty—and you haven't elected the right benefits or named the right beneficiaries, you might leave your family with heartbreak and a financial mess.

And if you never take advantage of what's offered, you're basically leaving money on the table.

Rookie Mistakes That Can Haunt You Later

Let's keep it real. Here are the top money mistakes rookies make in their first 5 years:

- Buying the "badge car" (a brand-new truck or Charger you can't afford)
- Living off overtime like it's guaranteed forever
- Ignoring credit, debt, or student loans until it's too late
- Not contributing anything outside the pension
- Not protecting their income with disability insurance
- Racking up credit card debt to keep up with veteran coworkers

- Living like they'll always feel young, healthy, and unstoppable

You've seen rookies flame out for attitude, for ego, for overconfidence. The same happens financially.

Stay humble. Stay sharp.

Systems Over Stress: Start Strong with the Basics

Let's walk through the essentials every first responder should build during their rookie years:

1. Start a Budget

This doesn't mean living cheap. It means knowing your numbers. Apps like YNAB, Mint, or a simple spreadsheet can keep you honest.

Track:

- Rent or mortgage
- Groceries
- Gas (you'll drive a lot)
- Minimum debt payments
- Savings goals
- Random stuff (dinners, dates, Amazon runs)

2. Create an Emergency Fund

Aim for $1,000 to start. Then build to 3–6 months of expenses. This is your financial turnout gear—ready when life catches fire.

3. Understand Your Pension

Learn:

- When you're vested
- How it's calculated
- What happens if you leave early
- If it includes COLA (cost-of-living adjustment)
- What you'll *actually* get at retirement

Pensions are great—but they aren't everything.

4. Open a Roth IRA or 457(b)

Start small—$50/month if that's all you can do. Set it to auto-debit. Time and compound interest are your backup crew here.

5. Check Your Credit Report

Go to annualcreditreport.com. Make sure there are no surprises. Good credit opens doors. Bad credit makes everything harder.

6. Get Adequate Insurance

Department policy might not be enough. Consider:

- Term life insurance (especially if you have kids)
- Disability insurance (because your body is your paycheck)
- Umbrella liability coverage (especially if you own a home or side business)

Real Talk: What Happens If You Get Hurt Off Duty?

Most rookies don't think about it. Until they fall off a ladder cleaning gutters or get in a motorcycle crash.

If you're hurt and can't work, you could lose your paycheck. Fast.

This is where:

- Short-term and long-term disability matter
- Emergency savings matter
- Having a side hustle or passive income stream matters
- Getting your paperwork (beneficiaries, wills, directives) in place matters

You train for worst-case scenarios on the job. **Train your finances the same way.**

Rookie vs. Veteran Mindset

It's easy to get caught up trying to live like the 20-year guys do—cars, boats, vacations.

But you're not there yet.

Let them do their thing. Focus on building a foundation.

Veterans with money peace did one thing early: **they started.** Not perfectly. But consistently.

Don't get trapped in the "I'll do it later" cycle.

Because later… shows up fast.

End of Chapter Wrap-Up

You've made it through academy, orientation, and your first few weeks on shift.

Now, take ownership of your money.

Not someday. **Today.**

You don't need to have it all figured out. You just need to take the next smart step.

Encouragement:

You've made it through harder things than budgeting. You've got this.

Reminder:

Financial planning isn't about being perfect. It's about staying prepared.

Takeaway:

Smart first responders don't guess with money—they train for it, just like anything else.

Prompt to Revisit:

Revisit this chapter every 6 months. Update your budget. Review your goals. Adjust your plan.

Because your life will change—and your money should keep up.

Chapter 2: Your First Paycheck – Understanding Taxes, Overtime, and Union Dues

You've done the work. The early mornings, the late nights, the sweat, the mental stress. You graduated the academy, made it through field training, and now you're on the job—earning that first real paycheck.

And then… you see it.

Not the gross pay, but the *net*. The part that hits your account. And you're thinking:

"Wait, where did all my money go?"

You're not alone. Every rookie has that moment of shock. Let's break it down, piece by piece, so you know exactly what's happening—and how to make it work for you, not against you.

Gross vs. Net: The First Lesson of the Job

Your **gross pay** is what your employer says they're paying you. Your **net pay** is what you actually take home.

The difference? A list of acronyms and deductions longer than a precinct roll call:

- Federal income tax
- State income tax (in most states)

- Social Security and Medicare (FICA)
- Retirement contributions (pension or 457(b))
- Health, dental, and vision premiums
- Union dues
- Life and disability insurance
- Deferred comp (if you've enrolled)
- Any voluntary deductions

So if your base salary is $60,000/year, don't plan your life around $5,000/month. That's not what you'll actually see.

Instead, get in the habit of **budgeting based on your net pay**. That's your real-world income. Everything else is just paperwork.

Understanding Federal and State Taxes

Federal Taxes

The IRS takes a cut based on how much you make and how you fill out your **W-4**. If you didn't adjust your withholdings, you might be over- or under-withholding right now.

Use a paycheck calculator and consider adjusting if:

- You're getting a huge refund (you're overpaying all year)
- You're writing a huge check in April (you're underpaying and may owe penalties)

State Taxes

Some states don't tax income (like Texas, Florida, and Nevada). Others tax aggressively (like California or New York). Know your state's rules. That "state tax" line on your pay stub isn't random—it's shaping your net income.

Social Security, Medicare, and the Special Rules for First Responders

Most employees pay into **FICA**, which funds Social Security and Medicare. But for **some first responders**, especially firefighters or police in certain municipalities, this works differently.

You may:

- **Not pay into Social Security at all**
- Have **a public pension plan instead**
- Still owe **Medicare taxes** but not Social Security

This matters. If you don't pay into Social Security, you won't qualify for full benefits later—unless you earn enough quarters elsewhere. That's why it's *critical* to understand **what your retirement will actually include**.

Talk to HR. Read your pension booklet. Ask other veterans. Don't assume anything.

Overtime: The Hero and the Trap

Overtime is one of the fastest ways to boost your income—but it comes with hidden costs.

The Upside

- Extra cash to pay off debt
- Boost your savings or investment accounts
- Fill financial gaps without a second job

The Downside

- **Higher tax liability**—OT can push you into a higher bracket
- **Burnout risk**—more hours = more physical and emotional fatigue
- **Lifestyle inflation**—you start spending like that OT will always be there
- **Dependency**—you plan your life around income that isn't guaranteed

Smart first responders treat OT like a **bonus**, not a baseline. Save it. Invest it. Use it to build leverage—not more bills.

Union Dues: What You're Paying For (And What You Should Be Getting)

When you see a deduction labeled "**Union Dues**", understand what you're paying for.

Unions often provide:

- Contract negotiation and representation
- Legal coverage for on-duty incidents
- Access to disability insurance
- Retirement advocacy
- Training resources and benefits info
- Political lobbying for first responder rights

If you're paying into a union, **use it**. Ask for help. Attend meetings. Read the newsletters. Leverage the benefits. This isn't just a deduction—it's a service you're funding.

And don't forget: some dues may be **partially tax deductible**, depending on your situation. Ask your CPA.

The Pay Stub: Your Financial X-Ray

Take 10 minutes and pull your last pay stub. Don't just glance at the deposit amount.

Look at:

- **Gross earnings** (base + OT + holiday pay + shift differentials)
- **Taxes withheld**
- **Retirement contributions**
- **Insurance deductions**
- **Other voluntary withholdings**
- **Year-to-date totals**

This is your roadmap. Don't ignore it. Set a calendar reminder to review your pay stub at least **once per quarter**.

Real Talk: When You Work 100 Hours and Still Feel Broke

Let's play out a real scenario.

You picked up OT, covered a shift, stayed late for a report, worked a holiday. You grossed $8,000 this month.

You expected to feel rich.

But after taxes, dues, deductions, and the higher tax bracket from that OT bump... you see maybe $5,100 hit your account.

Then rent, car payment, gas, groceries, child support, and a few takeout meals?

Gone.

That's not failure. That's reality. But it *does* mean you need a plan.

A budget built around your **base income**.

Savings goals that don't rely on OT.

A financial structure that **respects the grind—but doesn't depend on it**.

Action Steps: What You Can Do Right Now

1. **Print and Review Your Pay Stub**
2. Circle every line you don't understand. Ask someone in HR or your union rep to explain it.
3. **Estimate Your True Monthly Net Pay**
4. Take your average take-home pay for the last 3 months. Use *that* number to create your budget.
5. **Set Up Separate Accounts**
6. One for bills. One for savings. One for spending. Automation helps eliminate the mental load of juggling it all.
7. **Track OT Hours and Income Separately**
8. Log them each month. Build a spreadsheet. OT income should be a tool—not your crutch.
9. **Know Your Withholding Status**
10. Check your W-4. Adjust it if necessary to avoid owing the IRS or giving them an interest-free loan all year.
11. **Educate Yourself on Your Retirement Contributions**
12. Are you enrolled in a 457(b)? Are you contributing beyond the pension? Do you get matching? Learn the rules now.

Final Thoughts: Respect the Check

That paycheck you're earning? You fought for it. Trained for it. Put your life on the line for it.

Now it's time to **respect it.**

Don't just spend it.

Don't just survive on it.

Build with it.

Because this job is hard enough. Your money shouldn't be the part that keeps you up at night.

Encouragement:

You've already done the hard part—showing up and earning it. Now you just need to make it work for you.

Reminder:

The paycheck is just the beginning. What you *do* with it—that's where wealth is built.

Takeaway:

First responders who take time to understand their pay are more likely to build lasting financial peace.

Prompt to Revisit:

Check your pay stub every 3 months. Revisit your W-4 annually. Don't set it and forget it.

Chapter 3: Banking Basics – Setting Up Checking, Savings, and Emergency Accounts

Welcome to a chapter about something deceptively simple—**banking**.

You'd think by the time you're carrying a badge, driving an engine, or responding to medical calls, you'd already have this handled.

But the truth is, many first responders are walking around with checking accounts that leak money, savings accounts that earn pennies, and no real plan if life hits the fan.

So let's fix that.

This chapter isn't about becoming a banker. It's about learning how to use **basic tools**—checking, savings, and emergency funds—in a way that fits your shift life, your stress levels, and your goals.

Because you can be a tactical genius in the field and still be completely unarmed at the ATM.

Let's change that.

Why This Chapter Matters

You know what happens when gear isn't stored right?

When backup isn't ready?

When protocols get ignored?

It creates chaos, delays, and dangerous gaps.

Your **money** is the same way.

Without clear systems—especially around where your money goes when it hits your account—you'll always feel like you're playing catch-up.

Banking isn't just about *where* your money sits.

It's about building **structure and control** in a career where so much is unpredictable.

This chapter will show you how to:

- Build a paycheck system that actually works
- Set up a savings structure that doesn't get raided
- Create an emergency fund that buys you time, space, and dignity when life turns sideways

First Step: Build the Banking Framework

Let's get this out of the way: **you don't need fancy apps, six bank accounts, or crypto portfolios to be financially solid.**

What you *do* need is a **basic system that protects your money from yourself**, gives every dollar a job, and can handle the ups and downs of your first responder income.

We'll break it into three primary accounts:

1. **Checking Account** – For bills, spending, and direct deposit
2. **Savings Account** – For short-term goals and peace of mind
3. **Emergency Fund** – For life's "oh sh*t" moments

Some people do this all at one bank. Others spread it across different institutions to keep their money organized (or harder to touch). Either way—**clarity is key.**

Checking Account: Your Base Camp

Think of this as your financial command post. Your paycheck lands here. Your bills leave from here. Your day-to-day spending lives here.

What You Need:

- No monthly maintenance fees
- Free ATM access or ATM fee reimbursements
- Online/mobile access (so you can manage it between shifts)
- Optional: bill pay system or check-writing if needed

Pro Tip:

Avoid using this as your "everything" account.
That's how people lose track, overspend, and bounce payments.
Instead, **automate and separate**. Treat this account like a pass-through—not a piggy bank.

Savings Account: Where Your Short-Term Goals Live

Your savings account is *not* where you keep your emergency fund (we'll get to that in a minute). This is where you stash cash for:

- Travel
- Gear upgrades
- Car maintenance
- Property taxes
- Back-to-school supplies
- Union dues or professional recertification

What You Want in a Savings Account:

- **Online or high-yield savings** (don't settle for 0.01%)
- No minimum balance
- No fees
- Easy transfer access from your checking

Pro Tip:

Name your savings goals. Literally.
Most banks let you nickname your accounts:

- "Vacation Fund"
- "Truck Tires"
- "Kids' Sports Fees"

It's harder to spend what's labeled "Emergency Brake Replacement" on a last-minute concert ticket.

Emergency Fund: Your Financial Turnout Gear

This is your buffer. Your cushion. Your protection from life's surprises.
When your engine goes down, you've got a backup.
When your body breaks down—**do you?**

What It's For:

- Sudden medical bills
- Time off due to injury
- Unexpected travel
- Car repairs
- Appliance breakdowns
- Job loss or burnout-related leave

How Much?

Start with $1,000. That's your base.

Then build toward **3–6 months** of living expenses—especially if you're the primary earner or your household depends on your paycheck.

Where to Keep It:

- Separate from checking
- Easy enough to access in 24–48 hours
- Far enough away that you won't drain it on impulse

Online-only banks like Ally, Capital One 360, or Discover offer **high-yield savings accounts** ideal for this purpose.

System Setup: Your "3-Bucket" Paycheck Plan

When your paycheck hits, here's a structure you can live by:

1. **70–75% to Checking**

- For bills, food, gas, daily life

1. **10–15% to Savings Goals**

- Automatically routed to specific savings accounts

1. **10–15% to Emergency Fund or Investment**

- Build the buffer or start growing long-term wealth

This isn't perfect math. But it's a starting system. And the key is **automation**.

If you don't trust yourself to manually transfer money after a 48-hour shift or back-to-back OT, **set it and forget it**.

Pros and Cons of Online vs. Brick-and-Mortar Banks

Online BankLocal Credit Union/Branch Bank

Pros

Higher interest rates, lower fees, easy automation

Face-to-face service, faster transfers, tailored to first responders

Cons

Slower transfers, no physical presence

Lower savings rates, possible fees

Your Move?

Use both.

- Keep checking and short-term savings local
- Park your emergency fund online to make it harder to touch

Common Mistakes First Responders Make With Banking

1. **Using one account for everything** – Makes it impossible to track
2. **Mixing personal and side-hustle money** – Blurs tax lines
3. **Overdrafting** – Often from not separating bills from spending
4. **Raiding savings too easily** – Because it's "right there"
5. **Never checking their bank statements** – Fraud, fees, and mistakes happen

Real-Life Scenario

Let's say you just worked 60 hours of OT this month. You bring home an extra $2,000.

Option A:

It all sits in checking. You feel flush. You spend freely. Next month you're back to normal pay—and broke.

Option B:

You move:

- $1,000 to savings
- $500 to your emergency fund
- $500 stays in checking for life

Which version of you will feel better when your car battery dies, your kid's team wants $200 for uniforms, or you're too injured to work for a month?

Exactly.

Build Your Financial "Go Bag"

As a first responder, you wouldn't go into a call without your gear ready.

So don't do it with your money.

Your **financial go bag** includes:

- A solid checking system
- Named savings accounts
- An emergency fund with breathing room
- A list of beneficiaries for all accounts
- A budget built around net—not gross—income

Action Steps: Do This Now

1. **Open (or review) your checking account**

- Check for fees. Ask about overdraft protection and ATM access.

1. **Open a separate savings account**

- Start with one. Automate $50/month if that's all you can do.

1. **Open an online emergency fund**

- Use a different bank from your checking. Automate transfers after payday.

1. **Label your accounts**

- Call them what they are. Names create accountability.

1. **Set calendar reminders**

- Check your balances every payday. Set a quarterly review.

Encouragement:

You don't need to be rich to be ready. You just need structure.

Reminder:

Checking, savings, and emergency funds are your base. You can't build wealth on a shaky foundation.

Takeaway:

First responders who automate their banking don't just survive the job—they build financial resilience along the way.

Prompt to Revisit:

Every 6 months, review your accounts. Are they serving your life—or creating confusion?

Chapter 4: Understanding Credit Scores – What They Are and Why They Matter in This Job

When you first signed up for this career, you probably expected to deal with emergencies, high-stress decisions, long shifts, and public pressure.

What you probably didn't expect was how much your **credit score** could affect your career—even off the clock.

Whether you're applying for a mortgage, co-signing for your kid's student loan, buying a vehicle, or renewing your department-issued liability coverage, your credit score is the quiet gatekeeper behind the scenes. It's like an unofficial performance review that follows you everywhere.

And in a job where **trust, responsibility, and discipline** are the baseline—you can't afford to ignore it.

This chapter is your real-world breakdown of credit. No lectures. No scare tactics. Just facts, clarity, and strategy.

Why Credit Matters—Especially for First Responders

Let's get this straight from the jump: **your credit score isn't just about borrowing money.**

It affects:

- Your ability to **buy or refinance a home**

- What **interest rate** you'll pay on your car
- Whether you can **rent an apartment** without a cosigner
- Your **insurance premiums** (yes, your credit can raise your car insurance)
- Your ability to **qualify for a small business loan**
- Whether you get **flagged in a background check** for a promotion, transfer, or security clearance

As a first responder, your credibility matters. Whether it's fair or not, **bad credit can raise red flags** about your reliability, risk level, and personal discipline.

What Is a Credit Score—Really?

Your credit score is a three-digit number—between **300 and 850**—that sums up how trustworthy you appear to lenders.

It's not a judgment on your character. But it is a measurement of your **financial behavior over time**.

There are two major types:

- **FICO Score** – The one most lenders use
- **VantageScore** – Also popular with some banks and credit cards

Different versions exist (auto, mortgage, personal loan), but they're all based on the same core information.

What Makes Up Your Score?

Here's the breakdown for a **FICO Score**:

1. **Payment History (35%)**

- Do you pay your bills on time?

- Even one 30-day late payment can ding your score.

1. **Credit Utilization (30%)**

- How much of your available credit are you using?
- Keep it below 30% of your total credit limit.

1. **Length of Credit History (15%)**

- How long have your accounts been open?
- The longer, the better.

1. **New Credit (10%)**

- Did you just apply for a bunch of loans or credit cards?
- Too many "hard inquiries" can hurt your score.

1. **Credit Mix (10%)**

- Do you have a healthy variety (credit cards, auto loan, mortgage, etc.)?
- Not essential, but it helps.

Real Talk: What Hurts First Responders Most

You're working long hours. You forget a payment. You miss a notice. You swipe the credit card to cover a trip, equipment, or emergency—thinking you'll catch up next month.

Here's where most first responders trip up:

- **Missing payments during busy shift cycles**
- **Letting credit cards creep up due to irregular income**
- **Ignoring collections notices on old medical bills**
- **Co-signing for someone who doesn't pay**

- **Using OT money to justify overspending—and falling behind when OT dries up**

The job doesn't make it easy to stay on top of this stuff. But that's why having a **credit strategy** is even more important for you than most people.

Building Credit from Scratch (or Rebuilding After Mistakes)

Whether you're brand new to credit or trying to fix past damage, here's a simple plan:

Step 1: Get a Starter Credit Card

- Choose a card with **no annual fee**
- Use it for small recurring charges (like Netflix or gas)
- **Pay it off in full every month**
- Don't max it out—stay under 30% of your limit

Step 2: Check Your Credit Report

- Visit AnnualCreditReport.com
- Check for errors, fraud, or surprise accounts
- Dispute anything inaccurate—this matters

Step 3: Set Up Auto-Pay

Even if it's just for the minimum payment, this protects your score if life gets hectic.

Step 4: Avoid Opening Too Many New Accounts

One or two credit cards are enough. Don't get lured into every store card at the mall.

Step 5: Don't Close Old Accounts

Length of history matters. Even if you don't use an old card, keep it open with a zero balance.

Real-World Credit Scenarios in the First Responder World

Scenario 1: The Lease vs. Loan Dilemma

You're a rookie and want to lease a new truck. But your credit score is 620. The dealership says you need a cosigner or you'll face a 12% interest rate.

Lesson: **Your credit affects your freedom.** Raise your score and negotiate like a boss.

Scenario 2: Promotions and Background Checks

You're up for a federal agency transfer. They pull your financials. They see multiple collections and a 590 score.

Even if your field performance is stellar, **bad credit can raise concerns about stress, judgment, or vulnerability**.

Lesson: **Your credit is part of your personnel file, whether you realize it or not.**

Scenario 3: Divorce, Debt, and Damage Control

You went through a tough split. The bills were in your name. Your ex didn't pay. Now your score's in the 500s.

Lesson: **Financial protection is personal protection.** Clean it up.

Own it. Rebuild.

The Credit/Insurance Connection

Here's a shocker: **some insurance companies use your credit score to set your premiums.**

That's right—**your credit can make your car insurance go up** even if you have a clean driving record.

It's called a "credit-based insurance score." And it affects:

- Auto insurance
- Homeowners insurance
- Umbrella coverage in some states

Keeping your credit clean literally saves you money across the board.

Co-Signing: A Hidden Risk

You want to help your kid, your spouse, or your buddy.

You co-sign on:

- A car loan
- A student loan
- A credit card

Then they miss payments. Or ghost. Or struggle.

Guess what? **It hits your credit score, not theirs.**

Lesson: **Only co-sign if you're willing—and able—to make the payments yourself.**

Action Steps: Build Credit Like a Pro

1. **Pull Your Credit Report Today**
2. Go to AnnualCreditReport.com. It's free.
3. **Set Up Alerts on All Accounts**
4. Use your bank's app, Credit Karma, or another tool to stay informed.
5. **Automate Your Minimum Payments**
6. Never miss a due date, even when your schedule is chaos.
7. **Use Less Than 30% of Any Card's Limit**
8. Ideally, stay under 10% for the best score boosts.
9. **Use a Secured Card if You're Rebuilding**
10. Put down $200–500 and use it to rebuild responsibly.
11. **Freeze Your Credit if You're Not Applying for Anything**
12. It protects you from fraud and identity theft—especially with department breaches or public exposure.

Encouragement:

You've faced harder challenges than rebuilding a credit score. This is just a process—and you're the type to finish what you start.

Reminder:

Credit isn't a status symbol. It's a **tool**. Use it wisely, and it will work for you.

Takeaway:

Smart first responders protect their credit like they protect their gear—because both matter in every situation.

Prompt to Revisit:

Check your credit report every 6 months. Set reminders. Keep it clean. Keep it growing.

Chapter 5: Getting Your First Credit Card (Without Digging a Financial Grave)

You just finished your first month on the job. The badge is starting to feel natural. You've got your direct deposit flowing. And now that steady income makes something else possible:

Your first credit card.

For a lot of people, that little piece of plastic feels like freedom. Until it doesn't.

Because if you're not careful, your first credit card becomes your **first financial fire**, and nobody's coming to put it out but you.

This chapter is about **getting it right from the start**. Not just applying for a credit card—but **managing it like a pro**, avoiding the traps, and using it as a stepping stone to build your credit, not bury your finances.

What a Credit Card Is—and What It Definitely Is Not

Let's be clear:

A credit card is not:

- Free money
- A solution to bad budgeting
- A reward for getting hired
- A cash machine with no strings

A credit card *is*:

- A **tool** to build credit history
- A **bridge** for temporary cash flow—not a lifestyle
- A **test** of discipline in a system that wants you to fail
- A **liability** if it's not used wisely

If you're carrying a badge, people assume you're disciplined. So let's bring that mindset into your wallet.

Why First Responders Need to Be Especially Careful

You work long shifts. You're under stress. You miss bills by accident. You swipe more when you're burned out.

You also might get targeted for high-limit cards because of your public service career. Banks know you have steady income—and they're hoping you'll carry a balance.

The system is not designed for your success. It's designed for your *compliance.*

So you need a plan.

Choosing Your First Credit Card: What to Look For

There are hundreds of credit cards out there. The wrong one can cost you big. The right one can open financial doors.

Features to Prioritize:

- **No annual fee**
- **Low interest rate (APR)**—you'll still pay it off monthly, but just in case
- **Cash back** on groceries, gas, or basic purchases
- **No hidden fees** (late fees, foreign transaction fees, etc.)

Good Starter Card Options:

- A **secured card** (if you're building or rebuilding credit)
- A **student or first-time user card**
- A card through your **credit union or bank**—they may offer better terms

Don't apply for three or four at once. One card. That's it.

How Credit Cards Work (The Real Version)

Let's say your card has a $1,000 limit.

You buy:

- $60 in gas
- $150 for groceries
- $40 at a restaurant

You've spent $250. The **statement balance** is $250.

If you **pay it in full** before the due date, you owe **zero interest**. That's the goal.

But if you only pay the **minimum** (say, $25), the **rest starts to rack up interest**—often 20% or more.

That's the trap. Not the spending. The *carrying*.

Interest is where people fall behind and credit cards stop being tools—and become burdens.

Common Rookie Mistakes (That Will Bury You Fast)

1. **Only paying the minimum** – That's how a $500 purchase turns into $900 over time
2. **Using it like a debit card** – It's not. It's a *loan*, every time you swipe
3. **Missing payments** – One 30-day late ding can cost you 100+ points

on your credit
4. **Maxing it out** – Using 90–100% of your limit hurts your score, even if you pay it off
5. **Closing it too soon** – You want long-standing accounts to help your credit age
6. **Using it to "float" expenses** – This only works until you fall behind

Smart Ways to Use Your First Credit Card

- Set up **one automatic charge per month** (Netflix, Spotify, etc.)
- Set an **auto-payment** for the full balance
- Keep your **utilization under 30%** of the limit (preferably under 10%)
- Use your **credit card like a debit card**—only spend what you can pay immediately
- Treat any balance as an **emergency situation**, not a routine occurrence

Think of it like your department-issued gear: it's powerful, useful, and effective—but if misused, it can get you hurt.

The Psychology of Plastic: Why Good People Go Broke with Cards

Here's what they don't tell you: Credit cards are designed to feel **less painful** than using cash or a debit card.

You don't see the money leaving your account. You don't feel the loss. That makes it easier to justify:

- Fast food after a long shift
- Last-minute gear upgrades
- A "deserved" vacation
- Picking up the tab for a group dinner

The badge brings pride. The credit card brings the illusion of wealth.

You can have both—**but only if you stay disciplined**.

Real-World Scenario: Rookie Firefighter, Real-Life Trap

You're a new firefighter. You just moved into your own apartment. You buy a couch, a TV, and some basic furniture—all on a card.

It feels manageable... until your rig breaks down and you have to put $800 on the card for a repair.

Then you get hit with back-to-back shifts. You miss the payment. That late fee hits. Interest starts piling up. The balance balloons. Now you're paying $150/month just to tread water.

That's how it starts. Quiet. Then compounding.

Be smarter than the system.

Pros and Cons of Having a Credit Card

Pros:

- Builds your credit history
- Helps with travel and rentals
- Emergency tool when managed wisely
- Offers cash back or points
- Better fraud protection than debit

Cons:

- Easy to overspend
- Late payments crush your credit
- High interest rates
- Can lead to long-term debt
- Used against you in insurance and employment screens if mismanaged

Credit Card Red Flags to Avoid

- "Guaranteed approval" cards with high fees
- Store cards with 29% APR
- Cards that push you to carry a balance
- Introductory offers that expire and jump interest to 25%+
- Credit repair scams disguised as card offers

What If You've Already Messed Up?

You're not alone. But it's time to clean it up:

1. **Stop using the card immediately**
2. **Make at least minimum payments on time**
3. **Pay more than the minimum whenever possible**
4. **Call the issuer and ask for a lower interest rate**
5. **Track your balance weekly**
6. **Avoid opening more cards until this one is stable**

Credit recovery takes time. But every month you pay on time, you're rebuilding. One step at a time.

Action Steps: Your First Card, the Right Way

- Choose a **no-fee card** with reasonable terms
- Set up **autopay** for full balance
- Keep spending **under 10% of your limit**
- Review your **statement every month**
- Use an app like **Credit Karma** or your bank's app to monitor activity
- Commit to **never carrying a balance unless it's a true emergency**

Encouragement:

You've trained to keep people alive. You can absolutely keep your credit card in check.

Reminder:

A credit card is a tool. Like your gear—it's only dangerous when you're careless with it.

Takeaway:

Smart first responders don't treat credit cards like a paycheck. They treat them like a scalpel—precise, intentional, and with purpose.

Prompt to Revisit:

Check your card usage every payday. If your balance is growing—pause, assess, adjust.

Chapter 6: Budgeting on a Public Servant's Starting Salary – Making Every Dollar Count

Let's be real: most people don't become firefighters, cops, or paramedics for the money. You do it because you want to serve, because you're called to something bigger, because you believe in stepping up when others freeze.

But while the mission is noble, the paycheck—especially when you're starting out—isn't exactly life-changing.

That's why this chapter matters.

Because if you don't get intentional about budgeting early on, you'll wake up one day ten years into the job wondering where all your money went, why you're still living paycheck to paycheck, and how you're supposed to retire on pride alone.

Let's change that. Let's build a simple, bulletproof plan to help you **maximize your income**, **reduce stress**, and **put your money to work—even if it's not a lot right now**.

This Is About Strategy, Not Sacrifice

This isn't one of those "cut lattes and never eat out again" chapters.

We're not here to shame you for treating yourself after a 14-hour shift.

We're here to build **a financial operating system** that respects:

- The unpredictable nature of your job
- The reality of public-sector pay
- The fatigue that makes you want to swipe and forget

Budgeting isn't about punishment—it's about **purpose**. It's about taking control in a career where control is often the first thing you lose.

The Rookie Reality: Where Every Dollar Goes

Let's paint the scene.

You're making $45,000–$60,000 as a starting firefighter, patrol officer, or paramedic. That's before taxes, insurance, retirement contributions, and union dues.

After all that? You're taking home maybe $3,200 a month—give or take.

Here's what that has to cover:

- Rent
- Utilities
- Groceries
- Gas
- Car payment
- Insurance
- Phone
- Uniform costs
- Union dues
- Gear not covered by the department
- Student loans
- Family support (if you've got kids or help your parents)

It's tight.

Which means **you need a plan**, not just willpower.

Step 1: Build a Budget That Honors Your Reality

Let's ditch the spreadsheet for a second and talk **categories**.

A solid first responder budget has these core buckets:

1. **Fixed Costs** – Rent, car payment, phone, insurance, union dues
2. **Variables** – Gas, groceries, eating out, shifts at the station
3. **Savings** – Emergency fund, short-term goals, long-term investing
4. **Debt Payments** – Credit cards, loans, anything you owe
5. **Discretionary** – Gym, entertainment, gifts, travel, that new flashlight you "need" but really just want

Use the **70/20/10 rule** as a starting point:

- 70% for needs and living expenses
- 20% for savings and investing
- 10% for fun, flexibility, and small indulgences

If 70/20/10 doesn't work? Build your own ratio—but **make sure every dollar has a job**.

Step 2: Align Your Budget with Your Pay Schedule

Public service pay often comes **biweekly** or **semi-monthly**. Your budget should match that.

Here's the mistake rookies make: they budget monthly—but forget they're getting paid **every two weeks**, not on the same date each month.

That causes overdrafts, missed bills, and "how am I broke again?" moments.

Solution:

- Write down your **next 3 pay dates**
- Assign each check to cover **specific expenses**
- Build in room for the "three-paycheck months" (those are your budgeting bonus rounds—don't waste them)

Step 3: Don't Budget Based on Overtime

You're tempted to build your lifestyle around OT. We get it. The pay bump feels good.

But overtime is **not guaranteed**. It's **not dependable**. And it's **not worth the stress** of being one injury away from broke.

Base your budget on your **regular salary only**.

Treat overtime as **bonus income**—used for:

- Paying down debt
- Building your emergency fund
- Investing
- Taking care of irregular expenses

If you use it to finance a bigger car, a bigger house, or a bigger lifestyle, you're setting yourself up for burnout and regret.

Step 4: Use "The Four Account System" to Stay in Control

Set up four separate accounts:

1. **Bills Account** – For rent, car, insurance, etc. Automate your payments here
2. **Spending Account** – For groceries, gas, daily life
3. **Savings Account** – Emergency fund and goals
4. **Overflow Account** – Where OT or unexpected money goes first

This setup gives you **mental clarity** and **built-in guardrails**.
It also means you're not trying to do math at 2 a.m. after a 24-hour shift.

Step 5: Budget for the Unexpected (Because That's Your Life)

You don't get the luxury of calm schedules and predictable costs. You live in a world of:

- Flat tires
- Call-outs
- Sick kids
- Uniform replacement
- Family emergencies
- Burnout leave

So **your budget must flex with your life**.
That's why you build:

- A buffer
- An emergency fund
- A category for "weird sh*t that always happens"

Expect surprises. Build for them. Don't let them knock you off track.

Real-World Scenario: A Rookie's Budget Breakdown

Let's say you're bringing home $3,200/month.
Here's how a **lean but livable budget** might look:

- Rent: $1,000
- Car Payment + Insurance: $500
- Gas: $200
- Groceries: $350

- Utilities + Phone: $250
- Union Dues/Work Costs: $100
- Minimum Debt Payments: $200
- Emergency Fund Contribution: $150
- Roth IRA: $150
- Fun + Life: $300

Total: $3,200

You won't get rich off this—but you'll get stable. And that's the win.

Budgeting with a Family? It's a Team Operation

Whether you're married, divorced, or co-parenting, **budgeting isn't a solo mission**.

Sit down with your partner and:

- Set shared goals
- Divide responsibilities
- Make a plan for "surprise" costs
- Agree on limits for personal spending

This isn't about control—it's about **communication and clarity**.

Pros and Cons of Common Budgeting Apps and Systems

System Pros Cons

Pen & Paper

Free, hands-on

Time-consuming, easy to forget

Excel/Google Sheets

Customizable

Manual, requires effort

YNAB (You Need a Budget)

Great for zero-based budgeting, shift-friendly
Small monthly fee
Mint
Easy to link accounts
Can feel clunky, not built for first responders
Envelope Method (cash)
Good for overspenders
Not practical for shift workers or digital bills

Find what works for you. The best budget system is the one you'll actually use.

Action Steps: What to Do Right Now

1. **Write down your take-home pay**
2. **List all your fixed monthly bills**
3. **Track your last 30 days of spending**
4. **Set up a separate account for savings**
5. **Decide on a budgeting method**
6. **Schedule a 30-minute money check-in every payday**

Encouragement:

You've made it through worse. Budgeting is just a drill. Once you run it a few times, it becomes second nature.

Reminder:

There's no perfect budget—just consistent adjustments.

Takeaway:

Smart first responders don't guess where their money went. They give it orders.

Prompt to Revisit:

Review your budget every 6 months—or every time your pay, goals, or responsibilities change.

Chapter 7: Buying or Leasing a Vehicle on a First Responder's Salary

You're a few months into the job. You've got the badge, the shift rotation memorized, and the pride of doing something that actually matters. But now the old beater you've been driving since academy days is starting to rattle like a callout tone at 3 a.m.

You need a new ride.

Now comes the decision that catches way too many first responders off guard:

Do you buy, or do you lease?

Do you lock into a multi-year loan and own the vehicle outright?

Or do you lease something shiny, manageable, and brand new—knowing you'll be handing it back?

This chapter unpacks it all—the money, the mindset, the real costs beneath the sticker price—and helps you make a smart decision that won't wreck your budget or sabotage your long-term financial game.

Why This Chapter Matters

You work hard. Your schedule's brutal. Your vehicle is your escape, your off-shift getaway car, your mobile locker, and for many of you, your most expensive purchase outside your home.

The car lot can smell your OT check from across the lot.

They'll say:

"You deserve it."
"Let's stretch the term to 84 months."
"Zero down, zero interest!"
"Lease it now, worry later."

What they don't say is:

"Let's see how this fits your long-term financial strategy."

That's where we come in.

Leasing vs. Buying – The Real Talk

Here's what you've probably heard:

Leasing is like renting. Buying is like owning.

And that's technically true—but there's more to it. Especially when you factor in:

- Department mileage
- Commute to/from station
- Off-duty gigs
- Shift life wear-and-tear
- Budgeting with OT
- Long-term financial goals

Let's break them down.

Leasing a Vehicle: The Basics

Leasing means you're essentially renting the car for 2–4 years. You'll have a mileage limit, you'll be responsible for any damage, and you'll never own the car.

At the end of the lease, you either:

- Give it back and lease another
- Buy it out at a pre-set price
- Walk away and start over

Pros of Leasing:

- Lower monthly payments
- New car every few years
- Little or no money down
- Typically covered by warranty (fewer repair costs)
- No worries about resale value

Cons of Leasing:

- You don't own the vehicle
- Mileage caps (often 10,000–15,000/year)
- Fees for damage, wear, or going over miles
- No equity when the lease ends
- Can't modify or customize
- Early termination fees are steep

Who leasing works best for:

- First responders with short commutes
- Those who prefer a newer car with fewer repairs
- Those who *budget meticulously*
- People who rotate vehicles every few years anyway

Buying a Vehicle: The Basics

When you buy, you either pay cash (rare) or finance with a loan.

Once the loan is paid off—you own the car outright. You can keep it, sell it, give it to your kid, or drive it into the ground.

Pros of Buying:

- It's yours when paid off
- No mileage restrictions
- You can modify it, wrap it, load gear in it
- It holds resale value
- Eventually—no monthly payment
- Better for long-term cost savings

Cons of Buying:

- Higher monthly payments
- Maintenance costs rise over time
- Needs more cash up front (especially if you don't want to roll in taxes, fees)
- You take on depreciation

Who buying works best for:

- First responders with longer commutes
- Those who want to keep a vehicle long-term
- Anyone focused on long-term wealth over short-term flash
- Budget-conscious professionals who want equity

Total Cost of Ownership (Not Just the Monthly Payment)

When a dealership talks to you, they're talking in one language: **monthly payment.**

But you need to speak a different language: **total cost of ownership**.

That includes:

- Down payment
- Sales tax

- Monthly payments
- Insurance premiums (leasing usually requires more)
- Gas and mileage
- Maintenance
- End-of-lease fees (if applicable)
- Future value (resale or equity)

The **cheapest car on paper** isn't always the cheapest car in reality.

Real-World Scenario: Rookie Cop, New Car Temptation

You're 26, on your first patrol job. You've been eyeing that Dodge Charger since day one.

You've got a steady paycheck now. OT on the weekends.

Dealership says: "$399/month. No money down. You in?"

You bite.

You're three months in when you get hit with:

- High insurance because you're leasing a performance car
- You're already pushing the mileage cap
- You scuff a rim pulling out of the station lot
- You realize the monthly note doesn't leave much room for saving

Suddenly that "affordable" ride is **owning you**.

How Much Car Can You Afford?

Rule of thumb:

Your monthly car cost (payment + insurance + gas) should be **no more than 15%–20% of your net monthly income**.

If you're bringing home $3,000/month, that's **$450–$600 max**.

That's all-in—not just the loan.

Too many first responders get sucked into $800/month vehicles—because they "can afford it."

But "afford" isn't the same as "smart."

Should You Buy Used?

In many cases—**absolutely.**

Used vehicles:

- Avoid the first 2–3 years of depreciation
- Let you get more car for your money
- Can be financed with lower payments
- May be cheaper to insure

Just be sure you:

- Get a full inspection
- Pull a vehicle history report
- Look for certified pre-owned options
- Budget for repairs

When Buying or Leasing Becomes a Problem

- You're using OT to justify a bigger loan
- You're upside down (owe more than it's worth)
- You can't afford routine maintenance
- You're skipping savings to make the car payment
- You bought for the badge, not the budget

The goal isn't just to have wheels. It's to have **financial flexibility**.

Action Steps: Making a Smart Vehicle Decision

1. **Get pre-approved** for financing from your credit union or bank
2. **Price out the total cost of ownership** (not just the monthly payment)
3. **Run the numbers** using both lease and loan calculators
4. **Test your budget**—can you make the payment without OT?
5. **Don't sign anything the same day you test-drive**
6. **Avoid extended warranties, paint packages, or "add-ons"**
7. **Treat the dealership like a crime scene: trust no one until verified**

Encouragement:

You've got the discipline to run into chaos. You can handle a car decision with clarity.

Reminder:

Cars are tools—not trophies. They get you to work, but they shouldn't keep you there financially.

Takeaway:

Smart first responders don't drive broke. They drive smart. They buy what fits, not what flexes.

Prompt to Revisit:

Revisit your vehicle decision every time your job, commute, family size, or income changes. Your ride should evolve with your life—not control it.

Chapter 8: Should You Rent or Buy a Home as a Rookie?

You finally graduated. You're out of the academy. Your first few checks have cleared, your schedule is dialed in (mostly), and you've got just enough breathing room to ask the question:

"Should I keep renting—or should I buy a home?"

You've probably already heard the pressure:

"You're throwing money away on rent."
"You should buy now—prices are going up."
"A mortgage is better than paying someone else's."
"If you don't buy now, you'll never get in the market."

But here's what no one's asking you:

"Do you have an emergency fund?"
"How stable is your current assignment?"
"Are you ready for roof repairs and property taxes?"
"Can you handle this without needing OT to make it work?"

This chapter isn't about telling you which path is "better." It's about showing you how to think like a first responder with a **mission-driven financial strategy**, not an emotional reaction to pressure, hype, or bad advice.

Why the Rent vs. Buy Debate Feels So Heavy in This Profession

There's a lot wrapped up in this decision:

- A sense of pride
- Stability after a chaotic academy or training phase
- Wanting to "feel like an adult"
- Showing your family you're progressing
- Getting out of roommates or your parents' house
- Pressure from coworkers who just bought homes themselves

And let's be real—homeownership is often seen as a badge of responsibility, especially in this line of work.

But just like responding to a call, the right move isn't the most aggressive—it's the most informed.

Renting: What It Really Means

Renting doesn't mean you're failing financially. It means you're **buying flexibility**.

When you rent, you:

- Don't pay for repairs
- Can relocate easily if you're reassigned or want a transfer
- Know your monthly costs (no surprise water heater breakdowns)
- May have lower upfront costs (just security + first month's rent)
- Can take more time to build savings and credit before buying

For rookies still finding their footing, renting gives you **time to stabilize**, get to know your department, and learn how much the job is really going to cost you—physically and financially.

Pros of Renting:

- No maintenance or repair bills
- Flexible if your job shifts
- No property taxes or homeowners insurance
- Easier approval than a mortgage
- Can live closer to work without the buying pressure

Cons of Renting:

- No equity
- Rent can increase annually
- You're subject to landlord rules
- Can feel temporary or less "yours"

Renting is the right move if you need more time to:

- Build your emergency fund
- Increase your credit score
- Pay down other debts
- Decide if your department/city is long-term
- Avoid stress while still adjusting to shift life

Buying: What It Really Means

Buying can be an amazing move—if you're truly ready.
It gives you:

- A place that's yours
- Predictable mortgage payments (if you have a fixed-rate loan)
- The ability to build equity over time
- A forced savings mechanism
- Potential long-term wealth building

- Stability if you're planning to raise a family

But it also ties you down, increases your responsibilities, and introduces **a whole new category of unexpected costs**.

Pros of Buying:

- Long-term cost savings (if you stay in the home 7+ years)
- Ability to renovate or upgrade
- Tax benefits in some cases (mortgage interest deduction)
- Potential asset to pass on or rent out later
- Sense of ownership and pride

Cons of Buying:

- High upfront costs (down payment, closing costs, inspections)
- Maintenance and repair costs
- Property taxes, HOA fees, homeowners insurance
- Less flexibility if reassigned, injured, or need to move
- Risk of negative equity if the market dips

Real-World Scenario: Rookie Paramedic with Ambition

You're 25. You just passed probation. You're single. You've got a decent credit score, a bit of savings, and the bank says you're pre-approved for $300,000.

Your gut says: **"Buy now. It'll be an investment."**

But you're not sure how long you'll stay in this department. You're still figuring out whether you want to move closer to family. You've got a nagging student loan. And OT has been covering your budget gaps.

Buying might feel like progress—but in reality, it might be **premature pressure dressed up as success.**

Key Questions to Ask Before Buying

1. **Do you plan to stay in this job and this city for at least 5–7 years?**
2. If not, renting likely makes more sense.
3. **Do you have at least 3–6 months of expenses saved?**
4. If not, you're not ready for homeownership. Period.
5. **Will this home cost more than 25–30% of your take-home pay (including taxes, insurance, and maintenance)?**
6. If yes, it will stretch you thin—especially if OT slows down.
7. **Will you still be able to contribute to retirement, save, and live without financial strain?**
8. If buying forces you to pause all other goals, it might not be the time.
9. **Is your credit in a place where you'll get a favorable loan?**
10. Buying with a bad rate costs you thousands in interest over time.

Rookie Mistakes to Avoid When Buying

- **Confusing pre-approval with affordability**
- Just because they'll lend you $300,000 doesn't mean you should borrow it.
- **Ignoring closing costs**
- These can run 3–6% of the home price. That's $9,000–$18,000 on a $300K home.
- **Underestimating repairs**
- Water heater breaks? That's $1,200. New roof? $10,000. Don't buy unless you can handle these hits.
- **Counting on OT to make the mortgage**
- Never build your life on income that's not guaranteed.

Renting as a Wealth Strategy (Yes, Really)

You can still build wealth while renting if you:

- Keep housing costs manageable
- Max out your retirement contributions
- Invest in index funds or a Roth IRA
- Stay mobile and career-flexible
- Avoid bad home deals or debt traps

Renting doesn't have to be a forever thing. But it can be a *for now* thing that makes later wealth more realistic.

When Buying Might Be the Right Move—Even as a Rookie

It's not all caution tape.
Buying might make sense if:

- You have a steady assignment and want to build roots
- You're married or raising kids and want stability
- You've run the numbers and know your budget can handle it
- You're buying below your max—not at it
- You're not afraid of maintenance or managing a property
- You have enough savings that a repair won't wreck you

Action Steps: Making the Right Move for You

1. **Track your real expenses for 90 days**
2. Know what you truly spend—not what you *think* you spend.
3. **Meet with a trusted mortgage broker AND a financial advisor**
4. Not just a realtor.
5. **Run the numbers: rent vs. buy calculators**
6. Use conservative estimates.

7. **Build or beef up your emergency fund**
8. Aim for 6 months before buying.
9. **Don't rush.**
10. Take the pressure off. The goal isn't to keep up—it's to stay strong and steady.

Encouragement:

There's no shame in renting, and no glory in buying too soon. Make the move that protects your future—not just your pride.

Reminder:

A house should give you shelter—not stress.

Takeaway:

Smart first responders don't just chase ownership—they build readiness, options, and strength in every decision.

Prompt to Revisit:

Every year, check your financial situation. When the numbers—and your life—say you're ready, then start the house hunt.

Chapter 9: Understanding Your Employee Benefits – Health, Dental, Vision, and More

You signed the offer. You started the job. You made it through the academy or field training. And now someone hands you a benefits packet that's 30 pages long, filled with terms like deductible, coinsurance, PPO, HSA, and "Voluntary Supplemental AD&D."

You're tired, you're hungry, and your first instinct is to check a few boxes, sign the bottom, and hope for the best.

Don't do that.

This chapter is your walk-through. Because your benefits aren't just paperwork—they're part of your **compensation**, your **safety net**, and in many cases, your **family's entire financial foundation**.

If you're going to run toward danger for a living, you need to know what's covering you when life punches back.

Why Your Benefits Matter More Than You Think

Let's be clear: You don't get into this job for the perks. You do it for the purpose.

But your benefits? They're part of the **actual dollars and value** you're getting from your department.

And in a job that's physically demanding, unpredictable, and high risk, these benefits are more than "nice to have." They're essential.

They impact:

- Your take-home pay
- Your long-term financial planning
- Your ability to recover from injury or illness
- Your family's protection
- Your quality of life on and off shift

So let's unpack them, one layer at a time—plain language, no fluff.

Start Here: What's in a Typical First Responder Benefits Package?

Depending on your department or union contract, you may have access to:

- Medical (Health) Insurance
- Dental Insurance
- Vision Insurance
- Life Insurance
- Disability Insurance (Short- and Long-Term)
- Health Savings Accounts (HSA) or Flexible Spending Accounts (FSA)
- Employee Assistance Programs (EAP)
- Supplemental Benefits (hospital indemnity, accident, critical illness)
- Retirement Plans (457(b), pensions)
- Legal or identity protection
- Paid time off (sick, vacation, comp time)

This chapter will focus on the first four: **health, dental, vision, and related benefits** that you'll start using immediately.

Health Insurance: What to Know (and What to Watch)

Health insurance is your front line when something goes wrong—on the job or off.

Most departments offer at least one plan, often through a larger city or municipal system. You may get to choose between:

- **PPO (Preferred Provider Organization)** – More flexible, higher premiums
- **HMO (Health Maintenance Organization)** – Lower cost, more restricted network
- **HDHP (High Deductible Health Plan)** – Lower premiums, higher out-of-pocket costs

Key Terms You Need to Understand:

- **Premium** – What comes out of your paycheck for coverage
- **Deductible** – What you pay out-of-pocket before insurance kicks in
- **Copay** – Flat fee for doctor visits or prescriptions
- **Coinsurance** – The percentage you pay after the deductible
- **Out-of-pocket max** – Your financial ceiling for the year

Rookie Trap:

Choosing the cheapest premium because it feels like "less taken out of your check"—then getting wrecked by a $5,000 deductible when you break your ankle on vacation.

Pro Tip:

If you're young, healthy, and disciplined, a **high-deductible plan + HSA** can save you money and help you build wealth long-term. But you need to be ready to **cover that deductible at any moment**.

HSA vs. FSA: Which One Makes Sense?

If you have a high-deductible plan, you're eligible for an **HSA (Health Savings Account)**.

- **HSA Pros**:
- Contributions are tax-deductible
- Money rolls over year to year
- Funds can be invested
- You can take it with you if you leave the job

If your plan is traditional (PPO or HMO), you might have access to a **FSA (Flexible Spending Account)**.

- **FSA Pros**:
- Also tax-advantaged
- Can be used for medical, dental, vision expenses
- But: **Use it or lose it**—funds often expire annually

For long-term wealth and flexibility, **HSA wins**—but only if you can afford the higher deductible.

Dental Insurance: Don't Brush This Off

Dental often feels optional. Until you're sitting in a chair with a cracked molar, facing a $1,200 crown you didn't budget for.

Dental plans typically include:

- **Preventive care** (cleanings, x-rays): Usually covered 100%
- **Basic procedures** (fillings, extractions): Covered 70–80%
- **Major services** (crowns, root canals): Covered 50% or less
- **Orthodontics**: Often not included unless you pay extra

Watch For:

- **Annual maximums** (e.g., $1,500/year in coverage)
- **Waiting periods** for major work
- **Network limitations** (out-of-network dentists may cost more)

This is a **low-cost, high-value benefit**. Use it. Go to your cleanings. Budget for what insurance won't cover. Dental debt is a silent killer for a lot of rookie budgets.

Vision Insurance: A Small Cost That Pays Off Big

Vision insurance isn't just about glasses. It's also about eye health—and early detection of issues like diabetes or high blood pressure.

Typical coverage includes:

- Annual eye exams
- Discounts on frames/lenses
- Contact lens allowances
- LASIK discounts (sometimes)

Even if your eyes are 20/20 now, **get the exam**. Especially if you work nights, drive long shifts, or need sharp focus for safety.

Life Insurance: Protecting Your Family From the Worst-Case Scenario

Most departments include **basic group life insurance** (e.g., $25,000–$100,000) for free or low cost.

But here's the question: **Is that enough?**

If you have a spouse, kids, a mortgage—or just someone who depends on you—probably not.

What You Need to Know:

- Group life often ends when you leave the job
- You may be able to purchase **voluntary supplemental life** (usually up to 3–5x your salary)
- You may want to buy a **separate term life policy** outside your job

Why term life?

- It's cheap
- It lasts 10–30 years
- You choose the amount
- It covers the years when people rely on your income the most

Rule of thumb: If anyone depends on you financially, life insurance is not optional. It's part of your duty to protect.

Disability Insurance: What Happens If You Can't Work?

You've got life insurance if you die. But what if you survive—injured, off the job, unable to earn?

That's where **short-term and long-term disability** come in.

Your department may offer:

- **Short-term disability (STD)** – Covers a portion of your salary for a few months after an injury or illness
- **Long-term disability (LTD)** – Kicks in after STD and can last for years

What to Ask HR:

- What's the waiting period before benefits begin?
- What percentage of my income does it replace?
- Is it **taxable** or **non-taxable**?
- Does it coordinate with workers' comp or pension disability?

This is especially important for first responders—because your injury risk is higher than average.

Don't rely on hope or heroism. Get coverage that steps in when your body can't.

Other Benefits You Might Not Know You Have

Employee Assistance Programs (EAP):

Confidential help for:

- Mental health
- Legal issues
- Family counseling
- Substance use
- Grief or trauma

Use it. These services are built for people in high-stress jobs. No shame. Just support.

Critical Illness, Accident, Hospital Indemnity Plans:

These are **supplemental plans** you can opt into. They pay **you** if something big happens (e.g., cancer, heart attack, hospital admission).

Think of it as **cash for chaos**. Not essential, but helpful—especially if your savings are thin.

Real-World Scenario: Rookie Firefighter, Rookie Mistake

You're 24. You opt for the lowest-cost health plan. No dental. No disability. You figure you're young, healthy, and invincible.

Two months later, you:

- Crack a tooth eating off-duty
- Pull a muscle during PT
- Have to miss work for two weeks

You're paying out-of-pocket for everything. No paycheck, no coverage, no backup plan.

Lesson: You don't know what's coming—but you can prepare anyway.

Action Steps: What You Can Do Today

1. **Request a full benefits summary** from HR or your union
2. **Read every section**—highlight what you don't understand
3. **Compare health plan options**—run real-life scenarios
4. **Set up an HSA or FSA** (if available)
5. **Sign up for dental and vision—even if you think you won't need them**
6. **Get a quote for term life outside your employer**
7. **Check if you have long-term disability coverage—and add it if you don't**
8. **Bookmark your EAP contact info**—you never know when you'll need it

Encouragement:

Reading your benefits doesn't make you soft—it makes you smart. The toughest responders are the ones who prepare before the storm.

Reminder:

Your benefits are part of your paycheck. If you ignore them, you're leaving money—and protection—on the table.

Takeaway:

Smart first responders don't just clock in and clock out. They build a system around themselves that supports them when the job—or life—goes sideways.

Prompt to Revisit:

Every open enrollment season (usually once a year), review your benefits. Life changes, and so should your coverage.

Chapter 10: Term Life and Disability Insurance – Protecting Your Family Early

You've made it through the academy. You've got your gear, your station assignment, and your first few direct deposits. You're young, tough, and finally earning a steady paycheck.

The last thing on your mind?

What happens if you die—or can't work—tomorrow.

Let's talk about that anyway.

Because one day, someone you love might depend on you not just showing up to the next shift—but on what you've set up in case you never return.

This chapter isn't about fear. It's about **preparation**.

It's about protecting your family, your paycheck, your lifestyle, and your future—even if life throws a curveball you never saw coming.

Why Life and Disability Insurance Matter Now, Not Later

Most first responders wait too long to get serious about insurance.

They think:

"I'm healthy."

"I don't have a spouse or kids yet."

"I'm still getting settled."

"I'll deal with that when I'm older."

Here's the truth:

- Emergencies don't wait for you to be ready
- A career-ending injury can happen in your 20s
- Your family will still have bills—even if you don't make it home
- Delaying coverage makes it more expensive (or sometimes impossible to get) later

If you protect others for a living, it's time to protect the people and paycheck that matter most—**yours**.

Term Life Insurance: The Straightforward Way to Protect Your Family

Let's start with life insurance.

The kind that matters most for first responders is called **term life insurance**.

You pick a:

- **Coverage amount** (like $250,000, $500,000, or $1 million)
- **Term length** (10, 20, or 30 years)

If you die during that time, your family gets the payout.

If you outlive the term, the policy ends. That's it.

Simple. Powerful. Affordable.

Why Term, Not Whole?

You'll hear about "whole life" or "permanent life insurance." It's sold as an investment. But here's what they don't always tell you:

- It's 10x more expensive than term
- Most people cancel it early and lose money

- It's better to separate insurance from investing

Unless you have a complex estate or dependents with lifelong needs, **term life does the job better and cheaper**.

How Much Life Insurance Do You Actually Need?

Here's a rough guideline:

- **10x your annual income** if you have a spouse and/or kids
- Enough to cover:
- Debt (student loans, mortgage)
- Kids' college
- Funeral costs
- Years of income your family would miss

If you're single with no dependents? You might just want enough to cover:

- Your funeral
- Any cosigned debt
- A little cushion for your parents or siblings

But if you're married or raising kids? **You don't need life insurance. Your *family* needs it.**

Where to Get It: Through Work vs. On Your Own

Group Life Insurance (offered by your department or union):

- Easy to get—no medical exam
- Usually covers 1–3x your salary
- Often doesn't go with you if you leave the job
- Might not be enough for your full needs

Individual Term Policy (you own it):

- You choose the amount
- You choose the term
- You keep it no matter where you work
- You may need a medical exam
- Premium stays fixed for the entire term

Pro move:

Use group life as a free or cheap baseline. But get **your main protection through a personal term life policy**—ideally before you have health conditions that raise your rates.

Disability Insurance: When You're Alive—but Can't Work

If life insurance is for protecting your family when you die, disability insurance is for **protecting your paycheck when you don't.**

And this one? It's even more important—because **you're far more likely to be injured or disabled than to die early.**

Especially in this profession.

Two Types of Disability Insurance You Need to Know

1. Short-Term Disability (STD)

- Covers part of your salary (usually 60–70%)
- Begins after a waiting period (e.g., 7–14 days)
- Lasts a few months (often 3–6 months)

2. Long-Term Disability (LTD)

- Kicks in after short-term ends
- Can cover 50–60% of your pay
- May last until age 65, retirement, or return to work
- Can be tax-free if you pay the premiums yourself

What Disability Insurance Actually Covers

It depends on your policy.
Good disability coverage should:

- Replace a **significant portion of your income**
- Cover **both on- and off-duty injuries** (confirm this)
- Pay even if you can't return to your specific job—not just *any* job

Ask HR or your union:

- "Is disability insurance part of my benefits?"
- "Is it *own occupation* or *any occupation* coverage?"
- "What percent of my salary does it replace?"
- "How long is the elimination (waiting) period?"

Rookie Mistake: Relying on Workers' Comp Alone

Yes, you're covered for **on-duty injuries** through workers' comp.
But:

- It doesn't pay your full salary
- It may not cover off-duty injuries
- It often involves delays, paperwork, and fights
- It doesn't protect your long-term lifestyle

If your injury happens at the gym, on vacation, or playing with your kid in the backyard—you may be totally unprotected without private disability coverage.

Real-World Scenario: The Off-Duty Injury No One Saw Coming

You're 32, a seasoned paramedic. You twist your knee at a weekend pickup basketball game. It turns into surgery and six months of rehab.

It didn't happen on the job. Workers' comp won't help.

Your department's short-term disability barely covers rent.

Your emergency fund is drained by month three.

You're skipping retirement contributions and putting groceries on a credit card.

You don't need to die to lose your financial footing.

That's why disability insurance is **just as important as life insurance**—maybe even more.

The Cost of Coverage (And Why It's Worth It)

Term Life Insurance:

- A 30-year-old healthy non-smoker might pay:
- $15–20/month for $250,000
- $30–40/month for $500,000
- $50–70/month for $1 million

That's less than a tank of gas. Less than a dinner out.

Long-Term Disability:

- Premiums usually cost 1–3% of your salary
- You can sometimes pay through work
- Or get a private policy tailored to your job risk

It's not cheap. But it's cheaper than being broke for a year... or a decade.

Action Steps: Lock In Your Protection Today

1. **Check what coverage you already have** through your department
2. **Get a quote** for a personal term life policy (20 or 30 years)
3. **Get a disability insurance quote** if not offered through work
4. **Ask HR what happens if you're injured off duty**
5. **Name and update your beneficiaries** (and tell your spouse where your policy info is)
6. **Add coverage as your income or family size grows**

Encouragement:

You've seen the worst happen to good people. Taking care of your family isn't about paranoia—it's about honor. You've already proven you'll put yourself on the line for others. Now it's time to protect what matters most when you're not on the clock.

Reminder:

You don't need to be "older" to need life or disability insurance. You just need people who love you, bills that won't disappear, or a paycheck you can't afford to lose.

Takeaway:

Smart first responders plan ahead. They get coverage when it's cheap, simple, and available—before they need it.

Prompt to Revisit:

Revisit your coverage every 1–2 years, or after any major life change (marriage, kids, promotions, divorce, etc.).

PART II: BUILDING YEARS – Growing a Career and a Financial Base (Years 6–15)

The rookie years are behind you. You've proven yourself. The station knows your name, the rhythm of the job feels familiar, and your paycheck is starting to reflect your experience, promotions, and hard-earned overtime. But with more stability comes new complexity—and new pressure.

Part II is where you shift from survival mode to strategy.

These are the years when your financial choices start to compound. You might be raising kids, buying a home, paying off student loans, taking on side work, investing in retirement, or helping aging parents. You're being pulled in a dozen directions—and your money needs to keep up.

This section helps you:

- Avoid lifestyle inflation as your income grows
- Maximize benefits like pensions, 457(b)s, and deferred comp plans
- Make informed decisions about buying a home, investing, and protecting your family
- Build a solid emergency fund—and stop relying on overtime to patch the gaps
- Understand the financial impact of marriage, divorce, kids, and caregiving
- Create systems that serve your future, not just your present

These chapters don't lecture. They meet you in the kitchen after shift, or on the tailboard after a call—walking through real-life financial decisions with clarity, respect, and honesty.

This is where your career takes shape.

This is where your wealth-building begins.

This is where you stop just working your money—and start making your money work for you.

Let's build something that lasts.

Chapter 11: Promotions, Raises, and Overtime – What to Do with the Extra Money

Let's talk about the moment that catches a lot of people off guard—not when they get a financial setback, but when they finally get a break.

You get promoted.

Your step increase hits.

Your overtime checks start stacking up.

And for a minute, it feels like you can finally exhale.

But here's the question no one warns you to ask when the money starts flowing:

"Now what?"

This chapter is your blueprint for what to do when the money gets better—so it doesn't slip through your fingers just as fast as it arrived.

Because we've all seen it: The firefighter who picks up every OT shift for a new truck. The officer who gets a raise and suddenly feels rich—but is living check to check again three months later. The medic who worked every holiday and still can't figure out why nothing changed.

Let's talk about how to make those raises, bonuses, and extra hours actually move your financial life forward.

What "Extra" Really Means

First, let's reframe something:

That extra money? It's not **bonus money.**

It's not **fun money.**

It's not **"I deserve this" money.**

It's **leverage**. It's **momentum**. It's your **chance to build faster**.

If you treat raises and OT like a payday splurge, it disappears.

If you treat it like an opportunity, it builds everything else you want—peace of mind, freedom, a real future.

Promotions and Raises: Why They Don't Always Feel Like More

You finally get promoted. Rank goes up. Pay goes up. But somehow your stress goes up, too—and your bank account doesn't.

Why?

1. Taxes

As your gross pay increases, you may enter a higher marginal tax bracket—especially if OT pushes your income up fast. That "10% raise" might feel like 5% after deductions.

2. Lifestyle Inflation

You buy a nicer car. Upgrade your wardrobe. Take more expensive vacations. Suddenly your new paycheck just meets your new bills.

3. No Plan for the Difference

Without a system, every new dollar finds a new expense. If you don't decide what your raise will do for you, it will do whatever the world around you demands.

Step One: Know Your New Net Pay

Before you change your habits, run the numbers. Find your **take-home raise**—what's actually hitting your account after taxes, union dues, retirement contributions, and benefit adjustments.

If you just got:

- A $6,000 annual raise
- That's about $500/month gross
- But maybe only $325/month net
- That's still almost **$4,000 per year of new net money**—don't let it drift into thin air

Step Two: Divide and Direct

Use this moment to get intentional.

Use the 50/30/20 Rule (Raise Version):

- **50%** toward goals (debt payoff, investing, savings)
- **30%** toward future security (insurance upgrades, retirement contributions)
- **20%** guilt-free spending (yes, enjoy some of it—but cap it)

That means if your raise gave you $325/month net:

- $160 goes to building your future

- $100 shores up your protection and retirement
- $65 is yours to enjoy—without shame, without guilt, without going overboard

Overtime: The Trap and the Tool

Overtime can be a blessing. It's how many first responders hit their financial targets faster. But it's also where a lot of burnout and bad decisions hide.

Let's be honest: It's tempting to treat OT like a second job and a second paycheck.

But here's the key difference:

It's not guaranteed.

It's not permanent.

And if you build your life around it—you will eventually feel trapped.

Use OT for:

- One-time goals (emergency fund, car payoff, vacation savings)
- Catching up (paying off credit cards, building your Roth IRA)
- Boosting long-term investments—not for ongoing expenses

Don't use OT for:

- Affording a mortgage you couldn't cover without it
- Making the minimum payment on too many credit cards
- Stretching yourself to the edge of exhaustion

OT is fuel. Not foundation.

Real-World Scenario: The OT Spiral

A 37-year-old patrol officer has been working 60-hour weeks for years. OT covered his lifestyle. Now he's burnt out, his back is acting up, and cutting back means cutting bills.

No emergency fund. No passive income.

OT made life feel better—but never made life safer.

The lesson? Use OT while you can. But plan your life so you don't **have to.**

Step Three: Build Automatic Upgrades

You want the raise to stick? Automate it.

Here's how:

- **Split direct deposit**: Send a portion of each paycheck to savings or investment accounts
- **Auto-transfer on paydays**: $200 into your Roth IRA, $100 into your kids' college fund
- **Upgrade your retirement contributions**: If you went from contributing 5% to 8%, and you don't miss it? You win.

Use every raise as a moment to bump the system forward—not just the spending.

Step Four: Celebrate—Strategically

Yes, celebrate. You earned it.

But do it **within reason**, and **after you've taken care of the essentials.**

Examples:

- One-time bonus? Take 10–15% and spend it however you want

- Big raise? Go out for a great meal, but let the bulk of it go to wealth-building
- Promotion? Treat yourself, but also revisit your insurance, savings plan, and budget

Enjoy the reward—but build the legacy.

Pros and Cons of Common Choices

Buying a New Car with Your Raise

Pros:

- Feels good
- May replace an unreliable vehicle
- Can be used as a celebration of achievement

Cons:

- Raises your monthly fixed costs
- Insurance, taxes, and maintenance go up
- May cancel out every dollar of your raise

Better move? Buy reliable used with cash saved from OT. Or upgrade *after* other priorities are locked in.

Upgrading Your House or Taking on a Mortgage with OT

Pros:

- May reflect growing family needs
- Can feel like progress

Cons:

- OT isn't guaranteed
- A layoff, injury, or burnout could put you in financial crisis

Better move? Base your mortgage on your base salary. Use OT for down payment, moving costs, and to avoid PMI.

Increasing Retirement Contributions

Pros:

- Lower taxable income
- Long-term wealth building
- Passive growth and compounding

Cons:

- Feels invisible—no instant gratification

Better move? Start with auto-increasing contributions each year by 1% until you hit 15%–20% of your income.

Action Steps: What to Do When Your Pay Increases

1. **Know your new net pay**—not just gross
2. **Split the difference**—part for now, part for later
3. **Automate the upgrade**—savings, investing, protection
4. **Avoid locking into new monthly costs**
5. **Create a specific OT plan**—not "work more = spend more"
6. **Celebrate with intention—not regret**
7. **Adjust your budget**—and don't forget to revisit it annually

Encouragement:

You don't have to live like you're broke forever. You also don't have to go broke just because you got a raise. You've already earned the money—now it's time to let it work for you.

Reminder:

Lifestyle should rise slower than income. Let the gap build your future—not your stress.

Takeaway:

Smart first responders don't spend raises—they **deploy** them. They use OT like a scalpel, not a crutch.

Prompt to Revisit:

Every time your income increases—promotion, step bump, raise, or OT surge—ask yourself:

"How can I make this permanent progress, not temporary pleasure?"

Chapter 12: Understanding Your Pension – How It Works and Why It's Not Enough Alone

F*or the book: Financial Literacy For First Responders*

You took the job knowing it wasn't going to make you rich. But you were promised something else—**security**: A pension. A thank-you after 25 or 30 years of running toward danger.

But here's the thing no one ever said out loud at the academy:

Your pension won't be enough.

Not on its own. Not if you want options.

Not if you want peace. Not if you want freedom.

This chapter is the unfiltered, plain-English walk-through you never got when you were handed that benefits booklet on Day One. We're going to break it down—how pensions really work, why they're a gift but not a guarantee, and what you need to be doing now so you don't end up retired and worried.

What a Pension Is (And What It Isn't)

A **pension** is a defined benefit retirement plan. You work a certain number of years, contribute a portion of each paycheck, and when you retire, the system promises to pay you a monthly check for life.

Sounds simple. But there are **a lot of moving parts**, and the details matter.

What your pension depends on:

- Your years of service
- Your final average salary (often calculated over your last 3–5 years)
- A multiplier (usually 2%–3%)
- Your age at retirement
- Whether you retire early, with full benefits, or with reductions

Example:

Let's say:

- You work 30 years
- Your average salary at retirement is $80,000
- Your pension uses a 2.5% multiplier

Your formula would look like this:

30 years x 2.5% = 75%

75% of $80,000 = **$60,000/year pension**

You'll get $5,000/month before taxes for life.

That's solid. But is it enough?

Let's break it down.

Why a Pension Isn't Enough by Itself

1. No Cost-of-Living Adjustments (COLA)

Many pensions don't adjust with inflation—or they cap increases at 1–2%. That means your buying power drops every year.

2. Taxes Still Apply

You'll pay federal taxes on your pension (and maybe state taxes too). That $5,000/month could be closer to $4,200/month after taxes.

3. Healthcare Is Expensive

Most first responders retire before Medicare kicks in. You might be spending $1,000–$2,000/month on premiums and out-of-pocket health costs in your 50s and early 60s.

4. Your Lifestyle Might Have Grown

By retirement, you might have a mortgage, kids in college, or aging parents to support. That $60K pension? It might feel tight fast.

5. Pension Systems Can Struggle

Not every pension fund is healthy. Some are underfunded. Some change rules. You don't control the system—only your own backup plan.

So... What Should a Pension Be?

Think of your pension like a **base layer**. It's the foundation of your retirement income. But it's not the roof. It's not the whole house.

Your job is to:

- Understand exactly how your pension works
- Estimate how much you'll actually receive
- Build other streams of income around it

Know the Fine Print: What You Must Understand About Your Pension

Get These Questions Answered:

- What's the formula used to calculate my benefit?
- Is my pension based on my last year, 3-year, or 5-year average?
- What's my vesting period (how long until I qualify for benefits)?
- What happens if I leave before I retire?
- Can I buy service credits or military time?
- What are the survivor/spouse options if I die before or after retirement?

Get these answers in writing. Ask your HR. Ask your union. Don't guess.

The Pension "Drop-Off" Problem

You're used to a salary + OT + holiday pay + bonuses. By retirement, you've structured your life around $100K+ a year.

Then retirement hits.

And suddenly, your income drops by 30–40% overnight.

This is the gap that catches most retirees off guard.

And if you haven't built savings, investments, or side income—your pension might leave you secure... but stretched.

What You Can Do to Supplement Your Pension

Let's talk about **building the second layer** of retirement income. That way, when your pension check hits, it's not your only option—it's just the first.

1. Contribute to a 457(b) Plan

This is a retirement plan specifically designed for public employees.

Pros:

- Tax-deferred growth
- Higher contribution limits than IRAs
- Withdrawals are penalty-free if you leave the job

Auto-deposit a portion of each check and forget about it.

2. Open a Roth IRA

Fund it with post-tax dollars now. Take out tax-free income later.

Perfect for those earlier in their careers. And it's a great hedge against tax hikes in retirement.

3. Work OT for a Purpose

Use OT to fund your investment accounts, not your truck payment.

Let extra income build your freedom—not your debt.

4. Consider Income-Producing Assets

- Rental property
- A small side business
- Dividends from investments

These can create "third rail" income alongside your pension and retirement accounts.

Real-World Scenario: The Lieutenant Who Thought He'd Be Fine

He had 28 years in. Retired at 52. Pension was $68,000/year.
It sounded great—until:

- He had to pay $1,400/month for COBRA
- His spouse lost coverage too
- They had one kid still in college
- Inflation hit their grocery and gas bills hard

He didn't save enough outside the pension. Now he's working part-time at a hardware store—not because he wants to, but because he has to.

The pension wasn't the problem. The **lack of a plan** around it was.

Action Steps: Strengthen Your Future Today

1. **Get your pension estimate from HR or your union**
2. **Ask about vesting, years required, and early retirement penalties**
3. **Open a 457(b) and/or Roth IRA and automate contributions**
4. **Calculate your post-retirement budget—including healthcare**
5. **Map out what income you'll need *above* your pension**
6. **Don't rely on OT or DROP programs as your only backup**
7. **Talk with your spouse about retirement expectations now**

Encouragement:

You've already earned your pension—it's a gift most private-sector workers don't get. But don't treat it like a lottery ticket. Treat it like a powerful tool that needs a few more pieces to become a full plan.

Reminder:

Retirement isn't about a date—it's about having enough income to walk away without fear.

Takeaway:

Smart first responders use their pension as a base—but they build the rest themselves, with consistent contributions and calm, steady systems.

Prompt to Revisit:

Every 1–2 years, check your pension projection. Update your supplemental plan. Life shifts. Your pension won't. But your plan can.

Chapter 13: What's a 457(b), 403(b), Roth IRA, Traditional IRA?

Retirement Options Explained for First Responders

From the book: Financial Literacy For First Responders (Firefighters, Police, Paramedics)

You wear a uniform. You show up when things fall apart. You've earned every dollar that hits your account. But what happens when the job is behind you?

That's what this chapter is about: *retirement*. Not the fantasy. Not the daydream. The **real**, practical, build-it-yourself version that depends on more than just your pension.

Because here's the truth most first responders never hear until it's too late:

If your retirement plan starts and ends with your pension—you're probably going to come up short.

You need a second layer. Sometimes a third.

And luckily, that's exactly what accounts like the **457(b)**, **403(b)**, **Roth IRA**, and **Traditional IRA** are for.

Let's break them down clearly, one at a time.

No fluff. No jargon. Just straight answers.

Retirement Accounts in Plain English

Before we get into the names and acronyms, here's a big-picture truth:

All retirement accounts are simply **containers**.

They're buckets.

What makes each one different is:

- **Who can use it**
- **How it's taxed**
- **What the rules are for putting money in and taking it out**

Let's start with the one most first responders have access to but don't fully understand.

The 457(b): A First Responder's Secret Weapon

This account was made for public employees—exactly like you.

You contribute **pre-tax dollars** from your paycheck. That money grows tax-deferred, and you pay taxes only when you take it out in retirement.

Why it's powerful:

- Higher contribution limits than an IRA
- You can access the money *without a penalty* if you leave the job—**even before age 59½**
- Payroll deductions make it easy and automatic

Who gets it?

- Firefighters
- Police officers
- Paramedics
- Most public employees

Ask your HR rep or benefits coordinator if your department offers one.

If they do, you **should be using it.**

Contribution limits (as of this writing):

- Up to **$23,000/year** if under 50
- An extra **$7,500/year** if you're 50+

You can contribute tens of thousands *per year* and build serious wealth if you stick with it.

The 403(b): The 457(b)'s Quiet Cousin

You'll often see 403(b) plans offered by public school systems, hospitals, and nonprofits. Some first responders—especially those tied to municipal hospitals or training academies—may have access to both a **403(b)** and a **457(b)**.

Yes, you can contribute to both at the same time.

They work similarly:

- Tax-deferred growth
- Funded through paycheck deductions
- Limits are the same

The biggest difference is that **early withdrawals from a 403(b) may have penalties** before age 59½—**not true for the 457(b)**.

If you have both? Use the 457(b) first for flexibility.

The Roth IRA: Tax-Free Income Later

This is where things shift.

Unlike the 457(b), a **Roth IRA** uses *after-tax money*.

That means you don't get a tax break today—but everything it earns grows **tax-free**.

And when you retire, the money you take out? **Tax-free. Forever.**

That's huge.

Especially if:

- You expect to be in a higher tax bracket later
- You want to diversify your tax exposure
- You value control and flexibility in retirement

Who can use it?

Anyone with earned income **below the income limits** (ask your tax pro or check current guidelines).

2025 contribution limits:

- $7,000/year if under 50
- $8,000/year if 50+

You can't contribute as much as with a 457(b), but it's **yours**, not tied to your employer, and **it grows with you no matter where you go.**

The Traditional IRA: Old School But Still Useful

This is the **original** retirement account.

It works like this:

- You contribute **pre-tax** money (sometimes deductible, depending on your income)
- The money grows tax-deferred
- You pay taxes when you take it out

In many ways, it's like a mini 457(b)—but without the higher limits or the "no penalty withdrawal" option.

Most helpful if:

- You don't have a 457(b)
- You're self-employed or in a side business
- You want another bucket to save pre-tax

So Which One Should You Use?

That depends on:

- Your job
- Your income
- Your goals
- How much you want to save

Here's a simple, no-fluff game plan:

If You're a First Responder With a 457(b):

1. **Max out your 457(b)** to reduce taxes and build fast
2. **Open a Roth IRA** to give yourself tax-free income later
3. **Only then** consider a Traditional IRA or 403(b) if available

If You Don't Have a 457(b):

1. **Start with a Roth IRA**
2. Then **open a Traditional IRA**
3. Then look for other investment vehicles (brokerage accounts, real estate, etc.)

Why You Want Multiple Buckets

Let's say you're 60, getting ready to retire. You've got:

- A pension (taxable)
- A 457(b) (taxable)
- A Roth IRA (tax-free)

You can now **mix and match** your withdrawals.

Need extra cash one year? Pull from the Roth—no tax spike.

Pension income too low? Supplement from the 457(b).

It's called **tax diversification**, and it's one of the smartest moves you can make.

Real-World Scenario: The Fire Captain Who Used All Three

By age 40, a fire captain had:

- $220,000 in his 457(b)
- $90,000 in his Roth IRA
- $50,000 in a Traditional IRA

He retired at 55 with a pension and full healthcare.

Because he built *multiple accounts,* he:

- Took 457(b) withdrawals to bridge the gap until Social Security
- Used the Roth to pay for a daughter's wedding—tax-free
- Left the Traditional IRA alone until Required Minimum Distributions kicked in

He had options. And **options are what financial freedom feels like**.

Common Mistakes to Avoid

- Only relying on your pension
- Ignoring the Roth IRA
- Not contributing early enough
- Treating your 457(b) like a checking account
- Forgetting to update beneficiaries
- Letting your accounts sit in low-performing investments

Retirement savings is not just about *saving*. It's about **strategically using the tools available to you.**

Action Steps: Get Your Retirement Accounts Working for You

1. **Ask HR which retirement plans you're eligible for**
2. **Start contributing something—even $50/month—to your 457(b)**
3. **Open a Roth IRA online through a trusted provider**
4. **Automate your contributions** to both
5. **Review your investment options** within your plan
6. **Meet with a fiduciary financial advisor** to align your strategy with your goals
7. **Revisit annually**—increase your contributions as raises or OT increase

Encouragement:

Retirement doesn't come with guarantees. But every dollar you put aside now buys you freedom later. Even if it's small. Especially if it's consistent.

Reminder:

Don't wait until you're 50 to take this seriously. A 24-year-old firefighter putting away $200/month today will have more than someone who starts at 40 with $500/month.

Takeaway:

Your pension is part of the plan. But real financial independence comes from layering in other retirement accounts—and using them with purpose.

Prompt to Revisit:

Set a calendar reminder for every January and July. Check your balances. Revisit your contributions. Adjust to your life, your income, your future.

Chapter 14: Compounding: The Power Tool You Can't Afford to Ignore

Let's start with this: If you're reading this and you're under 40, this chapter is a gold mine. If you're over 40, it's still a gold mine—but now it's a little more urgent.

The most powerful force in your financial life isn't your pension. It's not your overtime. It's not your rank.

It's **compounding.**

And the earlier you understand how it works, the sooner you can put it to work for you.

What Is Compounding?

Compounding is when your money earns money—and then that money also earns money. Over time, your money doesn't just grow. It grows on itself. It multiplies.

Think of it like a fire:

- In year one, you light a match. Not much heat.
- In year five, you have a steady flame.
- In year fifteen, you're throwing off sparks.
- In year thirty, you've got a roaring blaze.

Compounding is the reason why starting small, early, and consistently can beat starting big but late.

Real-World Example: Two First Responders, Two Timelines

Firefighter #1 (Starts at 25):

- Invests $200/month into a Roth IRA for 10 years
- Then stops
- Total invested: $24,000
- Lets it grow until age 60

Firefighter #2 (Starts at 35):

- Waits until OT picks up
- Invests $200/month until age 60
- Total invested: $60,000

At a modest 7% annual return:

- Firefighter #1 ends up with **more money**
- Firefighter #2 invested more, for longer—and still ends up behind

Why? Compounding had more time to cook for Firefighter #1.
Time matters more than amount.

Where Compounding Works for You

1. Retirement Accounts (457(b), Roth IRA, etc.)

The earlier you contribute, the more time your dollars have to double.

2. Debt Repayment (But In Reverse)

Compounding works against you with high-interest debt. That's why credit card balances spiral—you're paying interest on interest.

3. Emergency Fund Interest (Even at Low Rates)

It won't make you rich, but even 3% in a high-yield savings account is better than 0% in a checking account.

The Rule of 72

This is a shortcut to understand how long it takes your money to double.

Take 72 and divide it by your rate of return.

If your investments earn 6%:

- 72 / 6 = 12
- Your money doubles every 12 years

So $10,000 becomes:

- $20,000 in 12 years
- $40,000 in 24 years
- $80,000 in 36 years

Without adding a single dollar more.

The OT Illusion vs. The Compound Effect

You can make a quick $1,000 in a weekend of overtime.

But if you invest $500/month for 25 years?

- At 7%, you'll have over **$380,000**

That's the long game. And the long game *always* wins.

Common Misunderstandings

"I'll start when I make more."

By then, you've lost your most valuable asset: time.

"I can't afford to invest right now."

You can't afford *not* to. Even $25/month gets the machine started.

"I'll work longer to make up for it."

That only works if you can. Health, burnout, family? Not always under your control.

Action Steps: Start Compounding Today

1. **Open a Roth IRA or 457(b)** immediately if you haven't already
2. **Automate** monthly contributions, even if it's small
3. **Avoid high-interest debt** like the plague
4. **Reinvest your earnings**
5. **Leave the money alone**

Don't try to outsmart the system. Let the system do its thing. Slowly. Steadily. Powerfully.

Pros and Cons of Compounding

Pros:

- Builds wealth passively
- Rewards consistency over brilliance
- Requires no special skill, just time and discipline

Cons:

- Takes patience
- Easy to interrupt with early withdrawals
- Doesn't feel exciting in the early years

But that's the point. It's **boring now so it can be amazing later.**

Real-World Scenario: The Medic Who Left Their Roth Alone

A 26-year-old paramedic starts investing $150/month into a Roth IRA. Never increased it. Never touched it. Just let it run.

By 60? It's over $240,000.

They forgot about it. But it didn't forget them.

Encouragement:

The most powerful financial tool you have isn't your income. It's your consistency.

Reminder:

Money that earns while you sleep is what gives you freedom while you're awake.

Takeaway:

Compounding isn't flashy. But it works 24/7, never calls in sick, and always shows up.

Prompt to Revisit:

Every year, increase your contribution by 1%. That's it. Set a calendar reminder and let the compound machine do the rest.

This chapter isn't just a financial strategy. It's a mindset.

First responders train. Compounding is your money training itself to work for you—day in, day out, without needing backup.

Put it to work. Let it grow. And watch how far it can take you.

Chapter 15: Marriage and Money: Merging Finances with a Spouse in a High-Stress Job

You carry trauma. You carry unpredictability. You carry long hours and missed holidays. And now, you carry a marriage too?

This chapter isn't about romance. It's about logistics. It's about making sure that when you build a life with someone, you don't let money become the wedge that breaks it apart.

Because here's the reality:

Many first responders split up *not* because they didn't love each other—but because they didn't know how to share money, manage stress, or plan together.

Let's make sure that's not your story.

Why Marriage and Money Feels Harder for First Responders

1. Your Schedule Is Demanding

- Days bleed into nights
- Missed birthdays and anniversaries
- You're not always there for money talks when they happen

2. You Carry Emotional Weight

- Calls that mess with your head
- Tragedies that stick with you
- You sometimes shut down at home to stay strong at work

3. Your Income Can Be Variable

- Base pay, OT, bonuses, extra-duty gigs
- Makes budgeting inconsistent

4. Your Spouse Might Not Understand the Culture

- The brotherhood/sisterhood
- The adrenaline
- The exhaustion

So you have to over-communicate. Especially about money.

Common Financial Clashes Between First Responders and Spouses

1. Different Spending Styles

One of you wants to save every dime. The other wants to enjoy life while they're still young. Both have a point. Both need compromise.

2. Combining Finances Too Soon (or Not Soon Enough)

You got married and just threw it all into one account without talking about it. Or you kept everything separate and now your spouse feels left out.

3. Unspoken Assumptions

You assumed your spouse would handle the bills. They assumed you would save for retirement. No one did either.

4. Power Struggles Over Income

If you make more, do you get more say? If they stay home with kids, are they still an equal partner? Yes, yes, and it still takes work.

Should You Combine Finances?

There's no one right answer. But you *do* need to agree on your system.

Option 1: Fully Combined

All money goes into joint accounts. Total transparency. Shared responsibility.

- Pro: Unified approach
- Con: Can lead to fights if one partner overspends

Option 2: Partially Combined

Shared household account + separate personal accounts

- Pro: Allows freedom within structure
- Con: Requires planning and boundaries

Option 3: Completely Separate

Each person pays a share of expenses and handles their own accounts

- Pro: Less conflict over spending
- Con: Can feel like roommates, not partners

Whichever path you choose, make sure it's mutual, clear, and revisited yearly.

Real-Life Scenario: Officer + Nurse = Confusion

An officer and his spouse, a nurse, both worked high-stress shift jobs. He handled day-to-day bills. She handled savings. They never talked.

Fast forward five years:

- Duplicate insurance policies
- Missed payments on student loans
- No shared retirement plan

All avoidable. If they'd had one financial check-in per month, they'd have been on the same page.

The Marriage Money Checklist

1. **Know Each Other's Numbers**

- Credit scores
- Student loans
- Monthly expenses
- Retirement balances

1. **Set a Shared Budget**

- Use software (YNAB, Mint) or paper
- Account for irregular income and OT

1. **Define Financial Roles**

- Who pays the bills?
- Who handles insurance?
- Who tracks investments?

1. **Have a Monthly Money Talk**

- Casual
- Short
- No blame

1. **Plan for Big Stuff**

- Kids
- Home buying
- Retirement goals
- Aging parents

1. **Write Down Goals Together**

- "Save $10K for a down payment"
- "Pay off credit cards by 2027"
- "Visit Italy for our 10-year anniversary"

Unique Challenges for Dual-First Responder Couples

When both spouses are in the job, it's even more complicated:

- Double pensions to track

- Rotating shifts with childcare stress
- Increased burnout risk
- Higher insurance needs

Have contingency plans. Build in more buffer. Check in more often.

Marriage and Financial Stress: Don't Let It Build Unspoken

Money fights aren't about dollars. They're about:

- Feeling heard
- Feeling safe
- Feeling in control

You wouldn't ignore an argument in the field. Don't ignore it at home. Therapy isn't weakness. Financial coaching isn't shame. Get help early.

Action Steps: Merge Your Financial Life Wisely

- Schedule a monthly "money roll call"
- Build a household budget with categories for self-care
- Agree on thresholds: "Anything over $300, we talk about it first."
- Designate one person to track goals, another to track bills
- Revisit your beneficiaries annually
- Create a shared financial folder: wills, insurance, account logins, emergency contacts

Encouragement:

You show up for your community every day. Show up for your marriage, too.

Reminder:

Marriage isn't just about love. It's about logistics. And shared logistics build lasting love.

Takeaway:

The strongest couples aren't always the ones who agree on everything. They're the ones who keep showing up, adjusting, and building a plan together.

Prompt to Revisit:

Make this chapter part of your anniversary tradition. Read it together. Update your plans. Dream a little.

Final Thought

Marriage in this job isn't easy. But neither is anything else you've done.

You ran into burning buildings. You responded to shootings, crashes, overdoses.

You can handle a money talk with your spouse.

Especially if it means a stronger marriage, a safer family, and a better future.

This isn't just about combining paychecks.

It's about building a life that honors the person you love *and* the person you serve alongside every day.

And that's a mission worth showing up for.

Chapter 16: Buying a Home as a First Responder: How Much Can You Really Afford?

If you're reading this, you might be thinking: "I'm ready to stop paying someone else's mortgage. I'm ready to buy my own place."

You're not alone. Most first responders, somewhere between year 3 and year 10 on the job, start thinking about homeownership. It feels like the next step. It feels like putting roots down. And in some ways, it is.

But here's what no one tells you: just because you *can* qualify for a mortgage doesn't mean you can *afford* that mortgage.

This chapter is about finding the difference between what a lender approves—and what your real life supports.

The Lender Doesn't Know Your Life

When a mortgage lender looks at your finances, they don't see:

- Your erratic overtime schedule
- Your shift fatigue
- Your kids' braces and summer camp
- The strain of back-to-back night shifts and side gigs

They see your base pay. Maybe your last two years of tax returns. They look at your debt-to-income ratio and tell you how much you "can borrow."

But you're not trying to borrow. You're trying to live.
Big difference.

Step 1: Know Your Real Budget, Not Just the Bank's

If the bank says you can afford $2,500/month... ask yourself:

- Can I still max out my retirement plan if I pay that?
- What happens if OT drops next year?
- What if I want to start a family? Or send kids to private school?

Homeownership isn't just the mortgage. It's:

- Property taxes
- Insurance
- Repairs and maintenance
- Furniture and utilities
- Emergency reserves for the water heater that dies during a blizzard

A Better Rule of Thumb for First Responders

The 28/36 Rule (Adjusted for Reality):

- **28%** of your gross income = max housing cost
- **36%** of your gross income = total debt payments (car, credit card, student loan, etc.)

But here's the adjusted version:

- Cap your housing at **25%** of *base* salary
- Don't count OT unless it's consistent and predictable
- Budget using your "low month" income, not your best-case scenario

Why? Because unpredictability is part of this job. Budget for reality.

Rent vs. Buy: The Hidden Costs and Hidden Freedom

Pros of Buying:

- Equity buildup over time
- Tax benefits (potentially)
- Stability if staying in one area
- Pride of ownership

Cons of Buying:

- Property taxes and maintenance
- Less flexibility if transferred or promoted to another district
- Large upfront costs (down payment, inspection, closing)
- Possible decline in home value

Pros of Renting:

- Flexibility
- Fewer responsibilities
- May be cheaper month-to-month depending on the market

Cons of Renting:

- No equity built
- Rent can go up
- Less control over space or upgrades

If your station assignment might change, or if your spouse might relocate for work, or if you're planning to start a business—you might want to rent a bit longer.

Real-World Story: Rookie Cop Buys Too Fast

A 25-year-old patrol officer, single, buys a $400,000 home at the top of his approval range. He's excited. It's new. It's close to the station.

Year 1: He can handle it, with lots of overtime.

Year 2: He tears a ligament during a call. Light duty. OT gone.

Year 3: Misses three mortgage payments. Foreclosure notice.

What went wrong? He bought based on *hopeful income*, not stable income.

Home Affordability Checklist

1. **Can you put down at least 10%?** (20% avoids PMI)
2. **Do you have 3-6 months of expenses saved post-closing?**
3. **Is your credit score above 680?** (lower rate = lower monthly)
4. **Will your monthly cost be under 25% of base income?**
5. **Can you still fund retirement and emergency savings after buying?**

If you answer NO to any of these, you may not be ready—yet.

Programs for First Responders

Look into:

- First-time homebuyer grants
- Local down payment assistance programs
- State programs for public servants
- VA loans (if you're a veteran)
- Good Neighbor Next Door (HUD)

These can reduce your upfront costs and improve terms.

But they still don't remove the need for a strong budget.

Don't Fall in Love With a House Before You're Financially Ready

Yes, the kitchen is perfect. The yard is great. The garage fits your squad car.

But if you stretch too far to buy it:

- You can't sleep at night
- You can't travel
- You can't say yes to overtime *without* needing it to survive

A home should be a blessing, not a burden.

Action Steps Before You Buy

- Check your credit and improve it if needed
- Track 6 months of spending
- Get pre-approved, but set your own cap
- Talk with a spouse or partner about long-term goals
- Build a 6-month emergency fund *before* moving in
- Don't rush. The housing market isn't going anywhere

Encouragement:

You don't need to own a home to be successful. You need to live below your means, invest early, and build a solid life plan.

Reminder:

A bank will always lend you more than you should take. Your job is to say no before it becomes a trap.

Takeaway:

The smartest first responders buy *less house than they can afford* and *more insurance than they think they need.*

Prompt to Revisit:

Review your housing goals each time your life changes—promotion, baby, divorce, relocation. Your strategy should evolve.

This chapter isn't anti-homeownership.

It's pro-readiness. Pro-freedom. Pro-you.

Because the person who runs toward danger deserves a home that brings peace—not pressure.

Chapter 17: Homeowners Insurance, Auto Insurance, and Umbrella Coverage—A First Responder's Liability Toolkit

You run toward burning buildings. Toward gunfire. Toward accidents and emergencies.

You don't flinch. But that doesn't mean you're bulletproof financially.

Your job puts you in the line of fire—physically, emotionally, and legally. One wrong move in your personal life, one accident off-duty, one lawsuit from a fender-bender or a neighborhood kid slipping on your porch—and your financial future could be toast.

This chapter is your shield. Your liability toolkit. Let's break down how you protect yourself, your family, and everything you're building with smart insurance.

Why First Responders Have Unique Liability Risks

You might be thinking: "I already have insurance through work." Sure. But...

- You drive more, and often at odd hours
- You're more visible in the community

- You might carry personal or professional liability
- You're a target in some civil suits just for being in uniform
- You work shifts that make it easy to miss details in policies or updates

So let's start from the top and build your toolkit right.

Homeowners Insurance: What You Need to Know

Whether you own a condo, a starter house, or a four-bedroom with a backyard, homeowners insurance is non-negotiable. But most first responders don't understand what it really *does.*

What It Covers:

- Your home's physical structure (roof, walls, etc.)
- Personal property (furniture, clothes, electronics)
- Liability if someone gets hurt on your property
- Living expenses if your home is unlivable after a disaster

What to Watch Out For:

- **Replacement cost vs. actual cash value**: Get replacement cost if you can. It pays what it costs to replace, not the depreciated value.
- **Coverage limits**: Don't underinsure. Rebuild costs may be higher than market value.
- **Deductibles**: Higher deductibles lower premiums, but could bite you in a storm.

Add-ons (a.k.a. Riders):

- Jewelry, collectibles, firearms (not always covered fully)
- Identity theft protection
- Sewer backup or flood insurance (not standard)

First Responder Tip:

If you keep gear at home—including duty boots, radios, or EMT equipment—make sure it's covered. Some policies limit coverage on "work equipment."

Auto Insurance: You're Not Driving Like Everyone Else

Long hours. Late nights. Early mornings. Secondary jobs. Training commutes.

Your vehicle is your second office, even if it's not a squad car.

Coverage Types:

- **Liability** (Required): Covers injuries/damage you cause to others
- **Collision**: Covers damage to *your* vehicle
- **Comprehensive**: Covers theft, vandalism, natural disasters
- **Uninsured/Underinsured Motorist**: If the other driver doesn't have enough coverage
- **Medical Payments (MedPay)** or **Personal Injury Protection (PIP)**: Covers your injuries

First Responder Risk:

You might face lawsuits even for minor fender benders—especially if someone recognizes you from your profession.

Don't skimp. $25,000 in coverage won't go far in a real accident.

Recommended Coverage Levels:

- Bodily injury: At least $100,000 per person / $300,000 per accident
- Property damage: At least $100,000
- Collision/comprehensive deductible: $500 or $1,000 depending on

emergency savings

Umbrella Insurance: Your Financial Kevlar

What Is It?

Umbrella insurance adds an extra layer of protection *on top* of your homeowners and auto policies.

Example:

You're in a car accident. You're sued for $600,000. Your auto policy only covers $300,000. Without an umbrella policy, you're personally responsible for the rest.

Why You Need It:

- You're in a high-visibility career
- You likely own a home, have savings, or plan to retire with a pension
- You have something to lose

Coverage Amounts:

- Start with $1 million
- Add more if your net worth climbs or you own rental properties

Cost:

Usually $150 to $300/year for $1M in coverage. It's one of the best deals in the insurance world.

Real-World Scenario: Off-Duty EMT Sued

An off-duty EMT hosted a backyard BBQ. A neighbor's kid slipped on wet pavement and broke an arm. Parents sued. Homeowners policy capped out at $300K. Verdict? $475K.

Umbrella policy? None.

He lost savings and part of his deferred comp.

This happens. It's not paranoia. It's prevention.

How to Build Your Liability Toolkit

Step 1: Review your policies

- Pull your homeowners and auto policies
- Check limits, exclusions, and deductible amounts

Step 2: Get quotes

- Contact your union rep, a broker, or online comparison tools
- Price out umbrella coverage today

Step 3: Update regularly

- New baby? New side hustle? New house? Update coverage
- Don't "set and forget" policies for 10 years. The world changes fast.

First Responder-Specific Discounts and Bundles

Ask for:

- First responder bundles
- Union or professional association deals
- Defensive driving course discounts

- Home security discounts (alarms, cameras, smart locks)

The Emotional Side: Insurance as Peace of Mind

You're the protector. But who protects you?

Your partner deserves peace of mind that if something goes wrong, they won't lose the house.

Your kids deserve to know their future isn't at risk because of one freak accident.

You deserve to sleep well after shift, knowing your bases are covered.

Final Checklist

- Is my home insured for rebuild cost, not market value?
- Do I have enough auto liability to avoid wiping out savings?
- Is my deductible an amount I could pay tomorrow?
- Have I priced out umbrella insurance?
- Do I review policies annually or after major life changes?

Encouragement:

You protect everyone else for a living. Taking one hour to protect yourself is a powerful act of leadership.

Reminder:

Insurance isn't about fear. It's about *function*.

Takeaway:

The smartest first responders don't just rely on their employer's policies. They build personal protection plans that hold up under pressure.

Prompt to Revisit:

Mark your calendar for an annual insurance checkup. If your life changes, your protection plan should, too.

Because when things go wrong, it won't be your badge that saves your finances. It'll be your preparation.

Chapter 18: Loan Forgiveness and Tax Strategies for First Responders

Let's sit down off-shift for a real conversation about two big topics that often confuse and overwhelm: student loans and taxes. You didn't get into this line of work for a windfall. You signed up to serve, to show up when others run the other way. But that doesn't mean you should sacrifice your financial security in the process.

This chapter is about putting two powerful tools in your toolkit—loan forgiveness and tax strategy—and showing you how they can support your long-term wealth building. Whether you're a rookie still figuring out how to read your paycheck stub or a seasoned officer juggling college tuition bills for your kids, this chapter will meet you where you are.

THE LOAN FORGIVENESS LANDSCAPE

Public Service Loan Forgiveness (PSLF): Your Golden Ticket (Maybe)

If you've got federal student loans and you work full-time for a government agency—police department, fire department, EMS unit, or even in certain nonprofit hospitals—you could be eligible for Public Service Loan Forgiveness (PSLF). Here's what that means:

- You make 120 qualifying payments (they don't have to be consecutive).
- You're on a qualifying repayment plan (like an Income-Driven Repayment plan).
- You work for a qualifying employer (most public employers qualify).
- You submit the PSLF Employment Certification Form regularly.

After those 120 payments (that's 10 years if you're making consistent monthly payments), the remaining balance on your federal Direct Loans is forgiven—tax-free.

Why You Should Care

A firefighter who started out with $80,000 in federal loans and paid $300 a month under an income-driven plan could potentially see over $50,000 forgiven after 10 years. That's life-changing.

But here's the catch: PSLF has strict documentation rules. Many first responders who thought they qualified got denied because they didn't fill out forms correctly or were on the wrong repayment plan.

TIPS TO STAY ON TRACK WITH PSLF:

- Submit your PSLF employment form every year—or anytime you change employers.
- Use FedLoan Servicing's PSLF Help Tool (until it fully transitions to MOHELA).
- Stick with Income-Driven Repayment (IDR) plans like PAYE, REPAYE, IBR, or ICR.

OTHER LOAN FORGIVENESS OPTIONS

Income-Driven Repayment Forgiveness

Even if you're not eligible for PSLF, sticking with an income-driven repayment plan can lead to forgiveness after 20 or 25 years (depending on the plan). The forgiven balance may be taxable—unless you qualify for one-time waivers or specific hardship provisions.

Perkins Loan Cancellation

If you have older Perkins loans, some public safety jobs (especially firefighters and law enforcement) may qualify for partial or full cancellation over time.

State and Local Forgiveness Programs

Several states offer student loan forgiveness or repayment assistance for law enforcement officers, firefighters, and EMTs. These can include grants, loan repayment assistance, or annual tax credits. Check with your HR department, union reps, or state education department.

TAXES FOR FIRST RESPONDERS: STRATEGY > SURVIVAL

Let's shift gears to taxes. Most first responders overpay their taxes—or underutilize deductions—because they were never taught the rules. And tax software isn't smart enough to understand the nuance of your life.

THE MOST COMMON MISTAKES:

1. Not adjusting W-4 withholding after OT or promotion.
2. Missing out on job-related deductions like union dues or uniforms.
3. Not tracking secondary income (like off-duty security or training gigs).
4. Filing married jointly when separately would reduce your student loan payment.
5. Ignoring HSA/FSA contributions that lower taxable income.

Let's fix that.

UNDERSTANDING YOUR TAX BRACKET

You're not taxed the same on every dollar. Your tax rate increases as your income goes up. This means the first $10K you earn may be taxed at 10%, the next $30K at 12%, and so on.

So what?

If you work a ton of OT and suddenly get bumped into a higher bracket, your next dollar earned is taxed more heavily. That's why a tax strategy isn't just for rich people—it's for people with variable income. Like you.

TAX TOOLS THAT WORK FOR FIRST RESPONDERS

Health Savings Account (HSA)

If your department offers a high-deductible health plan (HDHP), you may be eligible to contribute to an HSA.

- Contributions are pre-tax
- Earnings grow tax-free
- Withdrawals for medical expenses are tax-free

It's the only triple-tax-advantaged account in America.

Flexible Spending Accounts (FSAs)

Use it or lose it—but FSAs let you set aside pre-tax money for medical or dependent care costs.

Retirement Accounts

457(b) plans are built for public employees like you. Here's the short version:

- You can contribute up to $22,500/year (or more if over 50).
- Withdrawals are taxed, but you're deferring income today while in a higher bracket.
- 457(b)s allow penalty-free withdrawals before age 59 1/2 if you separate from service.

403(b) plans are similar to 401(k)s and are more common in nonprofit or educational EMS.

Roth IRA vs. Traditional IRA

A Roth IRA is taxed now, grows tax-free, and comes out tax-free later. Great if you think your future tax bracket will be higher. Traditional IRAs are tax-deferred. The right choice depends on your income today versus expectations later.

ACTION PLAN: 10 TAX MOVES TO CONSIDER THIS YEAR

1. Max out your HSA if eligible.
2. Contribute at least enough to your 457(b) to get your department's match.
3. Track your union dues, gear, and job-related continuing ed.
4. Log every side job and file estimated quarterly taxes if needed.
5. Adjust your W-4 after a big promotion or bonus.
6. Consult a CPA or EA who works with public safety professionals.
7. Review filing jointly vs. separately if your spouse has student loans or large deductions.
8. Evaluate Roth vs. Traditional retirement strategies based on your

income.

9. Keep a digital "tax binder"—W-2s, receipts, 1099s, insurance premiums, mortgage interest.
10. Review your past two years of returns for missed deductions.

REAL-WORLD SCENARIOS

Case Study 1: Police Officer in Year 7

You've been making IDR payments since graduation. You just realized you never submitted a PSLF employment form. Good news: you can retroactively certify past employment. That puts you back on track.

Case Study 2: Firefighter with a Side Hustle

You train rookies on the weekends and get paid cash. If you're not reporting it, you could be risking an audit. Use a separate bank account, report it as 1099 income, and write off your gear and mileage. Better to pay a little tax than face IRS penalties.

Case Study 3: Paramedic Approaching Retirement

You're maxing your 457(b), but your spouse doesn't work. Consider spousal IRA contributions to reduce your joint tax burden. And if you retire before age 59 1/2, remember you can tap your 457(b) without penalty.

PITFALLS TO AVOID

- Claiming deductions you can't substantiate
- Missing out on pre-tax benefits during open enrollment
- Letting your tax strategy be dictated by last year's refund
- Filing late or without reviewing for errors

FINAL THOUGHTS

You can't outrun taxes—but you can plan for them. And the same hustle, preparation, and grit you bring to the job can serve you well here.

Encouragement:

"You've made it through harder things than budgeting. You've got this."

Reminder:

"Financial planning isn't about being perfect. It's about staying prepared."

Takeaway:

"Smart first responders don't guess with money—they train for it, just like anything else."

Prompt to Revisit:

"Revisit this topic every 6 months. Your job evolves. So should your financial plan."

This is your blueprint. Now go take care of the financial house the same w

Chapter 19: Kids and College Savings: Starting Early with a 529 Plan

Your job is about showing up for other people—when the call comes in, you go. Fire, trauma, danger, medical emergencies, hostile situations, roadside chaos—you step into it, because that's what you signed up to do. But the same way your shift begins with preparation—checking your gear, your radio, your rig—your family deserves that same readiness when it comes to their financial future.

One of the biggest financial missions you may take on for your family is saving for your kids' college. It doesn't sound dramatic at first. But ask any parent staring down a $250,000 tuition bill how they feel, and you'll quickly realize this is one call that deserves early backup.

This chapter is about building that backup plan. Specifically, we're talking about 529 college savings plans—what they are, how they work, and why they can be one of the smartest, most flexible, and underused tools in a first responder's financial arsenal.

Why Saving for College Feels So Overwhelming

College isn't what it used to be. The cost of higher education has risen far faster than inflation or income. What was a $10,000-per-year public university cost when you graduated high school might be $30,000 by the time your kid enrolls—or more.

Add to that the unpredictable nature of shift work, overtime, promotions, and family emergencies, and it's easy to put off saving for college until "later." But here's the cold, honest truth: "Later" always shows up. And it usually brings stress.

That's why we plan early. Because you can't out-hustle compound interest.

Meet the 529 Plan: Your Financial Fire Hose

A 529 plan is a tax-advantaged investment account specifically designed to help families save for education. The basic idea is this:

- You put money in (after taxes)
- The money grows tax-free
- You can withdraw it tax-free to pay for qualified education expenses

That last part is huge. We'll break it down.

What Counts as "Qualified Education Expenses?"

529 plan funds can be used for:

- College tuition and fees
- Room and board (on-campus or off, if enrolled at least half-time)
- Books and supplies
- Computers, software, and internet access
- Some K-12 private school tuition (up to $10,000 per year per student)
- Trade schools and apprenticeships

This isn't just about four-year universities. You can use 529 funds for:

- EMT certification programs
- Fire academy tuition (if paid out of pocket)
- Technical colleges

- Culinary schools

Think of it as an education support system, not just a college fund.

The Tax Advantages of a 529

Here's why it matters so much:

- Your contributions grow tax-free
- You don't pay taxes when you take the money out (as long as it's for a qualified use)
- Some states give you a state income tax deduction or credit for contributions

If you invest $5,000 a year for 15 years and your account grows to $120,000, that growth is yours to use—not the IRS's.

What Happens If Your Kid Doesn't Go to College?

This is a common fear. What if they don't go? What if they get a scholarship? What if they join the military?

Good news:

- You can change the beneficiary to another child
- You can use it later for grad school
- You can use it for your own education
- You can leave it alone—529s have no time limit
- You can now roll over up to $35,000 into a Roth IRA for the beneficiary (with restrictions)

And if you take the money out for something unrelated? You'll pay income tax on the gains plus a 10% penalty—only on the growth, not the original contributions.

How to Open a 529 Plan

1. Choose a plan: Every state sponsors at least one. You don't have to choose your state's plan, but some give tax benefits for in-state use.
2. Open an account: Online, with a few pieces of info (your SSN, your child's SSN, address, etc.)
3. Choose your investments: Most plans offer target-date portfolios that get more conservative as your child gets closer to college.
4. Automate your contributions: Even $50 a month makes a difference.

Real-Life Example: Small Contributions, Big Payoff

Let's say you start when your kid is born. You put in $200 a month.

- That's $2,400 per year
- Over 18 years, that's $43,200
- At a 6% annual return, you'll have around $70,000

That's a car, tuition for a state university, or trade school + rent. It's options. It's freedom.

Why First Responders Should Pay Attention to This

You work long hours. You miss holidays. You put your body and mind on the line. The least your money can do is work just as hard. A 529 plan lets your dollars grow while you're on shift.

Also:

- It gives your family a conversation point about money and future planning
- It helps relieve pressure from you when college time comes
- It sets a legacy for financial thinking in your children

Action Steps

- Open a 529 plan this week
- Set up automatic monthly contributions
- Tell grandparents they can contribute for birthdays/holidays
- Revisit your contributions annually
- Learn your state's tax rules

Common Questions

Can I use it for student loans? Yes, up to $10,000 lifetime per person.

Can I use it out of state? Yes. You can use your home-state 529 at any accredited school in the country.

Is there a penalty if I use it for something else? Only on the investment earnings, and only if not for a qualified expense.

What if my kid joins the military? You can change beneficiaries, use it later, or withdraw with penalty.

What if I move? Your account goes with you.

Closing Thoughts

You don't have to save it all. You just have to start. The earlier, the better. Your child may not remember the day you opened that 529, but they will feel the impact when they're handed a college acceptance letter without a lifetime of debt attached to it.

In a job where unpredictability is the norm, planning ahead is one of the greatest gifts you can give your family.

Let your money stand at the ready, just like you do.

Chapter 20: Managing Financial Stress in a High-Risk Profession

Being a first responder is more than a career—it's a calling. It's waking up at 2:00 a.m. to help a stranger. It's dealing with trauma, making split-second decisions, and living with the aftermath. But behind the uniform, there's a paycheck that has to stretch across real-life demands—mortgages, kids, debt, insurance, groceries, and retirement planning. And unlike the stress of a tough call, financial stress doesn't clock out when your shift ends.

This chapter is for the firefighter worried about bills on top of burnout. For the police officer wondering if overtime is a blessing or a trap. For the paramedic juggling child support, credit card debt, and an aging parent's medical costs. Because in a high-stress, high-risk job, unmanaged financial pressure can become the weight that breaks you.

You've seen worse. You've been through worse. So let's talk about money—not from a place of judgment, but from a place of power. Because when you gain control over your financial life, you build peace in every other part of your world.

Why Financial Stress Hits First Responders Differently

Financial stress is common. But for first responders, it hits differently:

- **Irregular schedules and unpredictable income** (especially with

overtime, shift differentials, and side gigs)
- **High emotional toll** that can lead to impulsive spending, burnout-induced neglect, or strained relationships
- **Stigma** around asking for help—because you're supposed to be the strong one
- **Real consequences** like burnout, divorce, mental health decline, and even early retirement or disability

You might have signed up to protect your community. But protecting your wallet is just as important—because financial stress spills into your work, your health, and your family.

Section 1: Recognizing the Symptoms of Financial Stress

Financial stress doesn't always show up as an empty bank account. Sometimes it shows up as:

- Avoiding your bank statements
- Feeling a pit in your stomach every payday
- Living paycheck to paycheck despite good income
- Hiding purchases or debt from your partner
- Taking extra shifts to avoid thinking about your money problems
- Losing sleep, snapping at loved ones, or feeling constant low-grade anxiety

If you're nodding your head—don't panic. Awareness is the first step. You can't change what you won't confront.

Section 2: The Link Between Mental Health and Money

You already know your job comes with psychological trauma. But when financial stress piles on top, it becomes a dangerous cocktail. Studies show financial strain is one of the leading predictors of depression, anxiety, and even suicide.

And it becomes a cycle:

- You feel overwhelmed, so you procrastinate on bills.
- Bills pile up, so you feel more overwhelmed.
- You use spending, food, or alcohol to cope.
- Your financial situation worsens.

Breaking that cycle isn't about willpower. It's about structure.

Section 3: Building a Financial Triage Plan

When you're first on a medical scene, you assess and triage. Your finances need the same approach. Here's how to financially triage your life:

1. **Stop the bleeding:** Cancel unnecessary subscriptions. Pause spending. Stop taking on new debt.
2. **Stabilize the vitals:** Build a basic budget (more on that below). Create a simple emergency fund.
3. **Treat the wound:** Address root issues—overspending, under-earning, lack of insurance, no plan.
4. **Build resilience:** Automate savings. Start investing. Create long-term goals.

Quick Wins That Bring Quick Relief

- Cut cable and stream only what you need.
- Refinance high-interest debt.
- Ask your union or HR about financial wellness programs.
- Set up one weekly "money hour" to face your finances.

Section 4: Creating a Shift-Proof Budget

First responders often don't earn consistent pay. Overtime can balloon your check one week and disappear the next.

Here's how to budget around uncertainty:

- **Base your budget on your lowest take-home pay**, not your best-case check.
- **Split your bank accounts:**
- One for bills
- One for variable spending
- One for savings
- **Use windfalls wisely:** When OT or hazard pay hits, split it 3 ways:
- 50% to debt or savings
- 30% to future bills or goals
- 20% for guilt-free fun

Use the 70/20/10 Rule (Modified for You)

- 70% of your income = living expenses
- 20% = debt payoff and savings
- 10% = freedom fund / sanity money / family fun

Even if your percentages shift, the structure creates stability.

Section 5: Tackling Debt with Confidence

Debt doesn't make you bad at money. It makes you human. Especially when your profession often requires expensive training, delayed income, or unpredictable expenses.

Here's how to tackle it:

1. Face It All

Gather your balances, minimums, interest rates. Know what you owe.

2. Choose a Payoff Plan

- **Snowball:** Pay smallest debts first (great for motivation)
- **Avalanche:** Pay highest interest first (saves the most money)

3. Automate It

Set up recurring payments—even if small. Every dollar is a decision toward freedom.

4. Celebrate Progress

Track debt paid off. Reward yourself when balances disappear. This builds confidence.

Section 6: Talking to Your Spouse or Partner

Money stress can break a marriage—or strengthen it. But only if you talk.

Start with:

- "I've been thinking a lot about our finances. Can we talk without judgment or blame?"
- "I want us to feel more in control—not overwhelmed."
- "What do you need to feel financially safe?"

Create regular "money check-ins." It doesn't have to be hours long. Even 15 minutes every payday can change everything.

Be a team. Because resentment grows where communication is absent.

Section 7: When You Need Outside Help

You're used to being the help. But smart responders know when to call for backup.

You might benefit from:

- **A financial coach** (affordable and action-oriented)
- **A CFP (Certified Financial Planner)** if you want long-term strategy
- **A credit counselor** if your debt is overwhelming
- **Therapy** if money stress is damaging your mental health

It's not weakness. It's wisdom.

Section 8: Tools to Keep Stress Low Year-Round

Financial "Go Bag" Checklist

- Copies of your pay stubs, benefits, and pension statements
- Life insurance and disability policies
- Will and health care directives
- Budget template or app logins
- Emergency contact info for financial decisions

The First Responder Financial Calendar

- **January:** Review retirement contributions and insurance coverage
- **April:** Tax prep + plan summer spending
- **July:** Mid-year budget check-in
- **October:** Open enrollment + year-end planning
- **December:** Review progress, celebrate wins, set new goals

Consistency kills chaos.

Section 9: Teaching Your Kids About Money

Your stress can become their story—or their lesson. Start early.

- Let them earn money (chores, jobs)
- Teach them to save a portion
- Involve them in small financial decisions (grocery list, comparing prices)
- Be honest about money—not scared

You don't need to be perfect. Just intentional.

Section 10: The Long Game—Planning for Peace, Not Just Survival

You won't always be on the job. But the habits you build now shape what life looks like later.

- Retirement isn't a finish line. It's a new chapter—plan for it.
- Life insurance isn't fear-based. It's love in financial form.
- Estate planning isn't morbid. It's protection for the people you love most.

When you plan your money like you plan your calls—you reduce risk.

Final Encouragement: You've Fought Bigger Fires

You've had to hold the line under pressure. You've delivered CPR in chaos. You've calmed others in crisis.

Managing money isn't harder than that. It's just unfamiliar.

So treat it like a skill—not a character flaw.

Start today with one small move:

- Look at your last 3 bank statements
- Create a basic list of monthly bills
- Open a savings account and move $25

Then keep going.

This isn't about becoming a finance expert. It's about:

- Reducing stress
- Creating stability
- Protecting your family
- Retiring with options

You're not behind.

You're not alone.

You're not broken.

You're just not done yet.

And the best financial responders? They don't guess.

They train.

They plan.

They prepare.

Just like you've always done.

PART III: VETERAN YEARS – Maximizing Income, Benefits, and Long-Term Wealth (Years 16–25)

By the time most first responders reach years 16 through 25 of their service, they've seen a lot—on the job and at home. They've weathered financial storms, climbed the pay ladder, picked up more responsibility, and often carry the weight of both professional experience and family obligations. This phase of the book is about helping them leverage everything they've built so far—income, tenure, benefits, relationships, wisdom—and turn it into long-term financial strength, peace of mind, and generational impact.

This section is not about survival. It's about optimization. It's about making the most of your peak earning years while avoiding lifestyle creep, burnout, and financial complacency. Whether you're training the rookies now, eyeing the promotion to captain, or starting to think seriously about what retirement will look like, this part is for you.

You'll explore how to:

- Turn high overtime years into high-investment years.
- Use seniority to negotiate better benefits and protect your time.
- Max out your pension while still building outside retirement accounts.
- Plan strategically with a spouse as you enter your highest earning years.
- Balance the financial pull of college-aged kids and aging parents.
- Upgrade your insurance, estate planning, and asset protection strate-

gies.

- Begin designing your transition plan—on your terms, not the department's.

This part honors your years of sacrifice—and challenges you to be as disciplined with your money as you've been with your career. Because these are the years when smart financial systems can set you up not just for a solid retirement, but for a legacy that outlasts your final shift.

Chapter 21: Mid-Career Money Checkup: Are You on Track for Retirement?

You've made it past the rookie years. You know the weight of the badge, the back-to-back calls, the post-shift silence, and the family sacrifices. You've earned the patch, the respect, the seniority. But here's the question most first responders forget to ask in years 10 through 20 of their career:

Am I financially on track?

This chapter isn't about starting from scratch. It's about checking the map. It's about course correction. And if necessary, it's about speeding up, before the road starts turning downhill toward retirement.

If you're in your mid-career years, this is your gut-check moment. Not because you've done something wrong—but because you've still got time to make it right.

Let's go over everything you should be reviewing right now—and how to fix it if you're off-track.

1. Income Snapshot: Are You Using Your Peak Earning Years Wisely?

Most first responders see their highest earning potential between years 10 and 20. Overtime, special assignments, promotions, seniority raises—they all add up. But too often, that extra money gets eaten by lifestyle inflation. The bigger house. The newer truck. The name-brand everything.

Ask yourself:

- Has your savings rate increased along with your income?
- Is overtime helping you build wealth, or just cover new bills?
- Are you setting aside a percentage of every raise or bonus for your future?

Action Steps:

- Aim to save 15-25% of your gross income at this stage.
- Use bonuses or OT checks for one-third investing, one-third debt, one-third fun.
- Review your bank statements for spending leaks and auto-subscriptions.

2. Pension Reality Check: Don't Assume It's Enough

A pension is an incredible benefit—but it isn't a full retirement plan. Too many first responders assume their pension will replace their paycheck. It won't. Most pensions replace 40-60% of your income. And that's before taxes.

Ask yourself:

- Do you know what your pension payout will actually be?
- Have you estimated your retirement expenses with inflation in mind?
- Will you carry a mortgage or debt into retirement?

Action Steps:

- Request a pension projection from your HR department.
- Build a mock retirement budget based on today's dollars and inflate it by 3% annually.
- Start investing in a 457(b), 403(b), Roth IRA, or brokerage account to close the gap.

3. Retirement Account Checkup: Are You Contributing Enough?

This is the window where compound interest still works in your favor—

but the window is starting to shrink. The more you invest now, the less you have to scramble later.

Ask yourself:

- Are you maxing out your 457(b) or contributing at least 10-15%?
- Have you opened a Roth IRA (if income allows)?
- Are your investment allocations appropriate for your age and goals?

Action Steps:

- Increase your contributions by 1% every 6 months until it pinches.
- Rebalance your accounts annually.
- Don't just pick "target date funds" without reviewing what's inside.

4. Debt Load: Are You Managing or Drowning?

Debt is one of the biggest threats to mid-career financial stability. It creeps in quietly, often with good intentions: the second car, the home remodel, the kids' school supplies.

Ask yourself:

- What's your total monthly debt payment as a percentage of your income?
- Are you using debt strategically (0% interest, business use) or emotionally (stress spending, keeping up)?
- Do you have a clear plan to be debt-free before retirement?

Action Steps:

- Keep total debt payments (including mortgage) under 35% of your monthly income.
- Use the snowball or avalanche method to accelerate paydown.
- Avoid using OT to qualify for bigger loans—it won't be there forever.

5. Insurance Audit: Are You Protected If Things Go Sideways?

At this point in your career, you likely have a family, a mortgage, maybe aging parents. Are you covered if life throws a curveball?

Ask yourself:

- Do you have enough term life insurance to replace your income for 10-15 years?
- Do you have long-term disability insurance outside of work?
- Would an accident or off-duty injury derail your plan?

Action Steps:

- Get a term life policy equal to 10x your income, or enough to pay off your home and fund college.
- Check if your department's disability plan covers off-duty injuries.
- Consider an umbrella liability policy if your assets exceed $250K.

6. Estate Planning: Have You Put Your Wishes in Writing?

You know better than anyone—tomorrow is not promised. If you haven't done basic estate planning, now is the time.

Ask yourself:

- Do you have a will, power of attorney, and healthcare directive?
- Are your beneficiary designations up to date?
- Does your spouse/partner know how to access accounts?

Action Steps:

- Meet with an estate planning attorney for a basic package.
- Make a "financial go bag": account list, insurance info, emergency contacts.
- Revisit these documents every 3-5 years or after major life changes.

7. Mental Load: Is Money Stress Showing Up in Other Places?

Money stress doesn't always look like fear. Sometimes it looks like avoidance, irritability, insomnia, or overworking. Financial tension can strain your marriage, affect your health, or lead to burnout on the job.

Ask yourself:

- Do you avoid looking at your bank accounts or statements?
- Do money talks with your spouse end in arguments?
- Are you relying on overtime just to stay afloat?

Action Steps:

- Have a monthly "money meeting" with your spouse or accountability partner.
- Work with a financial planner who understands public service life.
- Don't ignore emotional spending triggers—they usually cost more over time.

8. Big Picture Check: Are You Building a Life You Want to Retire Into?

This is the moment where you ask not just about your money—but about your life. Are you building toward freedom? Or just treading water?

Ask yourself:

- What do you want retirement to actually look like?
- Will you be forced to get a second job in retirement just to make ends meet?
- Are you designing a legacy for your family, or just paying bills?

Action Steps:

- Write a retirement vision statement with your spouse or partner.
- Start tracking your net worth to measure real progress.

- Begin planning for post-retirement income: pensions, investments, possible part-time work.

Encouragement:

You've made it through harder things than a financial checkup. This is about control. Confidence. Clarity. No guilt. No shame. Just progress.

Reminder:

Financial planning isn't about being perfect. It's about staying prepared. Mid-career is your best shot to course-correct before the final approach.

Takeaway:

Smart first responders don't wing it with money. They run the drill. They check the gear. They prepare.

Prompt to Revisit:

Review this chapter every 6-12 months. Your career, your family, and your goals will evolve. So should your money game plan.

Because the job may be unpredictable.

But your future doesn't have to be.

Chapter 22: Advanced Investment Strategies: Index Funds, Brokerage Accounts, and Real Estate

For first responders, risk is part of the job. But when it comes to investing, the best strategy isn't running headfirst into complex trades or risky ventures. Instead, it's about building wealth with intentional systems that work while you sleep, rest, and serve your community. By the time you reach years 16 to 25 in the field, your investment strategy should reflect your maturity, responsibilities, and future goals.

Let's break down advanced investment strategies in a way that respects your intelligence and life experience—no fluff, no jargon, just tools you can use.

INDEX FUNDS: WHY SIMPLE STILL WINS

You don't need to be a stock picker to build wealth. In fact, most of the time, stock pickers don't even beat the market themselves. Index funds let you invest in the entire market—or a big slice of it—in one move. They track things like the S&P 500 or the total U.S. stock market.

Why Index Funds Work:

- **Low cost:** Fewer fees means more of your money stays invested.
- **Diversification:** You're not betting on one company or sector.

- **Passive performance:** Historically, they outperform most actively managed funds.

If you don't have time to babysit your investments (and let's be honest, you don't), index funds are your partner in growth.

Action Step:

Open or review your 457(b), Roth IRA, or brokerage account and make sure you're allocating at least part of your contributions to low-cost index funds like VTI (Total Stock Market) or FXAIX (S&P 500).

BROKERAGE ACCOUNTS: THE POWER OF TAXABLE INVESTING

Once you're maxing out your retirement accounts, it's time to start investing in a regular brokerage account. Unlike your pension, Roth, or 457(b), there are no contribution limits, early withdrawal penalties, or required minimum distributions. You get flexibility.

How Brokerage Accounts Work:

- You invest with after-tax money.
- You can buy stocks, bonds, ETFs, mutual funds, or REITs.
- You can withdraw anytime without penalties (though you may owe capital gains taxes).

This is your opportunity fund. Want to buy land later? Help your kids with tuition? Retire early? This account gives you options.

Action Step:

Set up automatic monthly investments in a brokerage account. Even $100/month, compounded over 20 years, can turn into a six-figure buffer.

REAL ESTATE: BUYING IN WITHOUT GETTING BURNED

Real estate is often pitched as a guaranteed way to get rich. But for first responders, time and bandwidth are already stretched thin. If you're going to own real estate, make sure it's a strategy—not a stressor.

Three Real Estate Routes:

1. **Your Primary Home:** Your biggest investment. Make sure it doesn't eat your entire paycheck.
2. **Rental Property:** Great for cash flow—but only if you can cover repairs, tenant turnover, and property management.
3. **REITs (Real Estate Investment Trusts):** A way to invest in real estate through the stock market—no maintenance calls or evictions.

Pros:

- Tangible asset
- Potential tax deductions and equity growth
- Passive income potential (eventually)

Cons:

- Big upfront costs
- Time and maintenance
- Market swings can hit local economies hard

Action Step:

If real estate is part of your strategy, talk to a financial planner or real estate advisor before pulling the trigger. Make sure the numbers work *after* taxes, vacancy rates, and emergency costs.

PUTTING IT TOGETHER: YOUR INVESTMENT GAME PLAN

Let's say you're in year 18 of service. You've got a pension on the horizon, some equity in your home, and kids heading toward college. Here's a smart split:

- 30% into 457(b) – tax-deferred growth
- 20% into Roth IRA – tax-free withdrawals later
- 30% into a taxable brokerage account – for flexibility
- 20% into real estate or REITs – for diversification

Adjust those numbers based on your goals and family needs, but the big idea is to build layers. Like turnout gear, you want protection, flexibility, and strength.

REAL-WORLD SCENARIO

Chris is a 42-year-old paramedic. Married. Two kids. He maxes his 457(b) and puts $300/month into a Roth IRA. He recently started putting $200/month into a brokerage account invested in an index fund. He and his spouse co-own a small rental property they bought using their HELOC five years ago.

He doesn't get fancy. He just shows up consistently.

Today, Chris has:

- $240,000 in retirement savings
- $80,000 in home equity
- $35,000 in brokerage investments
- A $300/month profit from their rental

He's not rich yet. But he's free.

ENCOURAGEMENT

You don't need to be a stock market genius. You just need a system. You already live by structure and routine on the job. Bring that same mindset to your money.

REMINDER

You're building a portfolio that won't just protect your future—it will give you the option to retire with choices, not just obligations.

TAKEAWAY

Investing doesn't have to be complicated. But it does have to be consistent. Keep it simple, stay the course, and don't chase shiny objects.

REVISIT

Check your investment strategy every 6-12 months. As your career evolves, so should your plan. Make adjustments with intention—not emotion.

And remember: even in a career where you run toward chaos, your financial plan should always move toward peace.

This is how you run toward wealth.

Chapter 23: Second Jobs and Side Hustles: Pros, Cons, and Tax Considerations

There's something about a first responder that just doesn't rest. Maybe it's the shift work rhythm. Maybe it's the adrenaline. Or maybe it's just a deep, embedded hustle mentality that says, "If I've got a few hours, I might as well be productive." That mindset leads many firefighters, police officers, and paramedics to pick up second jobs or side hustles. Some do it for extra income, some for passion, and some to build something beyond the badge. But before you throw yourself into a second job, let's talk money, time, burnout, taxes, and strategy.

Because not all side gigs are created equal. And not every extra paycheck helps your future.

WHY FIRST RESPONDERS SEEK SECOND JOBS

1. Income Boost in a Demanding Career

Let's be honest: entry- and even mid-level salaries in public service don't always match the risk, stress, or responsibility. For some, a second job is about covering basic needs. For others, it's about getting ahead—saving for a home, paying down debt, building a college fund, or investing.

2. A Need for Control

When your main job runs on chaos—alarms, calls, violence, trauma—a side hustle can give you a space where *you* make the rules. Whether it's woodworking, selling t-shirts, flipping real estate, or driving Uber, that sense of control and progress can be therapeutic.

3. Skill Diversification and Career Planning

No one wants to think about injury, burnout, or departmental politics ending their primary career too soon. But it happens. Side hustles can offer financial safety nets and create pathways to post-service life.

4. Building Wealth and Purpose

Some first responders use their second job to build generational wealth. They're not just hustling for today's bills—they're investing in a future business, real estate portfolio, or side brand that might outlive their pension.

THE PROS OF HAVING A SIDE HUSTLE

1. Extra Income Without Lifestyle Inflation (If Done Right)

This is key. If your second job just fuels more eating out, gadgets, or a bigger truck payment, you're not actually ahead—you're just working more to maintain more. But if you bank that income or use it strategically (paying off debt, investing, funding a Roth IRA), it can completely change your financial trajectory.

2. Resilience Against Job Loss or Injury

You're one injury, lawsuit, or departmental dispute away from a disrupted career. A side business with momentum can be the parachute that saves your financial future.

3. Identity Beyond the Uniform

Too many first responders wrap their whole identity in their job. A side hustle forces you to flex new muscles, try new things, meet new people, and remember that you're more than your badge number.

4. Entrepreneurial Tax Advantages

Self-employment (done right) opens doors to write-offs that can lower your tax burden: mileage, home office expenses, supplies, software, training, marketing, and even part of your phone or internet bill. More on this later.

THE CONS (AND COSTS) OF SECOND JOBS

1. Burnout Is Real

Your body is not a machine. Running 24s, flipping to a gig shift, then sleeping 4 hours and doing it again is a recipe for health problems, stress, poor decision-making, and resentment. If your second job is hurting your ability to do your first job—or show up for your family—you're paying a price that no side money can cover.

2. Taxes Can Be Tricky

Unlike your W-2 job where taxes are withheld, many side hustles pay gross income—meaning you're responsible for setting aside and paying your own taxes. And yes, the IRS expects its cut. Skip this and you could face penalties, interest, or worse.

3. Time Trade-Offs with Family and Health

What are you missing when you're at that second gig? Kids' games? Sleep? Mental rest? It's worth checking in: Are you buying financial security at the cost of your personal health or your marriage?

4. Legal Conflicts or Departmental Policy Issues

Some departments have strict rules about outside work, especially in security, private EMS, or anything that might involve your uniform or equipment. Make sure you understand your agency's off-duty work policies before you commit.

COMMON SIDE JOBS FOR FIRST RESPONDERS

- Teaching CPR, EMT, or fire science
- Personal training or wellness coaching
- Driving for Uber, Lyft, or food delivery apps
- Real estate sales or investing
- Carpentry, handyman work, or landscaping
- Creating and selling products online (Etsy, Shopify)
- Security detail or event security
- Consulting or public speaking

- Photography or videography

Each of these comes with different startup costs, time commitments, legal concerns, and income ceilings. Choose one that fits your skills, schedule, and goals.

TAX BASICS FOR SIDE GIGS

1. You're Now a Business Owner

Even if you don't file an LLC, the IRS sees you as a sole proprietor if you earn income outside your job. You're responsible for tracking revenue and expenses, estimating quarterly taxes, and reporting everything.

2. Keep Good Records

Use a separate bank account. Save receipts. Track mileage. Use bookkeeping software (even a spreadsheet will do if you're consistent).

3. Understand Self-Employment Tax

In addition to income tax, self-employed people pay the full 15.3% for Social Security and Medicare (your employer covers half of this for your main job, but here, it's all you).

4. Deduct Wisely and Honestly

Common deductions include:

- Office supplies
- Equipment
- Marketing costs
- Education or certification
- Business mileage
- Portion of your phone/internet
- Home office (if dedicated solely to business use)

Don't try to write off your personal pickup truck unless it truly qualifies. Be reasonable and accurate.

5. Use a CPA or Tax Pro

Once you start side work, taxes get complex fast. Find someone who understands small business taxes *and* public service income. They can help you avoid pitfalls and possibly save you thousands.

WHEN TO STOP THE SIDE HUSTLE

Yes, really. Here are red flags it might be time to press pause:

- Your family is always asking, "When are you home again?"
- You dread the side gig instead of enjoying it
- You're making money, but it's going to fast food and gas
- Your health, mood, or marriage is suffering
- You've hit your original financial goal

It's okay to use a side hustle as a short-term strategy. Not everything has to be a lifelong business. Know when to step back.

SYSTEMS TO MAKE IT WORK

If you decide to pursue a side job, treat it like a business. That means:

- **Schedule It**: Don't let it bleed into your whole life
- **Automate Savings**: Set a percentage to go straight into investments or debt payoff
- **Track Profit**: Revenue minus expenses—know your real earnings
- **Review Quarterly**: What's working? What's not? Adjust accordingly

QUESTIONS TO ASK YOURSELF BEFORE STARTING A SIDE JOB

- What am I trying to achieve?
- How much time do I realistically have?
- Is this hurting my main career or my family?
- Do I have a clear exit strategy?
- How will I handle the taxes?

CLOSING THOUGHTS

You didn't get into this line of work to get rich—you did it because you care, because you're tough, and because you wanted to serve. But that doesn't mean you can't build wealth, too.

A second job, done strategically, can change your life. It can be the extra push toward a debt-free life, a first home, an investment portfolio, or peace of mind.

But a second job, done reactively, can also grind you into the ground.

Don't just work more. Work smarter. Make your time serve your long-term goals.

Encouragement: You already do hard things every day. Managing a side hustle is well within your reach—as long as it serves *you*, not the other way around.

Reminder: Financial planning isn't about being perfect. It's about being intentional.

Takeaway: Don't just hustle harder—hustle with a purpose.

Prompt to Revisit: Review your side gig strategy every 6 months. Are you still aligned with your goals, or is it time to evolve?

This chapter isn't about glorifying nonstop work. It's about understanding how to turn extra effort into meaningful progress. You already serve your community.

Now let's make sure your money serves *you*.

Chapter 24: Estate Planning: Wills, Trusts, Guardianship, and Beneficiaries

Let's talk about what happens when the unthinkable happens.

Not in the heat-of-the-moment way you're used to on shift. Not in the "I got this" kind of way you say when someone's life is on the line and you rush in. I'm talking about your family's life—after you're gone.

This is estate planning.

It's not glamorous. It's not adrenaline-filled. It's not something you can slap a tourniquet on and call it good. But it's one of the most loving things you can do for the people who depend on you.

And make no mistake: if you wear a uniform, there is a higher-than-average chance that day comes sooner than you'd want. That's not morbid. That's math. And your job isn't to live in fear—it's to live prepared.

So let's break this down. What happens if you don't have a will? What's the difference between a will and a trust? Why is it dangerous to leave your pension beneficiary blank? And who's watching over your kids if something happens to you and your spouse at the same time?

Grab a coffee. This is going to feel heavy. But by the end, it'll also feel like peace of mind.

WHAT IS ESTATE PLANNING REALLY ABOUT?

Estate planning is just a fancy term for getting your legal and financial affairs in order so the people you love aren't left scrambling when you're no longer here. It ensures your money, your belongings, and your responsibilities go where you want them to—not where the court thinks they should.

It answers questions like:

- Who gets what?
- Who raises your kids?
- Who makes medical or financial decisions if you can't?
- How do you avoid legal fights among family?
- How do you protect your family from unnecessary taxes or debt?

And in the case of a first responder—it adds another layer: how do you ensure your service-related benefits, insurance payouts, and survivor pensions are distributed without delay?

THE CORE DOCUMENTS YOU NEED

1. **Will**
2. This is the baseline. It names:

- Who gets your stuff (your beneficiaries)
- Who handles the paperwork (your executor)
- Who takes care of your kids if they're minors (your guardian)

1. Without a will, the state decides. They use a generic formula, and it rarely aligns with what you would've wanted.
2. **Trust (Revocable Living Trust)**
3. A trust lets you pass assets outside of probate court (which can be expensive and time-consuming).

- It holds your property (home, accounts, etc.) while you're alive.
- You control it, but it has backup trustees if you pass.
- It can distribute assets on your terms—for example, "Pay my kids their inheritance in stages: 25% at age 25, 25% at 30, 50% at 35."
- It's private, unlike a will, which becomes public record.

1. **Power of Attorney (POA)**
2. If you become incapacitated, who pays your bills? Who can access your bank accounts? Your POA can.
3. **Healthcare Proxy / Medical Power of Attorney**
4. Who makes medical decisions for you if you can't?
5. **HIPAA Authorization**
6. If you want family to have access to your medical info, especially if they're not legally married to you, this lets the doctors talk to them.
7. **Beneficiary Designations**
8. These override your will.

- Retirement accounts (457, 403(b), IRA)
- Pension survivor options
- Life insurance

1. If your will says your daughter gets your life insurance, but the policy says your ex-spouse? Your ex gets it. Update these every few years or after major life events (marriage, divorce, birth).
2. **Guardianship Designations**
3. Especially critical for first responders with young kids. A will typically names a guardian, but you can also draft a standby guardianship form in some states to cover short-term emergencies.

WHAT HAPPENS IF YOU DON'T DO THIS?

- Your family enters probate court. That's a legal circus they'll have to endure while grieving.
- The state decides who raises your kids.
- Benefits can be delayed or lost.
- Your pension survivor benefits might not go to your spouse.
- The wrong people may get your assets.
- Family fights. Hurt feelings. Lifelong damage.

TRUSTS VS. WILLS: WHICH DO YOU NEED?

Use a **will** if:

- You have simple assets
- You don't mind your estate going through probate
- You just want a backup plan

Use a **trust** if:

- You want privacy
- You own property in multiple states
- You want to avoid probate
- You want more control over how and when assets are distributed

Most people benefit from both. A trust handles the big stuff. A will catches anything you didn't put into the trust.

ESTATE PLANNING MISTAKES FIRST RESPONDERS MAKE

1. **Leaving beneficiary forms blank**
2. Happens more than you'd think. Unclaimed benefits. Confusion. Court fights.
3. **Naming minor children as beneficiaries**
4. Minors can't directly inherit money. The court appoints someone to manage it—not always someone you'd choose.
5. **Assuming your spouse gets everything automatically**
6. That's not always how it works. Especially in blended families or second marriages.
7. **Not naming contingent beneficiaries**
8. What if your first choice dies before you?
9. **Forgetting to update documents**
10. Marriage, divorce, death, birth of children—every major life change is a reason to revisit your estate plan.
11. **Assuming your pension will take care of everything**

12. Pensions help. But they're not a plan. They're one piece.

REAL-WORLD STORY: THE BENEFICIARY FORM THAT WRECKED A FAMILY

Officer Dave passed away unexpectedly at 46. His department life insurance was worth $250,000. But he had never updated his beneficiary after divorcing his first wife. She got the check. His kids and current wife were devastated.

There was no will. No trust. The pension defaulted to his ex, too. No one could contest it because the forms were legally binding.

It took years to unravel, and the emotional scars never fully healed.

ACTION STEPS FOR FIRST RESPONDERS

- Get a will. Today.
- If you have kids or property, get a trust.
- Name guardians for your children.
- Review your beneficiary forms annually.
- Talk to your spouse about your wishes.
- Keep copies of documents in a fireproof box and with a trusted person.
- Tell your family where these documents are.
- Work with an attorney who understands public employee benefits and survivor pensions.

ESTATE PLANNING AS A FORM OF SERVICE

You serve others every day. But estate planning is how you serve your family when you can't be there physically.

It's quiet. It's responsible. It's not heroic in the public way.

But it's absolutely heroic for the people who love you.

This chapter isn't meant to scare you. It's meant to motivate you. To take action.

Not someday.

Now.

Because readiness isn't just for calls. It's for life.

And it's for afterlife.

Encouragement: You've seen people at their worst and still shown up. This is no different. You can handle this.

Reminder: Estate planning doesn't mean you're expecting to die. It means you're wise enough to plan.

Takeaway: If you don't make these decisions, the state will. And it probably won't get it right.

Prompt to Revisit: Revisit your estate plan after every major life change—marriage, divorce, birth, or home purchase. At a minimum, review it every 3 years.

Because financial readiness is part of operational readiness.

And your family deserves nothing less.

Chapter 25: How to Use Your Pension to Build Generational Wealth

Let's be honest. Most people see their pension as a finish line—a monthly check that kicks in when the gear is hung up and the alarm bell fades. But if you play it right, your pension isn't just the end of your career. It can be the beginning of your family's financial legacy. This chapter is about more than just collecting retirement income. It's about leveraging what you've earned through decades of service to build generational wealth.

For first responders, your pension is a reward for years of sacrifice. But what you do with that reward determines whether it dies with you or becomes a launching pad for the next generation. Let's get to work.

What Is a Pension Really Worth?

A pension is a promise. But like every promise, it's only as strong as the system behind it. Some first responders retire with a monthly benefit of $4,000 to $6,000. That might sound like a lot until inflation bites, healthcare costs rise, or you outlive your savings. That's why your pension should be one part of your larger strategy—not the whole plan.

Think of your pension as a steady stream. If you don't control where it flows, it'll trickle into expenses, taxes, and lifestyle inflation. If you harness it wisely, it can fund investments, protect loved ones, and create lasting security.

Using Pension Income Strategically

Your pension gives you something powerful: predictable cash flow. That predictability opens doors to:

- Real estate investments
- Life insurance policies with legacy benefits
- Gifting to children or grandchildren
- Funding a family trust
- Contributing to Roth IRAs (yes, even in retirement)

The key is to avoid using it all on day-to-day consumption. If you treat your pension like a paycheck, it'll be gone just as fast. But if you treat it like seed money, it can grow into an orchard.

Pros and Cons of Relying on a Pension

Pros:

- Predictable monthly income
- Often includes survivor benefits
- May be inflation-adjusted (COLA)
- Doesn't fluctuate like the stock market

Cons:

- Not always enough to cover all expenses
- May reduce or eliminate Social Security benefits
- Vulnerable to changes in local/state pension policy
- Usually stops after your spouse passes (unless you elected a survivor option)

Let's move beyond survival. Let's talk about how to build.

Step 1: Start with a Plan

Don't retire into uncertainty. By the time you're 5 years out from retirement, you should have a full pension strategy. That includes:

- Reviewing your pension payout options (single life vs. joint/survivor)

- Mapping out household expenses vs. pension income
- Calculating how much is left over to invest or gift
- Evaluating whether to use some pension income to buy life insurance for legacy

Action Step:

Schedule a pension counseling session through your department or union and bring your spouse, if applicable.

Step 2: Protect Pension Income with Insurance

You're not just protecting your income. You're protecting your family's financial future. One smart move?

Use a portion of your pension to pay for:

- Term or permanent life insurance
- Long-term care insurance
- An umbrella liability policy to shield assets

If you die early or need extended care, these policies protect the pension income you've built.

Step 3: Invest What You Don't Spend

Just because you're retired doesn't mean you stop growing wealth. If your pension covers your needs, you can:

- Invest in a taxable brokerage account
- Use a Roth IRA (yes, if you or your spouse still have earned income)
- Buy dividend-producing real estate

Action Step:

Automate investments from your checking account to your brokerage each month. Even $500/month compounds quickly.

Step 4: Create a Legacy Blueprint

If you pass away and your pension disappears, what are you leaving behind?

- Create a trust to hold assets for your kids/grandkids
- Name contingent beneficiaries on all accounts
- Ensure your will reflects your pension and post-retirement income

Don't just name a guardian for your kids. Name a financial steward.

Real-World Scenario:

Jason, a retired fire captain, has a $5,000/month pension. His house is paid off, and he and his wife live on $3,000/month. He takes the extra $2,000 and:

- Puts $1,000 into a trust for his grandkids
- Invests $500 into dividend stocks
- Pays $500/month for a life insurance policy that will leave $500,000 tax-free to his family

Jason didn't need a million-dollar salary. He just needed a plan.

What You Can Do Now:

- Run the numbers: How much will your pension actually be?
- Estimate your monthly needs (be honest)
- Identify the gap or surplus
- Decide how you want to use any surplus to benefit your family
- Talk with a financial planner who understands public service pensions

Encouragement:

You've done the hard part—surviving and serving. Now it's about building.

Reminder:

Your pension isn't just for you. It's a platform for your family's financial future.

Takeaway:

Smart first responders don't let their pension fade away. They turn it into a financial force multiplier.

Prompt to Revisit:

Check your pension planning and legacy goals every year. What you do with it today determines who benefits tomorrow.

You didn't serve your whole life to just get by in retirement. You served to leave something behind. Let your pension keep serving—for generations to come.

Chapter 26: Insurance Review – Disability, Long-Term Care, and Life Insurance Updates

You can be the toughest firefighter on your shift, the sharpest cop in the unit, or the steadiest paramedic when chaos hits—but if your insurance isn't up to date, one accident, illness, or missed detail can unravel the security you've spent years building. This chapter isn't about selling you anything. It's about showing you how to protect the things you've worked so damn hard to earn. It's about being a leader in your household the same way you are at the station, in the rig, or on the scene. Let's talk about coverage—the kind that steps in when you can't.

You're the Coverage. Who's Covering You?

When you're a first responder, people depend on you in every imaginable way. In the firehouse, on a call, at home. But who steps in if you're the one who gets knocked down? What protects your paycheck if your back goes out or you get hurt off duty? Who makes sure your kids are still eating, your spouse still has the mortgage covered, your family can stay afloat if you don't come home? That's what this chapter is about.

Insurance isn't glamorous. It doesn't get the adrenaline pumping. But it's the backbone of any solid financial plan—especially for people who live with real risk every single day.

We're going to walk through each of these with the clarity you'd expect from a training manual, but with the tone of a peer who's been there:

- Disability Insurance
- Long-Term Care Insurance
- Life Insurance (Term and Permanent)

Disability Insurance: Replacing Your Most Valuable Asset — Your Income

What It Is

Disability insurance pays you a portion of your income if you're too sick or injured to work. That could be a temporary situation, like a torn ACL or back surgery. Or it could be long-term—something career-ending.

Short-term disability usually covers the first few months. Long-term disability kicks in afterward and can last years, even until retirement.

Why It Matters

If your department offers disability coverage, that's a good start. But it might only be partial income or only cover on-the-job injuries. Off-duty accidents, illnesses, or chronic conditions might leave you uncovered.

You need to check:

- **What percentage of your salary is covered?**
- **How long is the elimination period?** (the waiting period before benefits start)
- **Does it cover off-duty incidents?**
- **Is it taxable income when paid out?**

Case Study: Kevin, Fire Captain

Kevin blew out his knee playing basketball with his son. It wasn't a line-of-duty injury, so his workers' comp didn't apply. His short-term disability only covered 60% of his income—and only for 90 days. He had to dip into savings to make ends meet and burned through his emergency fund. A supplemental long-term disability policy could've made that a non-issue.

Takeaway:

You insure your gear, your truck, your phone. Your income deserves the same.

Action Steps:

- Ask HR for a copy of your current disability benefits.
- If you don't have off-duty coverage, get a quote for private long-term disability.
- Know your policy's definition of "disability"—some only pay if you can't work *any* job, not just your current one.

Long-Term Care Insurance: Planning for the Years Ahead

What It Is

Long-term care insurance helps cover the cost of extended care when you're older and can't do basic activities—like dressing, bathing, or eating—on your own.

It helps with in-home care, assisted living, or nursing homes.

Why It Matters for First Responders

We're tough. We work through pain. We delay medical appointments. But aging and injury don't care about your toughness.

The truth? Many first responders retire early due to physical wear and tear. And many will need long-term care.

If you wait too long to get coverage, premiums will be sky-high or you won't qualify.

Case Study: Tina, Retired Police Sergeant

Tina retired at 55 after three decades of service. By 67, her arthritis and knee replacements made it impossible to live independently. She didn't want to burden her kids, so she hired in-home care—$6,000/month. Her pension covered some, but it stretched her budget. She wished she had bought a long-term care policy when she was younger and healthier.

Pros and Cons

Pros:

- Protects your nest egg from being drained by care costs.
- Eases the burden on your spouse and children.
- Pays for care in a setting you choose.

Cons:

- Premiums can be expensive if you wait until your 60s.
- Some policies have limits or exclusions.
- It's a use-it-or-lose-it scenario unless you get a hybrid policy.

Action Steps:

- Look into coverage in your late 40s to early 50s.
- Compare traditional long-term care vs. hybrid life/LTC combo policies.
- Consider inflation riders to keep up with rising care costs.

Life Insurance: Income Replacement for the People You Love

What It Is

Life insurance pays out a lump sum to your chosen beneficiaries when you pass away. It's your way of protecting your family's future, even when you're not there to do it yourself.

There are two major types:

- **Term Life Insurance**: Pure protection. Lasts for a set number of years.
- **Permanent Life Insurance** (Whole, Universal, etc.): Covers you for life and can build cash value.

Why It Matters

If someone depends on your income, you need life insurance. Period.

It doesn't matter if you're single with a mortgage or have three kids and a stay-at-home spouse. If your loss would cause a financial shock, then it's worth covering.

How Much Coverage?

A common rule of thumb: 10–15x your annual income. But that's just a starting point.

Consider:

- Mortgage payoff
- College for kids
- Final expenses
- Income replacement for your spouse
- Debts and obligations

Real Talk

You're in a high-risk job. You might have line-of-duty benefits—but those are limited and not instant. Don't rely on that alone.

Get a term policy that outlasts your mortgage and supports your family.

Permanent Life Insurance: When It Might Make Sense

Some permanent policies build cash value, which can be tapped later. They're more expensive, but in certain situations—like special needs planning or wealth transfer—they can be part of a long-term plan.

But don't confuse life insurance with an investment strategy. Your first priority is protection.

Action Steps:

- Get quotes for a 20–30-year term policy.
- Check your work coverage—it might not be portable if you leave.
- Name both primary and contingent beneficiaries.
- Review your policy every 3–5 years—or after a life event.

Annual Insurance Check-In: What to Review

Insurance isn't set-it-and-forget-it. Life changes. So should your coverage.

At least once a year—or after any major event (marriage, divorce, new baby, promotion, buying a home)—do an insurance audit.

Use this checklist:

- Do I have enough life insurance?
- Is my disability insurance covering the right income?
- Have I looked into long-term care options?
- Are my beneficiaries current?
- Is my insurance portable if I leave the job?

Coordination With Other Benefits

Many departments offer group insurance benefits—but they're not always enough. And if you switch departments or retire early, you may lose them.

That's why layering in personal policies is smart:

- **Department disability + private LTD**
- **Group life + personal term life**
- **No LTC? Get a hybrid policy.**

Make your insurance stack like your tactical gear—layers, backups, and a plan B.

Emotional Side of Insurance

Let's be honest. Talking about death or disability sucks. No one wants to think about it. But it's not about you.

It's about your spouse not having to panic.

It's about your kids not having to drop out of school.

It's about you—not being a financial burden on the people you love.

That's what insurance does. It turns chaos into calm.

Final Drill: Train for What If

You train for car fires, mass casualty incidents, active shooter events—not because they're likely, but because they're possible.

This chapter is your insurance drill. You'll hope you never need it. But if life knocks you down, your family will be covered.

Encouragement

You've faced tougher days than paperwork and premiums. You're built for this. You've got this.

Reminder

Insurance isn't about predicting disaster. It's about being ready when life throws you a curveball.

Takeaway

Don't assume you're covered. Verify it. Layer it. Protect your legacy.

Revisit

Recheck your insurance every year. Life changes—your coverage should, too.

Let's keep going. Because financial literacy for first responders isn't about theory. It's about putting systems in place that work when the lights are off and the sirens are quiet.

Chapter 27: Marriage, Divorce, and Financial Entanglements in the Line of Duty

In the firehouse, on patrol, or in the back of an ambulance, first responders face challenges that most civilians can't fathom. The adrenaline, the trauma, the long hours—it's all part of the job. But what happens when the stress of the profession seeps into personal lives, affecting marriages and financial stability? This chapter delves into the intricate relationship between the demanding nature of first responder work and its impact on personal relationships and finances.

Section 1: The Unique Strains on First Responder Marriages

1.1 The Nature of the Job

First responders often work irregular hours, face life-threatening situations, and witness traumatic events. This high-stress environment can lead to emotional exhaustion, making it challenging to maintain healthy relationships at home.

1.2 Emotional Suppression and Communication Barriers

To cope with their duties, many first responders learn to suppress emotions. While this might be necessary on the job, it can hinder open communication with spouses, leading to misunderstandings and emotional distance.

1.3 The Statistics

Studies indicate that first responders experience higher divorce rates compared to the general population. For instance, a study by The First

Responders Initiative shows that anywhere between 60-75% of their first marriages end in divorce .

Section 2: Financial Entanglements in Marriage

2.1 Combining Finances

Merging finances can be a complex decision. Some couples opt for joint accounts, while others maintain separate ones. It's essential to discuss financial goals, spending habits, and debt management to avoid conflicts.

2.2 Prenuptial and Postnuptial Agreements

These legal documents outline the division of assets in case of divorce. They can be especially beneficial for first responders who may have pensions or other significant assets .

2.3 Managing Debt Together

Debt can strain any relationship. It's crucial to have open discussions about existing debts and create a plan to manage them collectively.

Section 3: Navigating Divorce

3.1 Understanding the Process

Divorce involves legal, emotional, and financial challenges. It's vital to understand the process, from filing to finalizing, and to seek legal counsel familiar with first responder issues.

3.2 Division of Assets

Assets acquired during the marriage are typically divided equitably. This includes pensions, which can be a significant point of contention. Understanding how pensions are valued and divided is crucial .

3.3 Child Custody and Support

Irregular work schedules can complicate custody arrangements. It's essential to create flexible parenting plans that accommodate shift work and ensure the child's best interests are prioritized.

Section 4: Post-Divorce Financial Planning

4.1 Rebuilding Financial Stability

Post-divorce, it's essential to reassess financial goals, create a new budget, and plan for future expenses. This might include adjusting retirement plans and updating beneficiaries.

4.2 Seeking Professional Help

Engaging with financial advisors or therapists can provide guidance during this transition. Organizations like the Financial Therapy Association offer resources tailored to such needs .

4.3 Emotional Well-being

Divorce can take a toll on mental health. Accessing support groups or counseling services can aid in coping with the emotional aftermath.

Section 5: Preventative Measures and Strengthening Relationships

5.1 Open Communication

Regular discussions about finances, work stress, and personal feelings can strengthen relationships and prevent misunderstandings.

5.2 Financial Education

Understanding financial principles and planning can empower couples to make informed decisions together.

5.3 Support Networks

Engaging with peer support groups or counseling services can provide additional layers of support, especially tailored for first responders.

Conclusion: Navigating Personal and Financial Challenges

The life of a first responder is filled with challenges that extend beyond the job. By understanding the unique strains on relationships and finances, and by taking proactive steps, first responders can navigate these challenges more effectively, ensuring both personal and financial well-being.

Encouragement: You've faced countless challenges in your line of duty. Navigating personal and financial complexities is another mission you can accomplish with the right tools and support.

Reminder: Financial planning isn't about perfection; it's about preparation. Equip yourself with knowledge and resources to face any situation.

Takeaway: Open communication, continuous education, and seeking support are key pillars in maintaining both personal relationships and financial health.

Prompt to Revisit: Reassess your financial and personal plans every six months. As your career and life evolve, so should your strategies.

Chapter 28: Mental Health and Financial Health: Counseling, PTSD, and Financial Resilience

Every first responder knows that the job doesn't end when the shift does. The sirens may quiet, but the echoes of trauma, stress, and financial strain often linger. The intersection of mental health and financial well-being is a critical, yet frequently overlooked, aspect of a first responder's life. This chapter aims to shed light on this intersection, offering guidance and resources to navigate these challenges.

Section 1: The Psychological Toll of Service

First responders are routinely exposed to traumatic events—accidents, violence, disasters—that can lead to mental health issues such as PTSD, depression, and anxiety. Studies indicate that approximately 14.6% of emergency personnel experience PTSD, with paramedics showing the highest prevalence . The cumulative stress can impair decision-making, relationships, and overall quality of life.

Key Points:

- **Exposure to Trauma:** Regular exposure to traumatic incidents increases the risk of mental health disorders.
- **Stigma:** Many first responders hesitate to seek help due to stigma or fear of career repercussions.
- **Impact on Performance:** Mental health issues can affect job performance, leading to safety concerns for both responders and the public.

Section 2: Financial Stressors Unique to First Responders

Financial challenges are prevalent among first responders, often stemming from irregular hours, mandatory overtime, and the high cost of living in certain areas. These stressors can exacerbate mental health issues.

Common Financial Challenges:

- **Variable Income:** Overtime and shift differentials can lead to unpredictable earnings.
- **High Cost of Living:** Many first responders work in urban areas with elevated living expenses.
- **Lack of Financial Literacy:** Limited access to financial education can result in poor money management.

Consequences:

- **Debt Accumulation:** Without proper budgeting, debt can quickly escalate.
- **Retirement Insecurity:** Inadequate savings and reliance solely on pensions may not suffice for retirement needs.
- **Increased Stress:** Financial instability contributes to anxiety and can strain personal relationships.

Section 3: The Interplay Between Mental and Financial Health

Mental and financial health are deeply interconnected. Financial stress can lead to mental health issues, and vice versa. For instance, a first responder dealing with PTSD may find it challenging to manage finances effectively, leading to further stress and potential financial crises.

Strategies for Managing the Interplay:

- **Integrated Support:** Seek programs that address both mental and financial well-being.
- **Open Communication:** Discuss financial concerns with trusted individuals or professionals.

- **Regular Check-Ins:** Monitor both mental and financial health regularly to identify and address issues promptly.

Section 4: Resources and Support Systems

Numerous resources are available to assist first responders in managing mental and financial health:

- **Employee Assistance Programs (EAPs):** Offer confidential counseling and financial advice .
- **Peer Support Groups:** Provide a platform to share experiences and coping strategies.
- **Financial Counseling Services:** Organizations like FinancialCop offer financial education tailored to first responders .
- **Grants and Scholarships:** Programs like the Mental Health Resilience Scholarship assist with treatment costs .

Section 5: Building Financial Resilience

Developing financial resilience involves proactive planning and disciplined habits:

- **Budgeting:** Create a realistic budget that accounts for variable income.
- **Emergency Fund:** Aim to save 3-6 months' worth of expenses to cushion against unforeseen events.
- **Retirement Planning:** Diversify retirement savings beyond pensions, considering options like Roth IRAs or 457(b) plans.
- **Debt Management:** Prioritize paying off high-interest debts and avoid unnecessary expenditures.

Section 6: Cultivating Mental Resilience

Mental resilience is essential for coping with the demands of the job:

- **Therapy and Counseling:** Regular sessions can provide coping mechanisms and emotional support.

- **Mindfulness Practices:** Techniques like meditation and deep breathing can reduce stress.
- **Physical Health:** Regular exercise and proper nutrition contribute to overall well-being.
- **Peer Support:** Engaging with colleagues who understand the unique challenges can be therapeutic.

Section 7: Action Steps for First Responders

To proactively manage mental and financial health:

1. **Assess Your Situation:** Evaluate your current mental state and financial standing.
2. **Set Goals:** Define clear, achievable objectives for both areas.
3. **Seek Support:** Utilize available resources and don't hesitate to ask for help.
4. **Educate Yourself:** Continuously learn about financial planning and mental health strategies.
5. **Monitor Progress:** Regularly review and adjust your plans as needed.

Conclusion: Empowering First Responders for Holistic Well-Being

First responders dedicate their lives to serving others, often at the expense of their own well-being. Recognizing and addressing the intertwined nature of mental and financial health is crucial. By leveraging available resources, fostering open communication, and committing to proactive strategies, first responders can build resilience and secure a stable, fulfilling future.

Encouragement:

"You've faced challenges that most can't imagine. Taking steps to care for your mental and financial health is not just wise—it's essential. Remember, seeking help is a sign of strength, not weakness."

Reminder:

"Financial planning and mental health care are ongoing processes. Regular check-ins and adjustments are part of the journey."

Takeaway:

"By investing in your well-being today, you're ensuring a healthier, more secure tomorrow—for yourself and those who depend on you."

Prompt to Revisit:

"Set a reminder to review your mental and financial health plans every six months. As life evolves, so should your strategies."

Chapter 29: Helping Your Kids Avoid Your Money Mistakes

You've spent your life running toward danger. Kicking down doors. Holding the line. Clocking in for double shifts when everyone else clocked out. You've faced fires, trauma, bullets, and chaos—and you've stood tall through it all. But here's the part nobody trains us for: how to raise financially smart kids in a world that teaches them everything *except* money.

If you're like most first responders, you've had to learn money lessons the hard way—through trial, error, overdraft, and overtime. Maybe nobody taught you how credit works. Maybe you didn't have retirement on your radar until you hit your thirties. Maybe you're still digging out of debt from a divorce, or you're quietly hoping your pension will cover the gaps.

But now your kid is asking about getting their first car. Or maybe they just got their first job. Or they're headed to college and you're wondering how they're going to survive without swiping a credit card for pizza every night.

This chapter is about breaking that cycle—without shame, without lectures, and without pretending like you had it all figured out. Because the truth is, you don't need to be perfect. You just need to be intentional.

Start With Your Story

Kids listen to stories more than they listen to advice. And you've got stories—about payday loans, bounced checks, side hustles, and second chances. Don't hide those. Use them.

Tell your kid about the time you financed a car you couldn't afford. Or how you didn't understand interest rates until your credit card balance doubled. Let them know what you *wish* someone had told you. That's where the real teaching lives.

You don't have to scare them. You just have to be real with them. That's what earns their respect.

Teach in Real Time

Here's the problem with most financial advice: it's abstract. "Save money." "Invest early." "Don't get into debt."

But kids need *context*. They need to see how money works in the real world. That means letting them help with the grocery list and the budget. That means showing them how to pay a utility bill. That means pulling up your paycheck stub and walking them through the deductions.

Let them see the math. Let them sit with the consequences. Let them practice before they're on their own.

Let your kid plan a dinner night. Give them a $30 budget and let them decide what to buy, how to stretch it, and whether to skip dessert or get off-brand soda.

Let your teenager earn some money—then help them open a savings account. Better yet, help them open a Roth IRA if they have earned income. Let them see what compound interest looks like in action.

Lead by Example

You can't teach what you don't model. If your kid sees you blowing every dollar on Amazon, they'll do the same. But if they see you meal prepping, saving receipts, or turning down overtime because you budgeted smart—they'll learn that discipline is strength.

Tell them why you're contributing to your 457(b) or why you refinanced the house. Let them see you cancel a subscription you don't use. Let them hear you say, "We don't need that right now."

The way you talk about money becomes the way they talk to themselves about money. Are you modeling fear? Guilt? Scarcity? Or are you modeling clarity, control, and confidence?

Address the Pressure

Some kids of first responders grow up thinking money equals sacrifice. They've seen you come home late, leave early, take on holidays, and miss birthdays to keep the lights on.

They might think, *this is what you have to do to survive.* So talk to them. Help them understand that yes, your job is noble. But it doesn't mean you have to kill yourself for every dollar.

Let them know that money can be earned without martyrdom. That financial freedom is the goal—not just hard work. That they're allowed to say no. That rest is not a luxury.

Because when they see you choosing boundaries and smart strategy over burnout, they learn to do the same.

The Social Media Problem

Your kid is growing up in a digital world full of filters, fake wealth, and overnight success stories. They're seeing influencers lease luxury cars and pretend it's passive income. They're watching 19-year-olds flex crypto earnings without showing the losses.

Teach your kid to ask questions:

- Is that person showing the whole story?
- Is this real money or borrowed money?
- Is this a one-time win or long-term wealth?
- What are the risks behind that reward?

Help them understand that sustainable wealth rarely looks sexy. It looks like patience. Like savings. Like a used car paid off in full. Like not needing to post your paycheck to prove your worth.

Money Talks to Have with Your Kids (At Every Age)

Ages 4–10: Start with the Basics

- What money is (coins, bills, debit cards)
- Where money comes from (work)
- What money does (spend, save, give)
- The difference between wants and needs

Let them earn a small allowance. Use clear jars for spend/save/give. Take them grocery shopping and show prices.

Ages 11–14: Get Practical

- What a budget is
- How to compare prices
- Why credit cards aren't free money
- The magic of interest (good and bad)

Let them make small spending decisions. Open a joint youth bank account. Show them the electric bill.

Ages 15–18: Get Real

- What a paycheck looks like
- How taxes work
- Student loan pros and cons
- Credit scores and how to build one

Let them help fill out FAFSA. Show them how to check their credit. Talk openly about financial aid, scholarships, and work-study.

Ages 18+: Shift to Independence

- How to build a budget
- What insurance does
- How to invest for retirement
- How to avoid scams and predators

Encourage them to meet with a financial advisor. Get them on your credit card as an authorized user if you're paying on time. Show them how to file a basic tax return.

When You Messed Up—Teach That, Too

You made mistakes. We all did. Don't hide them. Use them.

Tell your kid about the time you:

- Bought a car with a 21% loan
- Got behind on child support because of overtime cuts
- Took a bad investment tip from a coworker
- Borrowed from your 401(k) and regretted it

Explain what you did next. How you recovered. What you learned. Make it clear: mistakes don't make you a failure—they make you wiser.

And then help your kid avoid the same landmines.

If You're Co-Parenting or Divorced

Money messages get messy when homes are divided. But your kid still needs stability.

Don't badmouth your ex's choices. Instead, lead with yours:

- "Here's how I handle money."
- "Here's why I think saving is important."
- "Here's how I budget with what I have."

If possible, align on the big stuff—college planning, major purchases, or savings accounts. But even if your ex is chaotic with money, your kid can still learn structure from you.

Action Steps

- Write down one money story from your life that you want to share with your kid.
- Open a savings or Roth IRA account with them.
- Let them plan a purchase with a set budget.
- Talk through the pros and cons of buying vs. financing.
- Teach them to read a pay stub and calculate taxes.
- Set up a time each month to talk money—casually, not critically.

Final Words

You won't get it perfect. That's not the point.

The point is to be present. To be honest. To make sure your kid leaves home with more financial armor than you had.

You've trained your whole career to run toward chaos and protect lives. Now train your kid to run toward *clarity* and protect their future.

You've got the tools. Use them.

You've got the heart. Lead with it.

And remember:

Smart first responders don't guess with money—they train for it, just like anything else.

So train your kids, too. They'll thank you later.

Encouragement: You've made it through harder things than budgeting. You've got this.

Reminder: Financial planning isn't about being perfect. It's about staying prepared.

Takeaway: Every financial mistake is a teaching moment in disguise. Use it.

Prompt to Revisit: Talk about money with your kids every 6 months. Let the conversation grow with them.

This is how you build a legacy—not just of service, but of wisdom, freedom, and wealth.

Chapter 30: Planning for Your Parents – Caregiving, Healthcare, and Multigenerational Planning

There comes a time in every first responder's life when the calls you answer aren't coming from dispatch—they're coming from your parents. A late-night fall. A confusing diagnosis. A missed mortgage payment. A silent phone you haven't heard from in too long.

And now you're not just protecting your community. You're protecting the people who raised you.

This chapter is about that next level of responsibility. Not the kind you train for at the academy—but the kind that hits harder than any shift. Because caring for aging parents while balancing your own family, career, and retirement isn't just emotional. It's financial.

We're going to talk about what that transition looks like, how to plan for it with clarity, and how to build a system that protects your parents *and* your own future. No guilt. No panic. Just straight talk and a real game plan.

The Quiet Shift: From Child to Caregiver

You might still feel like their kid—but life has a way of turning the tables.

Suddenly, you're:

- Driving your mom to doctor's appointments between shifts

- Explaining Medicare to your dad like he's the rookie
- Wondering if their house is still safe
- Managing bills and medications for someone who used to manage yours

It's hard. And it's often invisible. But it's also becoming the norm—especially for those in their 30s, 40s, and 50s working in high-stress, high-demand roles like yours.

If you're reading this and nodding, you're not alone.

Start the Conversation—Before the Crisis

Here's the truth: most families don't talk about money, health, or aging until it's too late.

Do this now. Not after the stroke. Not after the eviction notice. Not after the emergency surgery.

Have the tough talk.

Ask:

- "Do you have a will?"
- "What insurance do you have—and what does it cover?"
- "If something happened, where are your documents?"
- "Do you want to stay in your home as you age—or would you want help?"

And just listen. Let them know you're not trying to take over—you're trying to prepare. Because that's what professionals do. That's what you do.

The Essentials: What to Know About Your Parents' Situation

Make a checklist. Yes, like your shift bag. You need to know:

- Who their doctors are

- What medications they take
- What health insurance they have (Medicare? Supplement? Long-term care?)
- Where their legal documents are (will, trust, power of attorney)
- What their monthly income and expenses are
- What debts they have
- What kind of support system they have (siblings, neighbors, church, etc.)

This isn't snooping. This is preparation. And it could save you thousands—or more importantly, time and peace of mind—when a crisis hits.

Understanding Medicare and Long-Term Care

Most people assume Medicare covers everything. It doesn't.

Medicare covers hospital stays, basic doctor visits, some rehab—but NOT long-term nursing care.

That's where things get expensive—fast.

A private room in a nursing home? $8,000 a month or more.

Assisted living? $4,500 a month.

In-home care? $25 an hour, easily.

You need to know:

- Do your parents have long-term care insurance?
- Do they qualify for Medicaid or VA benefits?
- Do they have assets that could disqualify them from assistance?

Don't wait until they're in the ER. Talk to an elder law attorney or financial planner who understands long-term care planning *now*.

The Legal Forms That Matter

If your parent becomes incapacitated—even temporarily—you can't:

- Access their accounts
- Talk to their doctors
- Handle their bills
- Make medical decisions

Unless they've filled out the right documents.

Make sure these are in place:

1. **Healthcare Power of Attorney** – Allows you to make medical decisions if they can't.
2. **Durable Power of Attorney** – Lets you handle finances, sign checks, and manage bills.
3. **Living Will / Advance Directive** – Explains their wishes about end-of-life care.
4. **HIPAA Release Form** – Gives you access to their health information.

If they don't have these, help them get them. Or talk to an estate planning attorney who can guide you both.

Multigenerational Households: A Growing Reality

You're not just thinking about your parents. You're raising your own kids, too. That "sandwich generation" pressure is real.

Sometimes the answer is:

- Bringing mom to live with you
- Helping dad cover rent while saving for your child's tuition
- Rearranging your own work schedule to make room for caregiving

It's noble. But it can burn you out.

Create boundaries. Create systems. Know when to say "I need help." Whether it's home health aides, adult day care, or just a weekly check-in from a sibling—don't shoulder this alone.

You serve the community. But you're allowed to get support for your own family, too.

Pros and Cons of Financial Support

Should you pay your parents' bills?

Pros:

- Keeps them in their home longer
- Preserves family dignity
- May avoid predatory lending or scams

Cons:

- Drains your retirement savings
- Creates tension with siblings or your spouse
- Sets a precedent that's hard to undo

Ask yourself:

- Is this a one-time help or an ongoing need?
- Can I afford this without compromising my own family's future?
- Is there a government or community program that could step in instead?

Sometimes love means stepping in.

Sometimes love means setting boundaries.

Sometimes love means saying, "Let's talk to a professional."

Action Steps You Can Take This Month

- Schedule a "family financial summit" with your parents
- Locate or help them update their will and POA documents
- Review their insurance policies and identify gaps
- Research local senior services or state aging offices
- Create a binder or digital folder with all key documents
- Talk to your own kids about what they might need to know someday

What Happens If You Ignore This

Avoiding this planning doesn't just cost money. It costs time, peace, and options.

When families wait too long, they end up:

- Paying for emergency care out-of-pocket
- Rushing legal paperwork in the ICU
- Fighting with siblings over decisions
- Feeling lost, unprepared, and emotionally wrecked

You wouldn't go on a call without your gear.

Don't enter the second half of life without a plan.

Encouragement

You've already carried so much on your shoulders.

This is just one more thing—but you don't have to do it alone. Planning now means less panic later. It means honoring your parents *and* protecting yourself.

Reminder

Financial planning isn't just about wealth—it's about wellness. For you. For them. For the next generation.

Takeaway

Your badge doesn't make you invincible. But it *can* make you the leader your family needs.

Prompt to Revisit

Come back to this topic every 6–12 months. Health changes. Finances shift. Family dynamics evolve. Stay ready.

This chapter isn't about fear.

It's about freedom.

Because being the rock for your parents doesn't mean crumbling under the weight.

It means building a foundation strong enough to hold the next generation, too.

And that's what real wealth is.

Not just money—but peace, preparation, and protection—for everyone you love.

PART IV: RETIREMENT PREP – The Final Years Before You Hang Up the Badge or Helmet (Years 26–30+)

You've put in the years. The body's sore. The pager still buzzes—but the finish line is finally in sight. This section is about what comes next, and how to make sure you walk away with more than just memories and a pension.

For first responders in their final stretch—whether it's year 26 or year 35—retirement isn't just about clocking out for the last time. It's about transitioning with dignity, clarity, and control. *Part IV: Retirement Prep* is your no-BS guide to navigating the last few working years with smart, strategic steps so that retirement feels like a reward—not a regret.

We'll walk you through pension decisions, DROP plans, Social Security timing, taxes in retirement, healthcare coverage after the job, and the emotional realities of stepping away from an identity that has shaped your adult life. We'll talk about how to replace your paycheck, manage your time, and protect the wealth you've built.

We'll also tackle hard questions, like:

- Will your pension really be enough?
- Should you keep working part-time—or walk away completely?
- What if you want to move out of state?
- How do you handle retirement when your spouse is younger—or still working?

- What does your daily life look like after the uniform comes off?

This section is for the veteran firefighter who still knows the sound of every truck in the department, the seasoned paramedic who's seen it all, and the officer who's mentored the rookies and stood guard on every dark night.

You've spent decades running toward other people's emergencies. Now it's time to prepare for your own next chapter—on your terms. With peace of mind. With purpose. With a plan.

Because retirement isn't the end of your story. It's the next mission—and we're going to make sure you're geared up for it.

Chapter 31: When Can You Retire? Understanding Vesting, Service Credits, and Pension Math

Let's get real about retirement—the kind that doesn't come with a gold watch and a golf cart, but the kind that means walking away from the job with your head high, your pension intact, and your next chapter wide open.

But here's the thing: most first responders don't actually know *when* they can retire. Or if they can afford to. Or what their pension really pays. Because the system isn't always clear. And nobody hands you a playbook.

This chapter *is* that playbook.

It's for the 24-year-old firefighter who thinks retirement is 100 years away—and the 49-year-old officer who's wondering if they're close enough to start packing up their locker.

We're going to break down vesting, service credits, pension math, and the questions that will determine when—and how—you can retire. No jargon. No fluff. Just truth, systems, and strategy.

What Does "Vesting" Actually Mean?

Vesting means you've earned the right to receive benefits from your pension plan—even if you leave the job.

Most public safety pensions require you to work a certain number of years before you're vested. It might be five. It might be ten.

If you leave before that? You may get your own contributions back—but not the full pension.

Action step:

- Find out your vesting schedule. Don't assume. Ask your HR or pension board. Know the number.

What Are Service Credits—and Why They Matter

Your pension amount is based on **years of service**. That includes:

- Time worked full-time with your agency
- Potential prior service (military, other departments)
- Purchased service (in some cases, you can buy credits for prior eligible work)

The more credits, the bigger your benefit.

But beware: not all time counts. Some part-time work, unpaid leave, or lateral moves might not qualify.

Action step:

- Request a service credit report. Review it line by line. Correct any errors early—not five years from now.

The Basic Pension Formula

Most pensions follow a simple formula:

Final Average Salary x **Years of Service** x **Multiplier** = Annual Pension Benefit

Let's say:

- Final Average Salary (FAS): $75,000
- Years of Service: 30

- Multiplier: 2.5%

Then:

$75,000 x 30 x 0.025 = $56,250 per year

That's your gross annual pension benefit. But that's before taxes, insurance deductions, or any cost-of-living adjustments (COLAs).

Final Average Salary—What Counts?

Your FAS is usually calculated using your highest 3 or 5 years of salary. That might include:

- Base pay
- Overtime (in some plans)
- Holiday pay or bonuses

But not always. Some systems cap what counts. So if you're planning to "load up" in your last few years, make sure those dollars actually help your pension.

Action step:

- Ask what counts toward your FAS and if your plan has any salary caps or OT limits.

The Multiplier—How Big Is the Boost?

That 2.0% or 2.5% number? That's the multiplier. It's how generous your plan is.

A 3.0% multiplier is strong.

A 1.5% multiplier? Not so much.

Some plans reward more years with a higher multiplier—or reduce it if you retire early. Know what yours does.

Early Retirement Penalties

Thinking about retiring at 50 instead of 55?

Your plan might let you—but they might reduce your monthly benefit permanently for each year you leave early.

Example:

- Full benefit at 55
- You leave at 50
- 5 years early = 5 x 6% penalty = 30% reduction for life

That's a big hit.

Action step:

- Ask what your plan's "normal retirement age" is and what penalties apply for retiring early.

Cost-of-Living Adjustments (COLAs)

Does your pension go up with inflation? Maybe. Maybe not.

Some plans offer automatic COLAs.

Others require a vote—or offer none at all.

This matters. A $5,000/month pension today won't feel like the same $5,000 in 20 years if prices keep rising.

Action step:

- Find out your COLA structure. Know how often it's applied, and what it's based on.

Social Security—Will You Get It?

Some public safety workers don't pay into Social Security.

Others do.

If you do qualify, your benefit might be reduced by something called the Windfall Elimination Provision (WEP).

Action step:

- Call Social Security or check your online statement. Know what you're eligible for—and what might be reduced.

Health Insurance After You Retire

Your pension might look great—until you price health insurance.

If your department doesn't cover retiree medical, you could be paying $1,000/month or more out-of-pocket until Medicare kicks in.

Action step:

- Check your department's retiree health policy. Build this into your retirement math early.

DROP Programs—Good Idea or Trap?

Deferred Retirement Option Plans (DROP) let you "retire" on paper and keep working while your pension checks go into a separate account. Then, when you fully leave, you get a lump sum plus your monthly pension.

Sounds great, right?

But there are trade-offs:

- Do you lose out on future pension growth?
- Does it change your health benefits?
- What happens if you get hurt during DROP?

Action step:

- Meet with your pension board and ask every question. Get it in writing.

Real-Life Retirement Scenarios

Case 1: The 28-Year Vet

Maria, a firefighter, is in year 28. Her pension caps at 30 years. She's tired, but her final 2 years could increase her FAS by $5,000/year. That means an extra $3,750 annually for life—or $75,000+ over 20 years.

Case 2: The Officer Who Left at 18 Years

Derek left law enforcement at 18 years to run a business. He was vested—but his multiplier was lower. He gets a pension, but it's 40% smaller than if he'd stayed 25 years.

Case 3: The Medic Who Didn't Plan for Healthcare

Kim retired at 52 with a solid pension—but didn't realize her department didn't cover retiree health. Now she's paying $1,200/month until she's 65. It's crushing her budget.

Action Steps to Take This Year

- Run a pension estimate using your HR portal or pension board
- Book a retirement planning meeting with your department's benefits team
- Research healthcare costs if you left today vs. at Medicare age
- Double-check your beneficiary info and update it if needed
- Review your total retirement picture—pension, savings, investments

Encouragement

You've already made it this far. Retirement isn't some mystery you have to solve alone. It's a mission you can train for—just like you've trained for everything else.

Reminder

Don't wait until year 29 to start thinking about year 30. The earlier you get clear on your numbers, the more control you'll have.

Takeaway

Pensions are a tool—not a guarantee. The more you understand the system, the better you can work it to your advantage.

Prompt to Revisit

Recalculate your pension projection once a year—especially if your salary, service time, or role changes.

You know how to read a scene. Read your financial future the same way—with clarity, calm, and backup plans.

Because when the day comes that you hang up the badge or helmet, you don't want to be asking, "Can I afford to?"

You want to be saying, "I'm ready."

Chapter 32: The DROP Program – Deferred Retirement Option Plans Explained

You've put in the time. You're nearing retirement. But instead of walking away, your department offers you something different: a chance to "retire" on paper, keep working, and stack cash in a lump sum account while still getting your full paycheck. Sounds like a dream, right?

Welcome to the DROP program.

If you've heard other first responders talking about it, you might be wondering:

- What exactly is DROP?
- Who is it for?
- How does it really work?
- Is it worth it—or are there traps you're not seeing?

Let's break it all down like you're standing in the station kitchen, cup of coffee in hand, talking to the senior guy who's been through it.

What Is DROP?

DROP stands for **Deferred Retirement Option Plan**. It's a program offered by some public safety pension systems that allows eligible employees to "retire" officially, but stay on the job for a few more years. While you keep working and collecting your salary, your monthly pension benefit is calculated and paid into a special account in your name.

When you finish the DROP period and fully retire, you walk away with:

1. Your monthly pension checks (now paid directly to you)
2. A lump sum from your DROP account, representing all those "pension checks" that accumulated while you were still working

It's like hitting pause on your pension, letting it pile up, then cashing in when you're done.

How Long Can You Be in DROP?

Most DROP programs let you stay in for **3 to 5 years**. Some allow up to **8 years**. But once you enter, the clock starts ticking. You usually can't extend your DROP time later.

Action step:

- Check your plan rules. Every city and state is different. Know your limits.

When Are You Eligible?

Eligibility depends on reaching a certain combination of age and service. You usually have to:

- Be **vested** in the pension system
- Have reached **normal retirement age or years of service**

Example:

- Eligible after 25 years of service at any age
- Or age 55 with 20 years

DROP doesn't make sense unless you're already fully eligible to retire.

Action step:

- Ask HR or your pension board: "When am I DROP-eligible—and what's the deadline to enter?"

How the Money Adds Up

Say your pension would be $5,000/month.

You enter DROP and work 5 more years.

$5,000 x 12 months x 5 years = $300,000

That amount is credited to your DROP account. Some plans pay interest or investment returns on that balance. Others don't. Some may deduct fees.

When you retire, you get that $300,000 (plus/minus earnings) **in a lump sum**.

Sounds great, right?

Let's look deeper.

Pros of DROP

1. You Keep Earning a Paycheck

You're still working your regular job, pulling your regular salary.

2. Your Pension Stacks Up in a Lump Sum

Instead of just starting your monthly pension, it accumulates for years. That lump can be used for:

- Buying a home in retirement

- Paying off debt
- Investing
- Creating a legacy for your family

3. Clear Exit Plan

DROP gives you a definitive timeline. You know your retirement date in advance. That can be helpful mentally and financially.

4. Potential to Work Less Stressful Assignments

Some departments allow DROP participants to slide into training, mentoring, or admin roles. That's not guaranteed, but it's worth asking about.

Cons of DROP

1. You Stop Earning Pension Credit

The moment you enter DROP, your pension calculation is frozen. If you would've earned more by staying a few more years outside of DROP, you're giving that up.

2. You Can't Change Your Mind

Once you enter DROP, you've technically retired. There's no backing out. If you leave early or get injured, your payout could be smaller than expected.

3. You Might Lose Out on Future Pay Raises

Since your pension is calculated when you enter DROP, any raises or promotions afterward won't count toward your pension formula.

4. Tax Implications

A six-figure DROP lump sum sounds amazing—but it can trigger serious taxes if not handled carefully. You may need to roll it into a qualified plan (like an IRA) to avoid immediate taxation.

5. May Affect Health Benefits

In some jurisdictions, retirees lose active-duty health insurance. If you're technically "retired" while in DROP, you may need to switch to a retiree plan—which could cost more.

Action step:

- Ask HR: "Will my health benefits change during DROP? What are the costs and options?"

Real-World Scenarios

The Lieutenant Who Used DROP to Pay Off a Mortgage

Mike had 28 years on the job and a $4,500/month pension. He stayed in DROP for 5 years. That gave him a $270,000 payout, which he used to pay off his mortgage and fund a Roth conversion strategy.

The Officer Who Got Injured During DROP

James entered DROP at year 25. Two years later, he blew out his knee. He was forced to stop working—but because he hadn't completed his DROP period, his lump sum was smaller. His pension amount was also frozen at the lower FAS.

The Paramedic Who Waited Too Long

Kara was eligible for DROP at year 25 but stayed in active status. She got promoted at year 26, then entered DROP at year 27. The promotion bumped her pension—but she missed out on 2 years of DROP payments that could've grown a lump sum.

Who Is DROP Best For?

DROP is great if:

- You're ready to retire but still physically able and mentally prepared to keep working
- Your pension multiplier maxes out (i.e., more years won't grow your benefit)
- You want a lump sum to help pay off debt or fund retirement flexibility
- You're financially disciplined and won't burn through that lump sum too fast

DROP is *less ideal* if:

- You're still climbing the salary ladder and expect raises or promotions
- Your department allows you to earn more pension credits outside of DROP
- You might not complete the DROP period due to injury, burnout, or life changes

Action Steps Before You Enter DROP

- Get a pension projection with and without DROP
- Ask your department for a DROP guide—read every page
- Consult with a fiduciary financial advisor (not a product pusher)
- Review health insurance changes during and after DROP
- Make a plan for your lump sum—invest, pay off debt, fund future goals
- Discuss it with your spouse or partner. Your decision impacts them too

What to Do With the DROP Lump Sum

When you finish DROP, your lump sum options might include:

- **Direct deposit (taxable)** – not recommended unless you need the cash
- **Rollover into IRA or 457(b)** – tax-deferred
- **Combination of both**

Think twice before taking it all as cash. That could trigger a huge tax bill, possibly pushing you into the highest tax bracket for that year.

Action step:

- Plan your tax strategy before your DROP payout hits. Don't wait until April.

Encouragement

DROP isn't a magic fix. But it's a powerful tool if you understand it, prepare for it, and use it with a plan. You've worked hard to earn this option—now treat it with the respect it deserves.

Reminder

Every DROP program is different. Don't rely on locker room wisdom. Get your facts from your pension board, your HR, and a real advisor who works for *you*, not commissions.

Takeaway

You trained for emergencies. Now train for this opportunity. Use the DROP program to finish strong, walk away smart, and start the next chapter with real financial momentum.

Prompt to Revisit

Revisit your DROP timeline and strategy annually. Life changes. So should your exit plan.

The badge may come off. But your financial readiness? That sticks with you. Use the DROP plan to create not just an exit—but a launchpad.

You've earned it.

Chapter 33: Social Security and First Responders: What You're Eligible For (and What You're Not)

For the book: Financial Literacy for First Responders (Firefighters, Police, Paramedics)

You work 24s. You run toward danger. You miss holidays, birthdays, and too many family dinners to count. So when retirement comes around, most people assume you'll be getting everything you've earned—including Social Security.

But here's the truth: Not every first responder is eligible for it. Some get full benefits. Some get partial. Some get nothing at all—at least not without penalties.

Let's break it down, plain and simple. No fluff. No scare tactics. Just the real talk you deserve.

Why This Chapter Matters

You need to know whether Social Security will be part of your retirement income—or if it won't be. You need to understand why, and how to plan around it. Because relying on money that may never show up is a dangerous kind of hope.

If you've ever asked:

- "I don't see Social Security on my check—does that mean I won't get it?"

- "I paid into Social Security from my side job—do I get something?"
- "What's that Windfall thing they keep talking about?"
- Then this chapter is for you.

How Social Security Works (In Plain Language)

Social Security is a federal retirement program funded by payroll taxes. If you see **FICA** taken out of your paycheck, you're paying into it. Pay in for 10 years (or 40 "credits"), and you're considered *vested.* That means you qualify for retirement benefits—though how much you get depends on how much you earned over those years.

But here's the catch: Many public sector jobs—especially for police officers, firefighters, and some paramedics—*don't* pay into Social Security. If your department participates in a state-run pension instead, you may have been exempt from Social Security payroll tax.

Sounds like a win, right?

Not always.

Because opting out of Social Security can have long-term consequences—especially if you're counting on it as a "backup" for your pension.

Are You Covered?

Here's how to figure out if Social Security is even on the table for you:

Step 1: Look at your paycheck.

Do you see deductions labeled **FICA**, **Social Security**, or **OASDI**? If yes, you're contributing. If not, you're likely in a pension-only system.

Step 2: Ask HR or your pension board directly:

"Does our department participate in Social Security?"

(If they dodge the question, ask again. It's your future.)

Step 3: Check your Social Security statement.

You can log into ssa.gov and view your account. It will show how many work credits you've earned and what your projected benefit is—if any.

If your statement is blank or shows only a small number of credits, you're likely *not* fully covered.

The Windfall Elimination Provision (WEP)

If you worked a non-covered job (no Social Security) *and* a covered job (like a side hustle or early career), the government may reduce your Social Security check using something called the **Windfall Elimination Provision**, or WEP.

Here's the basic idea:

WEP was created to prevent people who didn't pay into the system consistently from collecting full benefits. In practice, it often reduces your monthly Social Security benefit by **up to $600/month**—sometimes more.

That's not a small amount. And it hits first responders particularly hard because many of you do have second jobs, or you switched careers before or after the department.

So if you've ever worked in the private sector, bartended, ran a business, or paid into Social Security for any period of time—WEP could apply.

And that's not all...

The Government Pension Offset (GPO)

Let's say your spouse is eligible for Social Security and you're hoping to receive spousal or survivor benefits one day.

There's a second rule you need to know: the **Government Pension Offset**, or GPO.

This rule says if you receive a government pension (like most public safety pensions), your spousal or survivor benefits may be reduced—or wiped out altogether.

In fact, the GPO can reduce your survivor benefit by **two-thirds** of your pension amount. That's a huge cut, especially for widows or widowers who were counting on dual income in retirement.

Real Talk: What It Feels Like

Imagine this:

You put in 30 years. You retire with a $4,000/month pension. You think, "Hey, I also worked a side job for 10 years—I'll get some Social Security too."

Then the WEP kicks in and slashes your benefit in half. Then you realize your spouse passed, and GPO cuts out the survivor benefit you were counting on. Now you're looking at a fixed income with fewer backup options than you expected.

This happens every single day to good men and women who simply didn't know.

Let's make sure it doesn't happen to you.

What You Can Do

1. Get Your Social Security Statement Now.

Go to ssa.gov. Create a login. Look at your earnings history. If you don't have 40 credits, you're not eligible yet. If you do, scroll to the estimated benefit—then remember, that number could get WEP'd down.

2. Understand Your Pension Rules.

Not all public pensions are the same. Some states don't trigger WEP or GPO. Some departments have "split" contributions—meaning you may pay into both systems. Ask. Read. Confirm.

3. Don't Count on Social Security Alone.

Even if you're eligible, it's rarely enough to retire on comfortably. It's a safety net—not a retirement plan.

4. Max Out Other Accounts.

If you're not paying into Social Security, you have even more reason to max out your **457(b)**, **Roth IRA**, or **403(b)**. These are your backup. These are your leverage.

5. Prepare Your Spouse.

GPO affects survivor benefits. If your family is counting on that income, they need to know what's actually going to show up—and what won't.

6. Talk to a Financial Advisor Who Knows WEP/GPO.

Many financial pros don't understand how these rules affect first responders. Don't settle for someone who says, "Hmm, I'll look into that." Find someone who already knows.

Real-World Scenarios

"I worked as a police officer for 25 years, but before that, I did construction and paid into Social Security for 10 years. I was expecting a small monthly check—but WEP cut it by half."

"My wife passed away. She had full Social Security benefits. I thought I'd get her survivor benefits—but I have a public pension, and GPO canceled them out."

"I moved from one department to another—first one didn't pay into Social Security, second one does. No one ever explained how that would work."

These aren't horror stories—they're caution signs. And with the right information, you can plan smarter than most.

Pros and Cons (of Being In or Out of Social Security)

Pros of NOT Paying In:

- Higher take-home pay during working years
- Often better pension benefits
- May retire earlier than Social Security allows

Cons:

- No Social Security income (or reduced)
- GPO wipes out spousal benefits
- Less diversification in retirement income

- Need to self-fund healthcare in retirement

Pros of Paying In:

- More predictable retirement income
- Access to Medicare Part A with no premium
- Spousal and survivor benefits available
- Social Security payments indexed for inflation

Cons:

- Lower take-home pay now
- Still subject to benefit reduction (WEP)
- Smaller pension in some dual-contribution systems

Action Steps

1. **Review your Social Security status at ssa.gov**
2. **Ask your department's HR whether your pension is covered or non-covered**
3. **Calculate how many credits you currently have toward Social Security**
4. **Review your pension summary to see how WEP/GPO might apply**
5. **Map out all your sources of retirement income—not just pension**
6. **Run a worst-case retirement income projection**
7. **Educate your spouse or partner about survivor scenarios**
8. **Create a backup retirement funding plan that doesn't rely on Social Security**
9. **Stay updated—these rules evolve. Check in every 6-12 months.**

Encouragement

You've made it through harder things than retirement math. You can handle this—especially now that you know what to look for.

Reminder

Financial planning isn't about getting it perfect. It's about staying ready. Knowing your eligibility (or lack thereof) is how you avoid surprises—and build real peace of mind.

Takeaway

Smart first responders don't guess with retirement. They ask questions, run the numbers, and build their plans like a structure fire—methodically, with clarity and confidence.

Prompt to Revisit

Check your Social Security and pension status again every 6-12 months, especially if your department changes, you take on side work, or your family situation shifts.

This isn't about what's "fair."

It's about what's *real*—so you can plan accordingly.

You've run toward danger your whole career. Let's help you run toward retirement with your eyes open, your plan locked in, and your family protected.

You don't just deserve a pension.

You deserve peace.

And that starts with knowing what's truly on the table.

Chapter 34: Healthcare in Retirement: Planning Beyond the Department Plan

You've been covered most of your career—whether by a city-sponsored plan, a union-negotiated package, or something else your HR department walked you through when you were 22 and barely listening. Maybe your healthcare plan wasn't perfect, but at least it was there. You had a badge, a job, and coverage.

But retirement is a different story.

And too many first responders are caught off guard when the department coverage stops but their medical needs keep going. Retire at 50 or 55 and you may be staring down a 10-to-15-year gap between your last shift and your first Medicare card.

This chapter is your prep guide. No jargon. No guessing. Just a straight-up conversation about how to make sure your retirement isn't derailed by healthcare costs.

Why Healthcare Is the Retirement Dealbreaker No One Talks About

Here's the truth: for a lot of first responders, retirement isn't about whether they've saved "enough."

It's about whether they can *afford to be uninsured.*

A $4,000/month pension sounds solid—until you realize COBRA continuation could run you $1,600 a month. And that's if you don't get sick. Add in prescriptions, copays, and out-of-network bills, and suddenly "retirement-ready" starts to look shaky.

And the worst part? It doesn't matter how tough you are. Healthcare is one of those things that doesn't care about your pension, your overtime, or your years of service.

If you're not ready, it'll eat your retirement alive.

When the Department Coverage Ends

Most departments offer some form of healthcare during your working years, but very few offer full lifetime retiree medical benefits anymore—especially not without strings attached.

Here's what typically happens:

- **You retire before age 65**
- Your department coverage ends after a short grace period (or continues under COBRA for 18–36 months)
- You're on your own for insurance until Medicare kicks in at 65

Some departments let you "buy into" coverage at full price—aka **retiree healthcare**. That's not the same as what you had while active. You're footing most, if not all, of the bill.

Others offer no post-retirement medical at all.

That means from age 50–65, you're shopping for coverage, paying full freight, and praying you don't get a diagnosis that wipes out your savings.

Your Options Between Retirement and Medicare

Let's break it down like a game plan:

1. **COBRA Continuation Coverage**

If your department coverage ends at retirement, COBRA lets you continue that plan for 18 months (sometimes 36, depending on circumstances).

Pros:

- Keeps your same doctors and network
- No gap in coverage
- Familiar structure and copays

Cons:

- You pay the full premium + 2% admin fee
- Very expensive (average is $1,500–$2,000/month for families)
- Ends after 18–36 months

COBRA is a short-term bridge, not a long-term plan. But it can buy you time while you research longer solutions.

2. **Spousal Coverage**

If your spouse is still working and has access to healthcare, you may be able to get on their plan.

Pros:

- Often cheaper than COBRA
- May extend to age 65

Cons:

- Only lasts while your spouse is employed
- Divorce or death can leave you uncovered
- Not always available if they work part-time or are also retired

Make sure you know what's available—and what's not.

3. **Marketplace/ACA Plans**

You can buy coverage through the Affordable Care Act (ACA) marketplace. Subsidies may apply based on income—but your pension counts as income.

Pros:

- Broad plan selection
- Guaranteed coverage, no denial for preexisting conditions
- Subsidies available if your income is low enough

Cons:

- Coverage varies by state and region
- Costs can skyrocket without subsidies
- Networks may be limited

This is where your retirement math starts to matter. A $5,000/month pension might sound good—until it disqualifies you from subsidies and makes ACA plans unaffordable.

4. **Health Sharing Ministries**

Some people opt into healthcare cost-sharing groups (usually religious or nonprofit). They're not insurance, but participants help pay each other's medical bills.

Pros:

- Lower monthly cost
- May provide catastrophic coverage

Cons:

- Not regulated insurance
- No guarantees on payment

- Limited on preexisting or ongoing conditions

This is a "last resort" option for those priced out of everything else.

5. **Part-Time Work With Benefits**

Some retirees take a lower-stress part-time job—at a hospital, school district, or even retail chain—to access affordable group health insurance.

Pros:

- Keeps you covered
- May include dental, vision, HSA eligibility

Cons:

- You're back on the clock
- Schedules may conflict with retirement lifestyle
- You may burn out or lose eligibility over time

Still, if the right gig shows up, this can be a smart play.

What About Medicare?

Medicare starts at age **65**—but it's not free, and it's not automatic unless you're already on Social Security.

Here's the quick breakdown:

- **Part A**: Hospital coverage — free if you (or spouse) paid into Social Security
- **Part B**: Doctor visits — monthly premium
- **Part D**: Prescription drugs — optional but recommended
- **Medigap or Medicare Advantage**: Covers the gaps

Just know: **you must sign up when eligible**—or you'll face permanent penalties. And Medicare won't cover everything, so you still need a plan.

If you retire early, you'll need to fill the 5–15 year healthcare gap before Medicare starts.

What This Costs

Let's talk numbers.

Most retirees will spend **$300,000–$400,000** on healthcare during retirement.

Even with Medicare, you'll face:

- Premiums for Part B, D, and Medigap
- Deductibles and copays
- Dental, vision, and hearing (not included)
- Long-term care (not covered at all)

This is why *retiree healthcare* isn't just a checkbox—it's a financial pillar.

Real Scenarios

"I retired at 52 and thought my wife's school district plan would cover us. But she went part-time and lost the benefit. Now we're paying $2,100/month in ACA premiums until I'm 65."

"I used COBRA for 18 months, then went uninsured for a year because the Marketplace was too expensive. I ended up in the ER after a bike accident and racked up $43,000 in bills. That shook me."

"My department offered retiree healthcare, but I didn't realize it was $900/month—and they'd drop me if I missed one payment. There's no margin for error."

Pros and Cons of Early Retirement from a Healthcare Perspective

Pros:

- More time freedom
- Chance to downshift before Medicare age
- Avoid physical burnout

Cons:

- High insurance costs
- Risk of gaps in coverage
- May erode pension or savings faster

Action Steps to Take Right Now

1. **Ask your HR or union rep about retiree healthcare options**
2. **Find out what COBRA would cost you and for how long**
3. **Check whether your spouse's plan is available to you if they keep working**
4. **Price out ACA plans for your zip code and income level**
5. **Run a Medicare cost projection for age 65+**
6. **Build healthcare into your retirement budget—not as an afterthought, but as a core line item**
7. **Create a plan for the gap years—especially if you plan to retire before 65**
8. **Explore HSAs if you're still eligible—they're powerful tools for tax-free healthcare money**
9. **Talk with a financial advisor who understands public safety retirements and medical planning**

Encouragement

You've survived fires, trauma, violence, and sleepless shifts. You can survive the complexity of retirement healthcare. You just need a plan—and a little time to put it together.

Reminder

Healthcare isn't a luxury in retirement. It's a necessity. Plan for it like you'd plan for your last alarm call: thoroughly, seriously, and with eyes wide open.

Takeaway

Smart first responders don't guess when it comes to medical costs. They build a plan, create backups, and make sure their health doesn't rob them of their wealth.

Prompt to Revisit

Revisit your healthcare plan every 6–12 months—especially before retirement and at age 64. The system changes. So should your strategy.

This chapter isn't about scaring you.

It's about preparing you.

You've earned your pension. You've earned your rest. But without a real healthcare plan, rest can get expensive fast.

Let's make sure that when the uniform comes off, your coverage stays strong.

Because even heroes need care.

And the smartest ones don't wait until it's too late.

Chapter 35: How to Turn Your Pension and Investments Into Monthly Income

You've been running full speed for decades—toward danger, into chaos, through fires, fights, trauma calls, and cardiac arrests. And now, you're thinking about slowing down. Retirement is in sight. You've earned that pension. You've contributed to your 457(b). Maybe you've even built up a Roth IRA, some savings, and a side business along the way.

But here's the question almost no one teaches you how to answer:

How do you turn that money into income you can actually live on?

You've been trained to respond to emergencies, not to structure monthly withdrawals from retirement assets. But now, this is your next mission—getting your retirement money to pay you like a job once did. Not just for a few years. For the rest of your life.

Let's talk about how to do that—with clarity, structure, and calm. Like two first responders figuring out the best way to prep a rig before the next shift.

Why Monthly Income Is the Real Goal

You don't retire on an account balance.

You retire on **income**.

$1 million in an investment account sounds great—until you realize you still have to figure out how much of it to use each month.

$5,000/month in guaranteed income? That's something you can plan around.

This chapter is all about building that monthly paycheck from your pension, retirement accounts, and personal savings—so you can live your life without constantly second-guessing every grocery bill, gas fill-up, or vacation.

You don't need a perfect plan.

You need a *repeatable, dependable system.*

Let's build it together.

Step 1: Understand What's Guaranteed and What's Not

Let's start by separating your retirement money into two buckets:

Bucket 1: Guaranteed Income

- Pension
- Social Security (if eligible)
- Annuities (if used)
- Rental income (if reliable and consistent)

Bucket 2: Flexible Assets

- 457(b), 403(b), or 401(k)
- Roth IRA or Traditional IRA
- Personal savings
- Inheritance or windfalls
- Cash reserves

Your job is to figure out how much guaranteed income you'll have coming in—and how much you need to pull from the flexible stuff to fill the gap.

Think of Bucket 1 as your base salary in retirement. Bucket 2 is your overtime, shift differential, or side hustle—you tap into it strategically.

Step 2: Know Your Monthly Number

Forget the headlines about "saving $1 million." What you really need to know is:

How much do you need each month to live the life you want—without going broke?

That means running a real retirement budget. Include:

- Mortgage or rent
- Utilities
- Groceries
- Gas
- Health insurance and medical expenses
- Travel or hobbies
- Family support (if you help kids, grandkids, etc.)
- Property taxes
- Insurance premiums
- Fun money (yes, you still need that)

Let's say your number comes out to $6,000/month.

You look at your pension and see that it pays $4,200/month.

Social Security might bring in $800/month at 67 (if eligible).

Now you're short about $1,000/month.

That $1,000 needs to come from your investment accounts.

We'll walk through how to do that *without* draining your accounts too fast—or sitting on the sidelines in fear.

Step 3: Understand the 3 Main Withdrawal Strategies

There's more than one way to turn a lump sum into monthly income. Let's look at the most common ones.

1. **The 4% Rule (Modified for Reality)**

This rule says you can safely withdraw 4% of your investment portfolio per year and have a decent shot of not running out of money over a 30-year retirement.

So if you have $500,000 saved, 4% is $20,000 per year—or about $1,667/month.

Pros: Simple, straightforward

Cons: Doesn't adjust for inflation, market crashes, or healthcare costs

Use this as a starting point—not a hard rule. Many advisors now recommend 3–3.5% to be safer, especially in volatile markets.

2. **The Guardrails Approach**

This strategy sets a "floor" and "ceiling" for withdrawals. If the market is doing well, you can withdraw more. If it's down, you reduce your spending temporarily.

Example:

- You plan to take $1,500/month from investments
- If the market drops 20%, you reduce to $1,200/month
- If it rises, you adjust back up to $1,500+

Pros: More flexible, better for market shocks

Cons: Requires discipline and adjustments—might not work for everyone

3. **The Bucket Strategy**

You divide your retirement money into time-based "buckets."

- Bucket 1 (1–3 years): Cash or conservative funds for immediate needs
- Bucket 2 (4–10 years): Moderate risk for mid-term income
- Bucket 3 (10+ years): Growth investments for long-term needs

As you spend from Bucket 1, you replenish it with gains from the others.

Pros: Smooths out market volatility, gives you peace of mind

Cons: Requires some initial setup and regular monitoring

Step 4: Decide on Withdrawal Order

Pulling money from the wrong account at the wrong time can cost you thousands in taxes. Here's a common sequence:

1. **Pension and Social Security (guaranteed money first)**
2. **Taxable savings or brokerage accounts**
3. **Tax-deferred accounts (457, Traditional IRA)**
4. **Roth IRAs last (they grow tax-free and don't have required withdrawals)**

If you're under age 59½ and withdrawing from retirement accounts, make sure you understand the **penalties and exceptions.** Public safety workers often get early access to their 457(b) plans *without* the 10% penalty.

Step 5: Prepare for Market Fluctuations

Markets go up. Markets go down. If you're retired and pulling income, that volatility can wreck your plan unless you're ready.

What to do:

- Keep 1–2 years of expenses in safer assets
- Don't panic-sell in a downturn
- Don't stop withdrawing altogether and starve your lifestyle
- Rebalance annually to stay within your risk comfort zone

Remember, you've seen chaos before. Treat the market the same way you'd treat a multi-car pileup: assess, act calmly, follow the plan.

Real-World Scenarios

"I retired with a $4,800 pension, but I still needed $800 more a month. I set up automatic transfers from my 457(b) and left the rest invested. It's been steady."

"I didn't realize taking too much from my IRA would bump me into a higher tax bracket. I adjusted by using a Roth conversion strategy in my early 60s."

"I created a three-bucket system. Even when the market dropped, I had cash for a year, so I didn't stress. That made all the difference."

Pros and Cons of DIY vs. Professional Planning

Doing It Yourself

Pros:

- Full control
- No advisor fees
- Works well if you're confident and disciplined

Cons:

- Easy to make costly mistakes
- Emotional decisions can derail strategy
- Tax missteps are common

Working With a Financial Advisor

Pros:

- Customized withdrawal plans
- Integrated tax strategy
- Can handle rebalancing and investment allocation

Cons:

- Cost (typically 1% of assets annually)
- Not all advisors understand first responder pensions or benefits

Find someone who gets your world—not just someone selling products.

Action Steps

1. **Run a full retirement income budget—down to the dollar**
2. **Add up your guaranteed income streams**
3. **Calculate the monthly gap you'll need to fill with investments**
4. **Choose a withdrawal strategy that fits your risk tolerance**
5. **Set up a 12-month cash cushion to avoid panic during market dips**
6. **Coordinate withdrawals with your tax bracket to avoid big surprises**
7. **Review and adjust your income plan annually—or after big life changes**
8. **Decide if you want to manage it yourself or partner with a trusted professional**

Encouragement

You've led teams. You've responded to disasters. You've handled life-threatening situations with focus and precision. This is just another version of that—except now, the mission is your own peace of mind.

Reminder

Retirement isn't about never working again—it's about choosing how you spend your time. A steady income stream gives you that freedom.

Takeaway

Smart first responders don't wait until they're out of the game to build their retirement paycheck. They plan ahead, build a system, and stick to it—just like every shift, every scene, every response.

Prompt to Revisit

Review your income plan every 6–12 months, and especially after market drops, big life events, or changes in your health.

Final Note

This isn't about retiring rich. It's about retiring *ready*.

With income you can count on.

With peace of mind you've earned.

With the freedom to live on your own terms—not just survive off what's left over.

You've run toward danger your whole career.

Now it's time to walk into retirement with confidence—and a monthly plan that's got your back.

Chapter 36: What Happens to Your 457(b) and IRA After Retirement

You've clocked out of your final shift. You've turned in the gear, packed your locker, said your goodbyes, and walked out the same doors you walked into years ago—green, hungry, and full of questions.

Now here you are, a few decades later. The uniform's off. The pension's in place. But there's a new question on your mind:

"What do I actually do with my 457(b) or IRA now?"

It's not just about how much you saved—it's about how you *use* it. How you take the money you spent years building and turn it into something you can live off of, protect, and pass on. You're no longer just a first responder. You're the chief financial officer of your own retirement. And the decisions you make now? They'll echo for the next 20 to 30 years of your life.

So grab some coffee, lean back, and let's talk—straight up—about what happens to your 457(b) and IRAs after you retire.

Your Accounts Don't Retire—You Do

First things first: your accounts don't know you're retired.

They don't magically turn into monthly paychecks. They don't start mailing you checks on their own. And they definitely don't get easier to understand just because you've stepped out of the station.

But what they do offer—if handled correctly—is flexibility, freedom, and leverage.

Handled poorly? They can turn into tax traps, income headaches, or forgotten tools gathering dust.

Let's make sure your 457(b) and IRAs keep working—so you don't have to.

Understanding the 457(b) in Retirement

Let's start with your 457(b)—a plan tailor-made for public sector workers like you.

What it is:

A tax-deferred retirement account where you likely stashed money over the years. Contributions came out of your paycheck pre-tax, and the account grew tax-deferred.

What happens now:

You can start taking withdrawals. And here's the key difference between 457(b)s and 401(k)s or 403(b)s:

There's no 10% early withdrawal penalty on a 457(b)—even if you retire before age 59½. That's huge.

So if you're 53 and you're done working, you can tap your 457(b) penalty-free (though you'll still pay income taxes).

That flexibility is part of what makes the 457(b) such a powerful tool for first responders.

Understanding IRAs in Retirement

You may have also built up:

- A **Traditional IRA**: tax-deferred, just like your 457(b)
- A **Roth IRA**: funded with after-tax dollars, grows and distributes tax-free if used properly

So what happens to these after you retire?

Traditional IRA:

- You'll pay ordinary income tax on any withdrawals
- You *can't* touch it before age 59½ without a penalty (unless you qualify for certain exceptions)
- You'll have to start taking Required Minimum Distributions (RMDs) at age 73

Roth IRA:

- Withdrawals are tax-free after age 59½ if the account's been open 5+ years
- No RMDs in your lifetime
- Great tool to leave to heirs or use in high-tax years without bumping your income bracket

Think of your Traditional IRA as a deferred paycheck—and your Roth IRA as a secret stash that gets better the longer you leave it alone.

Should You Consolidate Your Accounts?

Some retirees wonder whether they should roll their 457(b) into an IRA.

Here's the pros and cons:

Pros of Rolling Over to IRA:

- More investment options
- Easier to manage everything in one place
- Better for estate planning or Roth conversions

Cons:

- You lose the special 457(b) no-penalty rule
- Once it's rolled over, early withdrawals may be subject to 10% penalty

if you're under 59½
- Might complicate your tax strategy if not done correctly

Bottom Line:

If you're under 59½ and want access to that money without penalties, **keep your 457(b) intact for now.** You can always roll it over later.

Required Minimum Distributions (RMDs)

Starting at age 73, the IRS makes you start pulling money from your tax-deferred accounts. Why? Because Uncle Sam wants his cut.

Applies to:

- Traditional IRAs
- 457(b), 403(b), and 401(k) plans
- Not Roth IRAs (during your lifetime)

If you don't take your RMD, the penalty is massive—**up to 25% of what you should've withdrawn.** That's not a slap on the wrist. That's a financial knockout punch.

So mark the calendar. Know the rules. Plan your withdrawals intentionally.

Tax Traps to Watch For

1. Double Dipping Into the Same Bracket

If you're taking a pension, withdrawing from your 457(b), and drawing Social Security or other income—all in the same year—you may push yourself into a higher tax bracket without realizing it.

2. Big One-Time Withdrawals

Need a new truck? Want to do a home renovation? Pulling $40,000 all at once from your 457(b) could spike your taxes big time. Consider spreading withdrawals across years, or using Roth funds if available.

3. Roth Conversions Without Strategy

Converting money from your 457(b) or IRA to a Roth can be smart—but do it in a high-income year and you'll pay dearly in taxes. Always run the numbers.

What to Do With the Money Now

You've got three main options:

1. **Leave It Alone**
2. You can leave your accounts invested and untouched until you need them. This is great if you don't need the money yet and want to let them grow.
3. **Set Up Monthly Withdrawals**
4. Many retirees set up automated withdrawals—say, $1,000/month—from their 457(b) or IRA. This creates a "retirement paycheck" to supplement your pension.
5. **Move to an IRA and Manage More Actively**
6. If you want more control, or plan to use Roth conversions, you might move your 457(b) into an IRA. Just be strategic about when and how.

How Much Should You Take Each Month?

There's no magic number. But here are some principles:

- **Don't withdraw more than 4% annually**, unless you're planning for a shorter retirement
- **Adjust for market conditions**—cut back during downturns
- **Balance income with taxes**—keep your total taxable income in a manageable range
- **Use Roth funds for tax flexibility**—especially in years when income spikes
- **Maintain a cash cushion**—3–6 months of expenses in a money

market or savings account

Real-World Scenarios

"I retired at 56 and kept my 457(b) intact. I take $2,000/month from it and leave my IRA alone until I hit 60. So far, so good."

"My pension covered the basics, but I wanted more travel money. I use my Roth IRA to take $5,000 every other year—tax-free—and it doesn't mess with my tax bracket."

"I rolled everything into a Traditional IRA too early and got hit with penalties when I needed the cash. I wish I'd known about the 457(b) early withdrawal rule."

Pros and Cons

Keeping 457(b) Intact

Pros:

- Penalty-free access under age 59½
- Familiar structure
- Can draw income gradually

Cons:

- Limited investment choices
- May lack planning flexibility
- Might need to roll over eventually

Rolling to IRA

Pros:

- More investment options
- Better control over withdrawals and tax planning

- Roth conversion opportunities

Cons:

- Lose penalty-free access if under 59½
- Must follow stricter RMD rules

Action Steps

1. **Inventory every retirement account: 457(b), IRA, Roth IRA, etc.**
2. **Decide which accounts you'll use first—and which you'll delay**
3. **Avoid rolling over your 457(b) if you're under 59½ and need access**
4. **Set up an income stream if you need regular withdrawals**
5. **Map out your RMD dates starting at age 73**
6. **Run a tax forecast with all your income sources**
7. **Consider Roth conversions in low-income years**
8. **Keep a cash reserve outside of your retirement accounts**
9. **Review your plan every 6–12 months with a qualified financial advisor**

Encouragement

You've built these accounts over decades—through long nights, dangerous calls, and skipped holidays. You *can* figure out how to use them well. And you don't have to do it alone.

Reminder

These accounts are tools—not trophies. They're meant to be used. Don't be afraid to draw on what you've earned—just do it with clarity and strategy.

Takeaway

Smart first responders don't just save—they build systems. Turning your 457(b) and IRA into monthly income is a mission worth planning for.

Prompt to Revisit

Revisit your withdrawal and rollover strategy every year—especially if the market shifts, tax laws change, or your personal life evolves.

Final Note

This is the part where the job gets personal. It's no longer about shifts, structure fires, or trauma scenes. It's about your next chapter. Your freedom. Your choices.

Your 457(b) and IRA aren't just accounts—they're the fuel for your life after the job.

Let's make sure that fuel lasts.

Let's make it count.

Chapter 37: Taxes in Retirement – What You'll Still Owe Uncle Sam

So you're done with the late-night calls. The station coffee. The overtime shifts. The risk. The heat. The trauma. You've earned your pension, built your 457(b), maybe even padded an IRA or two. You've done what most never do—made it to retirement in one piece.

Now you're looking forward to the slower mornings, more time with grandkids, fishing trips, or that dream RV road trip you and your spouse keep talking about.

But there's one thing that never retires.

Uncle Sam.

Just because you're done working doesn't mean the IRS is done with you. And if you don't have a strategy—if you think retirement means your tax days are behind you—well... you're gonna learn the hard way.

Let's make sure that doesn't happen.

This chapter is a conversation—between you and someone who understands your world. Someone who knows what it's like to get dressed in the dark, eat lunch at 3:00 a.m., and wonder if your back will hold up one more year. We're going to break it all down in plain English, with no judgment and no fluff.

Because retirement isn't about dodging taxes—it's about being ready for them.

The Big Lie: "I Won't Owe Much in Retirement Taxes"

Here's what too many first responders believe:

> *"Once I retire, I won't make as much, so I won't pay much in taxes."*

That's only partially true.

If you live off *only* Social Security and have no pension, sure—you might owe very little. But most of you reading this? You're retiring with:

- A public pension
- A 457(b) or 403(b)
- Possibly a Roth or Traditional IRA
- Some side income (maybe from consulting, training, or part-time work)

You've done well. You've put in your time. But here's the kicker:

Every dollar of pension income is taxable.

Every withdrawal from your 457(b) or Traditional IRA is taxable.

And Social Security? That's partially taxable too—depending on your total income.

So if you're collecting $5,000/month in pension and pulling $1,500/month from your 457(b)?

That's $78,000 in annual income—not including Social Security or side gigs.

That's **taxable** income.

So let's get into it.

What's Taxable in Retirement—and What's Not

Let's keep this real simple.

Fully Taxable:

- Your public pension income

- Withdrawals from your 457(b), 403(b), or Traditional IRA
- Part-time job or consulting income
- Rental income
- Most annuity income
- Required Minimum Distributions (RMDs)

Partially Taxable:

- Social Security (up to 85% of it, depending on income)

Tax-Free (if done right):

- Qualified Roth IRA withdrawals (age 59½ + 5-year rule)
- Municipal bond interest
- Health Savings Account (HSA) withdrawals for medical expenses
- Life insurance death benefit payouts

The goal? Don't just focus on how much you have saved. Focus on how much of it you *keep* after taxes.

Your Retirement Tax Bracket

The U.S. tax system is progressive, meaning the more you make, the higher your rate on that last dollar.

As of this writing, here are some sample brackets for a married couple filing jointly:

- 10%: $0 – $23,200
- 12%: $23,201 – $94,300
- 22%: $94,301 – $201,050
- 24%: $201,051 – $383,900

You might think, "Well I'm not rich. I'll be in a low bracket."

But once you add pension + 457(b) withdrawals + Social Security + other income, you might be pulling in $80K–$120K/year in retirement—and sitting squarely in the 22–24% bracket.

That's not crazy rich. That's "did the job, put in the time, and built something" income.

And without a tax strategy, you'll lose thousands to Uncle Sam every year.

Understanding Social Security Taxation

Here's a real gut-punch for many retirees:

> *Up to **85% of your Social Security** can be taxed depending on how much other income you have.*

Here's how it works:

They calculate something called "**provisional income**":

- Your adjusted gross income
- half your Social Security
- any tax-exempt interest (like muni bonds)

Then:

- If you're **single** and your provisional income is over $34,000—or **married** and over $44,000—up to 85% of your Social Security becomes taxable.

So yeah. If you thought Social Security was a tax-free benefit, think again. For most retired first responders, **it's partially taxed.**

Required Minimum Distributions (RMDs)

Once you turn 73, the IRS starts making you take money out of your tax-deferred accounts—whether you need it or not.

That includes:

- 457(b)s
- Traditional IRAs
- 403(b)s and 401(k)s

You have to withdraw a certain percentage each year, and that money gets added to your taxable income.

Miss the deadline? The penalty used to be 50%—now it's 25%. Still brutal.

Many retirees get caught off guard by how much their RMDs bump their tax bill—especially when combined with pension and Social Security.

How to Lower Your Tax Bill in Retirement

Let's talk tactics—not theory.

1. Roth Conversions in Low-Income Years

If you retire at 55 but delay Social Security until 67, you've got a 12-year window where your income may be lower. That's prime time to start converting some of your 457(b) or IRA to a Roth—paying taxes now at a lower rate to avoid higher ones later.

2. Strategic Withdrawals

Don't wait until RMDs force your hand. Start taking small withdrawals from tax-deferred accounts earlier—especially if your pension isn't enough by itself.

3. Fill Your Tax Bracket, Not Blow Past It

If you're in the 12% bracket, see how much room you have before hitting the 22% bracket—and only withdraw up to that line. Don't accidentally jump brackets and pay more on every extra dollar.

4. Use Your HSA Wisely

If you have an HSA from your working years, it can be a secret weapon. Withdrawals for medical expenses are **completely tax-free.** That's one of the few places where you can spend tax-free in retirement.

5. Keep Roths for Later

Don't tap into your Roth IRA too early. Let it grow. Use it strategically in years when your tax bill spikes (like when selling a property or facing a big medical bill).

What If You Move Out of State?

Thinking of retiring to Florida or Texas? You're not alone.

Here's what you need to know:

- **Some states tax pensions. Others don't.**
- **Some states don't have any state income tax at all.**
- Even if your state doesn't tax Social Security, the *federal government still might.*

A move can lower your tax bill—but only if you've planned for it. Know the rules before you pack the truck.

Real-World Scenarios

"I retired at 60 with a $4,800/month pension and didn't realize it was taxable. The first year I owed $5,200 more in taxes than I expected."

"I converted $50,000 from my IRA to Roth in one year and pushed myself into the 24% bracket. I could've spread it over 3 years and paid far less."

"My RMD at age 73 added $25,000 to my income, bumped me into a higher Medicare bracket, and triggered a bigger premium. It was a domino effect I didn't see coming."

Action Steps

1. **Run a Retirement Tax Projection**—use your pension, estimated 457(b) withdrawals, and Social Security
2. **Learn your tax bracket**—and what income level pushes you into the next one
3. **Decide when to take Social Security based on tax impact—not just age**
4. **Start small Roth conversions early (if it fits your situation)**
5. **Calculate RMDs in advance** so you're not surprised at 73
6. **Meet with a tax-savvy advisor annually**—retirement is not the time to DIY your taxes
7. **Review state tax laws if considering a move**
8. **Update withholding elections on pension and IRA distributions**—so you don't get a nasty April surprise
9. **Keep tax-efficient investments in taxable accounts**—muni bonds, ETFs, etc.

Encouragement

You've made it through harder things than tax planning. Don't let this stress you. You don't need to know *everything*—you just need to know *enough* to ask the right questions and build a smart plan.

Reminder

Your job in retirement isn't to avoid taxes altogether—it's to avoid tax *surprises.* Predictability is power.

Takeaway

Smart first responders don't just train for emergencies. They train for everything—including taxes. Because the quieter your retirement tax story, the smoother the rest of the story runs.

Prompt to Revisit

Review your tax plan every year—or anytime your income changes. A smart tax move this year could save you thousands for decades.

Final Note

You protected others for decades. Now it's time to protect *yourself*—from taxes you didn't expect, brackets you didn't see coming, and penalties that can eat up your hard-earned peace of mind.

This isn't about fearing taxes.

It's about **leading your next mission with clarity**.

You've run toward danger.

Now run toward retirement—tax-aware, confident, and in control.

Chapter 39: Retirement Locations – Stay Local or Move? Cost-of-Living Considerations

You've finally reached the finish line. The pager's quiet. Your turnout gear is boxed up. You're no longer checking your phone for shift swaps or calls from dispatch. You're retired. But now, a different kind of decision is staring you down—the one most people don't talk about until it's too late:

Where are you going to live?

Not just "what's your zip code"—but *where will your money, your lifestyle, and your peace of mind stretch the furthest?*

Will you stay in the same city you've served for decades, where the neighbors know your name and your grandkids are a short drive away? Or do you pack up and move somewhere cheaper, quieter, warmer, or farther from the tax man?

This chapter isn't about fantasy retirement. It's about *real-life tradeoffs*. It's a conversation between peers—off shift, off duty, and finally thinking about what life looks like *after* the job.

Retirement Isn't Just About Income—It's About Where That Income Lands

Let's start here:

A $5,000/month pension looks a whole lot different in San Francisco than it does in Savannah.

It's not just what you *make*—it's what you *keep*.

Too many first responders build their careers thinking, *"Once I hit 30 years, I'm set."* But then they retire in a high-cost zip code, inflation kicks in, property taxes rise, and suddenly the pension that felt solid is stretched thinner than expected.

So the question isn't just *"Can you afford to retire?"*

It's *"Can you afford to stay where you are?"*

Why This Decision Matters More Than You Think

Where you retire determines:

- Your cost of living (housing, food, utilities, insurance)
- Your state income taxes (on pensions, Social Security, investments)
- Your access to healthcare (Medicare networks, specialists, rural hospital availability)
- Your proximity to family and your support system
- Your peace of mind—yes, that too

This is not just about dollars and cents. It's about *quality of life*.

Do you want to be near grandkids?

Do you want snow-free winters?

Do you want more bang for your retirement buck—or more familiarity and routine?

There's no one-size-fits-all answer. But there is a system you can use to make a smart decision.

Let's build that system together.

The Big Question: Stay Local or Move?

Staying Local

Pros:

- Close to family, friends, and grandkids
- Familiar doctors, stores, and routines
- No moving expenses
- You know the local risks—property taxes, insurance quirks, fire/flood zones, etc.
- Emotional attachment to the community you served

Cons:

- Higher cost of living in many metro areas
- Local taxes may bite into pension income
- Real estate/property taxes may rise faster than your income
- May not be the best healthcare access, depending on region
- Emotional familiarity can block objective financial decisions

Moving Elsewhere

Pros:

- Potentially lower taxes and housing costs
- Warmer climate or slower pace of life
- Stretch your retirement income further
- Start fresh—new hobbies, lifestyle, friends
- Better alignment with health needs (e.g., near VA hospital or specialists)

Cons:

- Farther from family and support system
- Risk of isolation or loneliness

- Less familiarity with local services (medical, legal, financial)
- Moving and relocation costs
- Starting over—church, barbershop, gym, grocery store, everything

This isn't just a spreadsheet decision—it's a lifestyle one. And you've got to weigh it from every angle.

Understanding Cost of Living (COL)

Cost of Living isn't just one number. It includes:

- Housing
- Groceries
- Utilities
- Property taxes
- Transportation
- Insurance premiums
- Healthcare costs

Your pension may stay flat. But those things don't. Especially healthcare. Especially taxes.

Use tools like COL calculators, but then go one step further. Call someone who *lives* in the area you're considering. Ask them about:

- Their utility bills
- Insurance costs
- Grocery prices
- Medical wait times
- What their property taxes look like

That's the real-world research that matters more than any Google search.

State Tax Considerations

Not all states treat your retirement income the same. Some don't tax pensions at all. Others tax part of them. Some hammer you with property taxes. Others make up for no income tax with higher sales taxes.

States with no income tax:

- Texas
- Florida
- Nevada
- Washington
- Tennessee
- South Dakota
- Wyoming
- Alaska

States that don't tax pensions or Social Security:

- Illinois
- Mississippi
- Pennsylvania
- Alaska
- Florida
- Nevada
- South Dakota
- Tennessee
- Texas
- Washington
- Wyoming

But don't just chase tax savings. A state may have no income tax but outrageous property taxes or insurance costs (looking at you, coastal Florida).

Balance tax policy with total cost of living.

Real-World Scenario

Bob – Retired Fire Captain, Age 56

Lives in New Jersey. Has a $6,000/month pension. Wants to stay near kids but is getting crushed by property taxes ($11,000/year). Groceries and gas are up. He's house-rich, cash-tight.

His Options:

1. Sell the house, move 3 hours away to Pennsylvania—drops his property taxes by 60%, same healthcare access
2. Stay put, but rent out the basement or downsize
3. Relocate to Florida near his brother, where housing and taxes are cheaper, but he loses weekly grandkid visits

There's no "correct" answer. But there is a *calculated* one. Bob runs the numbers, weighs the emotional impact, and chooses PA—still close to family, but with financial breathing room.

Emotional Ties vs. Financial Realities

Let's talk truth:

Some of you will want to stay where you raised your kids, where you coached youth ball, where you saved lives, fought fires, and built your identity.

And that matters.

But just like you used to tell rookies on scene: **emotions don't replace tactics**.

You can love your city and still decide to live somewhere else in retirement.

You can still visit. Still support local causes. Still be connected.

But your retirement money has to last.

And sometimes that means leaving behind the comfort zone so you can protect your long-term well-being.

Action Steps

1. **Get a true COL estimate for your current zip code AND any you're considering**
2. **Research state taxes on pensions, IRAs, and Social Security**
3. **Factor in moving costs, real estate fees, and home repairs if downsizing**
4. **Make a list of your non-negotiables: climate, healthcare access, proximity to family**
5. **Visit potential retirement locations during off-season—what's it *really* like?**
6. **Talk to a CPA or financial advisor about the tax impact of relocating**
7. **Run a "retirement budget" for 3 different locations**
8. **Think through long-term healthcare—are you close to the right facilities?**
9. **Revisit this question every 2–3 years—your needs will evolve**

Encouragement

You've spent your whole life helping others stay safe. It's okay to make a decision that protects *you* this time. You earned that.

Reminder

This isn't a forever decision—you can move once, twice, or not at all. But don't let habit or fear make the call for you. Make it with your eyes open.

Takeaway

Smart first responders know that where you live affects how you live. Retirement location isn't just about climate or cost—it's about lifestyle, health, access, and legacy.

Prompt to Revisit

Every couple of years, ask yourself: *Is where I live still aligned with how I want to live?*

Final Note

Whether you stay in the same zip code or retire two states away, the goal is the same:

Peace of mind. Room to breathe. Money that lasts.

You served others for decades. Now you get to serve *your future self*—with clarity, courage, and a well-mapped plan.

And wherever you land, remember:

You're not running from anything.

You're *moving toward* freedom.

Chapter 40: Retirement Hobbies That Pay – How Retired First Responders Can Consult, Teach, or Volunteer

You finally did it. You turned in your gear. No more 24-hour shifts, midnight trauma calls, or structure fire adrenaline dumps. You don't have to run anymore—at least not toward danger. You've got a pension, maybe some savings or a 457(b), and time on your hands.

But here's the thing they don't tell you about retirement:

It's not just about what you walk away from. It's about what you walk toward.

And if you've been wired to serve, to lead, to solve high-pressure problems your entire adult life—you're not just going to fade into the background. That's not how you're built.

The good news? You don't have to choose between doing meaningful work and having your freedom.

You can teach. You can consult. You can volunteer.

And yes—you can *get paid* doing it.

This chapter is about rediscovering purpose, passion, and peace of mind—while maybe pocketing a little side income on the way.

Retirement Doesn't Mean Irrelevance

Let's be clear: retirement doesn't mean you're done.

It means you're **free to choose** what you do next.

Some retired first responders take their knowledge and apply it to a second act:

- Teaching EMT classes
- Consulting for private security or fire protection firms
- Coaching leadership for new recruits
- Writing for trade magazines or blogs
- Serving in community emergency response teams (CERT)
- Volunteering at schools, camps, or nonprofits
- Becoming elected officials, advocates, or advisors

Retirement is your launchpad—not your end zone.

Why Paid Hobbies Are the Sweet Spot

There's something powerful about doing work you care about—with none of the politics, pressure, or pension worries attached.

Here's why hobbies that pay are gold in retirement:

- **They give you purpose without burnout.**
- **They let you leverage a lifetime of skill and credibility.**
- **They can provide supplemental income without messing up your pension.**
- **They connect you to others in ways that promote longevity and mental health.**

And here's the key: you don't have to grind anymore.

You're not building a career—you're enjoying a season. A season that you control.

Common Retirement Side Paths for First Responders

Let's break down some common—and lucrative—paths that retired firefighters, police, and paramedics walk into:

1. **Teaching and Training**

You've got decades of experience. That's worth something.

- Teach EMT, CPR, first responder certification courses at local colleges or training centers.
- Serve as an instructor for new hire academies or cadet programs.
- Offer in-service training or continuing education for departments needing updated certifications.
- Teach community first aid classes, home safety courses, or "Stop the Bleed" workshops.

How much can you earn?

Adjunct instructors often make $25–$75 per hour depending on the topic and region. Private classes can net even more.

2. **Consulting**

You know how to manage crisis, systems, operations, safety protocols, communication under pressure. That's consulting gold.

- Work with municipalities or private firms to evaluate their emergency plans.
- Help schools, hospitals, or large businesses improve their evacuation or incident response protocols.
- Support legal teams in cases involving first responder testimony, procedures, or liability.
- Assist new chiefs or department heads in leadership transitions.
- Review budgets and resource allocations as an outside eye.

How much can you earn?

Many consultants start at $50–$150/hour. Expert witness work or corporate consulting may fetch more.

3. **Writing and Speaking**

Got stories? Lessons? Opinions? Turn them into content.

- Write for trade publications, firefighter/police/EMS magazines, or niche blogs.
- Develop a book, memoir, or training manual.
- Speak at conferences, community groups, or school events.
- Host a podcast or YouTube channel on leadership, safety, or the life of a first responder.

It doesn't have to go viral. It just has to be *true*—and yours.

4. **Volunteer Roles That Open Doors**

Sometimes, giving your time opens new professional opportunities you never imagined.

- Join the board of a nonprofit that serves veterans, youth, or trauma victims.
- Volunteer at a fire museum, police outreach program, or community safety initiative.
- Mentor younger officers, paramedics, or cadets.
- Participate in disaster response drills or medical reserve corps events.
- Serve as a public information officer during local emergencies—on your terms.

You might not make money right away—but these roles often turn into consulting gigs, speaking invites, or part-time leadership posts.

Will It Mess Up My Pension?

For most state and municipal pensions, *outside income won't reduce your pension benefit*—as long as you're not returning to work for the exact same agency that employs you.

Still, know the rules:

- **Double dipping laws** may apply in your state if you return to public service in a similar role.
- **Earnings limits** could affect Social Security if you take benefits before full retirement age.
- If you're on a disability pension, **earning income may trigger a re-evaluation.**

When in doubt, talk to your pension office or a trusted advisor.

But don't let fear stop you from doing work that fills you up.

Real-World Examples

Lt. John – Retired Police Officer, Age 58

Teaches part-time at the police academy and consults with a local city council on neighborhood safety plans. Earns about $2,000/month working 10–15 hours/week. Says, "I'm still making a difference—without wearing the badge."

Maria – Retired Paramedic, Age 60

Volunteers with the local high school health careers club. Eventually gets asked to speak at a regional EMS conference. Now runs a small online course teaching paramedic test prep. Makes extra money, but more importantly, feels connected.

Ray – Retired Battalion Chief, Age 62

Starts a handyman business and helps other retirees fireproof their homes. Turns it into a niche safety consulting firm. Hires a part-time assistant. Says, "It never felt like work. It felt like I was still protecting people—just with a wrench instead of a hose."

Pros and Cons of "Paid Hobbies" in Retirement

Pros:

- Keeps your mind sharp and your calendar balanced
- Offers extra income without full-time pressure
- Lets you stay connected to your field or community
- Can improve emotional and psychological well-being
- Reinforces your identity, purpose, and usefulness

Cons:

- May trigger tax complications if not planned for
- Can distract from rest or travel if boundaries aren't set
- Requires self-promotion or networking if starting something new
- Risk of "accidentally" working full-time again
- May reduce government benefits (Social Security) if early

This is why structure matters. You don't want your "fun side gig" to become your second career—unless you *want* that.

Action Steps to Turn Passion into Pay

1. **Make a list of things you loved (and didn't love) about your career.**
2. **Write down three skills you'd like to share—outside the field.**
3. **Explore local opportunities—community colleges, nonprofits, CERT programs.**
4. **Talk to someone who's already consulting or teaching part-time.**
5. **Set a monthly time budget—how many hours you *really* want to work.**
6. **Decide if you want to make income or just impact—or both.**
7. **Create a simple resume or "one-sheet" about what you offer.**
8. **Check with your pension office or tax advisor to avoid surprises.**

9. **Try something on a trial basis before fully committing.**
10. **Revisit your engagement every 6–12 months to make sure it still fits your lifestyle.**

Encouragement

You didn't retire to sit still. You retired to live free. If you want to keep serving, teaching, or contributing—there's a place for you. And you don't have to choose between doing good and doing well.

Reminder

Work in retirement should *fit your life,* not run it. If you wake up dreading it, it's not a hobby anymore—it's a job. Set boundaries. Choose joy. Create impact.

Takeaway

Smart first responders don't just stop working. They *redirect* their purpose. And if that purpose happens to pay a little? Even better.

Prompt to Revisit

Reassess your retirement hobbies every 6 months. Are they still fun? Still meaningful? Still worth your time? If not, pivot. You've earned the right to explore.

Final Note

This chapter wasn't about getting rich. It was about staying *rich in purpose.*

Because after decades of service, your voice, experience, and leadership still matter.

Whether it's in a classroom, on a board, behind a camera, or across a kitchen table—you're not done giving.

And the world still needs what only you can offer.

You ran toward danger.

Now run toward *what lights you up.*

And if it happens to put a few extra dollars in your pocket?

Even better.

Chapter 41: Legacy Planning – Leaving More Than Just a Pension Behind

You didn't spend decades charging into danger just to leave behind a paycheck.

You served, protected, healed, trained, and led. You kept your promises—to your department, your crew, and your community. But now, in the quiet stretch after the final shift, another kind of leadership begins:

What will you leave behind?

Not just to your spouse or kids. Not just in your bank accounts or pension checks. But in your values, your name, your decisions, and your systems.

This is legacy planning.

And no, it's not just about a will. It's about creating order from chaos for the people who will carry your story forward. It's about clarity when they're grieving. Direction when they're lost. And peace of mind—because you handled things like the professional you've always been.

This chapter is your blueprint. Your final service plan. Your guide to building a financial and personal legacy that lasts.

What Legacy Really Means

Legacy isn't a luxury. It's not for "rich folks."

It's not something you do when you're 90 with nothing else to think about.

It's structure, values, clarity, and care—passed down with purpose.

And for first responders, legacy matters even more. You've lived a life where danger was normal, and sudden loss wasn't rare. So let's build the kind of legacy that protects your people long after your last call.

It starts with answering this question:

If something happened to me tomorrow, would my family know what to do?

If your answer is no—or even "sort of"—you're in the right place.

You Are More Than Your Pension

Let's break this down:

What most people leave behind:

- A pension (or survivor benefit)
- A house (maybe with a mortgage)
- A retirement account (457(b), IRA, etc.)
- A funeral bill
- A lot of confusion

What smart first responders leave behind:

- A clear estate plan
- Up-to-date beneficiary designations
- An emergency binder or "go bag" of financial documents
- Life insurance (if applicable)
- A list of passwords, accounts, and advisors
- Clarity about their values and final wishes
- A debt-free or manageable estate
- Confidence that their family will be okay

This isn't about money. It's about **reducing chaos during a crisis.**

You wouldn't walk into a structure fire without a plan.

Don't walk into retirement without one either.

Building a Legacy Plan, Step by Step

Step 1: Get Your Will, Power of Attorney, and Healthcare Directives in Place

These aren't just for "old people." They're for *prepared* people.

- **Will** – Who gets what, and who handles it
- **Financial Power of Attorney** – Who manages your accounts if you're incapacitated
- **Healthcare Directive/Living Will** – What kind of care you want (or don't want)
- **Healthcare Proxy** – Who makes medical decisions if you can't

Without these, your family may need to go to court, guess your wishes, or get stuck in red tape when time is critical.

Don't leave them in the dark. Put it in writing.

Step 2: Review Your Beneficiaries

This takes 15 minutes and could save your family months of legal battles.

Review the listed beneficiaries on:

- Your pension survivor option
- Life insurance
- 457(b), IRA, or other retirement accounts
- Union death benefits or department payout accounts
- Bank accounts with transfer-on-death options

Pro tip: Beneficiary designations override your will. So make sure they're correct—and updated if you've had a divorce, remarriage, or birth of a child.

Step 3: Create a Financial "Go Bag"

Just like your gear bag had everything you needed for a call, this one holds everything your family needs if something happens to you.

Include:

- Copies of your will, power of attorney, healthcare directive
- List of accounts and institutions (bank, credit union, pension board, etc.)
- Login info for key financial accounts (or instructions to access them)
- A contact list of your financial advisor, attorney, insurance agent, etc.
- Titles to property, vehicles, and insurance policies
- Instructions for funeral, cremation, or burial preferences
- Military paperwork if applicable (DD-214)

Put this in a fireproof safe. Tell your spouse or children where it is.

Pensions Aren't Bulletproof

You know this: pensions are strong—but not invincible.
What if:

- Your spouse doesn't get the full amount you did?
- You both die and the pension dies with you?
- The pension board changes rules in the future?

This is why legacy planning also includes:

- **Life insurance** (term, whole, or department-based)
- **Private savings and investments**
- **A Roth IRA or 457(b)** that can be passed to heirs
- **A trust** if you have minor children or complicated family dynamics

The pension is the base. But it can't be the whole plan.

Talk to Your Family—Even If It's Uncomfortable

This is the step that makes all the legal stuff *real.*

Sit down with your spouse. Your adult kids. Your sibling if they're your executor. Whoever needs to know.

Tell them:

- What your wishes are
- Where your documents are
- Who to call if something happens
- What you *don't* want them to stress over

They don't need a PowerPoint presentation. They need *your voice.*

You've faced death before. You've walked into uncertainty and come out stronger. This conversation might be hard—but it's not harder than leaving your family lost without answers.

Teaching the Next Generation What You Wish You'd Known

Legacy isn't just legal. It's emotional. Cultural. Educational.

Part of what you leave behind isn't a bank account. It's *wisdom.*

Write a letter to your kids or grandkids. Teach them what you wish someone had told you:

- How to build credit
- Why saving early matters
- What not to do with a windfall
- The dangers of lifestyle inflation
- How you got burned—and how they can avoid it

You don't need to be a financial planner. Just share what you learned the hard way.

That's legacy, too.

Real-Life Scenarios

"After Dad died, we didn't know where anything was. No will. No paperwork. We spent six months tracking down pension info and had to pay out-of-pocket for the funeral. I swore I'd never do that to my kids."

"I thought my pension covered everything. Then I realized my wife would only get 60% after I'm gone. We bought a small life insurance policy just in case."

"I wrote letters to my grandkids. Told them how I saved, why I worked so much OT, and what I hope they do with the house one day. They cried reading it. Said it meant more than the money."

Action Steps

1. **Write or update your will**
2. **Assign a financial and healthcare power of attorney**
3. **Review and update your beneficiary forms**
4. **Create or update your "go bag" with essential documents**
5. **Talk to your family about your legacy plan**
6. **Get basic life insurance if your pension doesn't provide full survivor protection**
7. **Meet with a financial advisor and estate planning attorney**
8. **Write a values letter to your loved ones (optional, but powerful)**
9. **Review all of this annually—or after a major life change**

Encouragement

You've already done the hard part—serving, saving, showing up. This is just the follow-through. And your family? They'll be grateful you thought ahead.

Reminder

Legacy is not about being rich. It's about being *ready.*

Takeaway

Smart first responders don't just leave a pension. They leave a plan. A system. A safety net. And a legacy that lasts.

Prompt to Revisit

Check your legacy plan once a year—or after a major event like retirement, divorce, new grandchild, or death in the family.

Final Note

You've protected others your entire career.
Now protect their future—even after you're gone.
Give them clarity. Peace. Direction. And dignity.
Because the real legacy isn't just the pension you earned.
It's the person you were—and the love you left behind.
Make it count.

PART V: SPECIALTY TOPICS FOR FIRST RESPONDERS – What Makes This Job Financially Unique

From the book: Financial Literacy For First Responders (Firefighters, Police, Paramedics)

Part V is where we step out of the generic financial advice lane and into the real-life, boots-on-the-ground reality of the first responder experience. This section addresses the financial issues that *only* firefighters, police officers, and paramedics face—the stuff that doesn't show up in mainstream personal finance books but impacts your money every single shift, every single year.

Here, we unpack the complex blend of public pensions, unpredictable overtime, injury risks, early retirement timelines, and survivor benefits that make your career—and your financial planning—different. We explore how high-stress jobs affect spending habits, how hazard pay and shift differentials can confuse your actual income, and what happens when your body gives out before your pension kicks in. We cover the rules, red tape, and nuances around Deferred Retirement Option Plans (DROP), vesting timelines, and why your Social Security eligibility may not look like your neighbor's.

This part also digs into the psychological side: the burnout, the "I'll deal with it later" mindset, the adrenaline-fueled spending, and the urge to spoil your kids because you missed their birthdays to work the job. It's about how trauma shapes how you handle money—and how to build systems that protect you and your family when life on the job gets messy.

If Parts I through IV laid the foundation, **Part V is the firehouse kitchen conversation**—raw, honest, and tailor-made for your world. It gives you the tools to plan not just for *a* retirement, but for *your* retirement. Not just for wealth, but for resilience.

This is where financial literacy stops being abstract—and starts being personal.

Chapter 42: Understanding First Responder Liability – Legal, Civil, and Financial Risks

You've trained for chaos. For trauma. For blood, fire, and bullets. You've practiced running toward the worst-case scenario.

But what happens when *you* become the one under scrutiny? Not in uniform. Not on scene. But in court. Or at the kitchen table trying to explain a letter that says, "You are being sued."

As a first responder, you face a level of personal liability that most civilians will never understand. One split-second decision under pressure can trigger legal consequences that chase you for years—long after the lights stop flashing.

This chapter is not about fear. It's about preparation.

Not about guilt. But **about guarding your future**.

Because the badge may shield your chest—but not your finances.

And if you're not protected properly, one lawsuit can blow up the life you've worked your whole career to build.

Let's break it down—clearly, calmly, like two shift partners over coffee, working through the realities of what this job can expose you to, and how to prepare financially for the storm that (hopefully) never comes.

Liability Is Not a Moral Judgment. It's a Legal One.

Let's start here:

Getting sued **doesn't mean you did something wrong.**

It means someone *claims* you did. That claim can be:

- Justified
- Exaggerated
- Totally bogus
- But either way—you now have a legal and financial problem to deal with.

Liability simply means: *Are you responsible for damages?*

And as a first responder, you're often the one in the crosshairs when someone is hurt, angry, or looking for accountability.

Three Types of Liability First Responders Face

1. **Criminal Liability**

This is rare—but not impossible. Especially for law enforcement.

If you break the law—on or off duty—you can be criminally prosecuted. Examples:

- Excessive force resulting in serious injury or death
- Perjury during testimony
- Sexual misconduct
- DUI while operating a department vehicle

Criminal cases can lead to jail time and the end of your career. But for most first responders, it's not the biggest threat.

2. **Civil Liability**

This is where the real financial risk lives. Civil suits mean someone is seeking *money* from you personally.

Common examples:

- Wrongful death claims
- Negligence during a medical call
- Fire suppression actions that "cause" property damage
- Delayed response time leading to loss
- Arrest-related injuries
- Inaccurate or falsified reports

Even if you were acting in good faith, if the court finds you deviated from standard procedure—or if your department distances itself from your actions—you could be on the hook.

You may be named personally in lawsuits **alongside** your department.

If the department settles or wins, you might still be liable for *your role.*

3. **Administrative or Professional Discipline**

Not a lawsuit—but it still hurts.

This includes:

- Internal Affairs investigations
- License revocation (for paramedics/EMTs)
- Demotion, suspension, or loss of pension
- Being placed on a Brady/Giglio list (for LEOs)

These can derail your career and limit your post-retirement job options—even if you're never sued.

What About Qualified Immunity or Sovereign Immunity?

You've heard the term: *"You're covered. You're immune."*

But here's the fine print:

- **Qualified immunity** doesn't apply to criminal acts or "clearly established" rights violations.

- **Sovereign immunity** protects government agencies, not always individuals.
- Even if immunity *applies*, it can take **years and tens of thousands in legal fees** just to get the case dismissed.

Translation? Immunity doesn't stop someone from suing you. It's just a defense you have to *pay to use.*

Real-Life Example

A police officer is involved in a high-speed pursuit. The fleeing suspect crashes into a third party. That third party sues:

- The city
- The police department
- The individual officer

Even though the officer followed protocol, he's personally named. If the department's legal team decides not to cover his defense—or later claims he "deviated from policy"—he could face legal costs out of pocket.

Even if he's cleared, he still pays legal fees, and may not recover lost wages during suspension.

Now imagine that officer was six months from retirement.

That's the kind of risk we're talking about.

Financial Exposure Points

If you're sued and **not** fully covered by your department or union, you're at risk of losing:

- Personal savings
- Retirement accounts (some are protected, some aren't)
- Home equity

- Vehicles or property
- Future wages or settlement income
- Your financial stability

That's why first responders **must think defensively** with their finances.

How to Protect Yourself Financially

1. **Carry Personal Liability Insurance or Umbrella Coverage**

If your department doesn't cover everything, a personal **umbrella insurance policy** can help.

- Usually covers $1M–$5M beyond your home/auto policies
- Costs about $150–$300 per year
- May protect you from liability on- or off-duty

Check if it covers work-related exposure. Some unions also offer **professional liability insurance** for paramedics, officers, and firefighters.

This is one of the **cheapest layers of protection you can buy**—especially if you own a home or have assets to lose.

2. **Keep Personal and Family Assets Legally Separated**

In some states, assets in a spouse's name may be shielded from lawsuits. You can explore:

- Putting the house title in your spouse's name
- Creating a revocable or irrevocable trust (with a qualified attorney)
- Titling bank accounts as joint with rights of survivorship or transfer-on-death

These are not loopholes. They're **legal risk shields**—but get professional legal guidance.

3. **Understand What Your Pension Protects—and Doesn't**

Most state pensions are protected from creditors and lawsuits.

But:

- Withdrawals from your pension can be garnished
- If you roll over funds into an IRA or 457(b), creditor protection may change
- Divorce, child support, or restitution can reduce or redirect benefits

Don't assume your pension makes you bulletproof. Know your state's laws.

4. **Have a Legal Go Bag**

Just like your financial go bag, create a legal version:

- Union contact
- Department legal counsel info
- Personal attorney (not the same as the department's)
- Professional liability insurance policy
- Any IA documents or past complaints
- Notes or reports that may become relevant later

Being legally organized is the first step toward staying financially protected.

Action Steps You Can Take Right Now

1. **Ask your union or department what legal protections you have—and what you don't.**
2. **Get a personal umbrella policy.** It's cheap. It's smart.
3. **Review your home and auto insurance liability limits—and increase if needed.**
4. **Talk to a financial planner about asset protection strategies.**
5. **If you work part-time, volunteer, or moonlight—check that your insurance covers *that* too.**
6. **Make a list of lawyers in your state who specialize in civil defense for first responders.**
7. **Create a "legal go bag" with contacts, insurance info, and docu-**

ments.

8. **Revisit these protections annually—or after any high-risk incident.**

Encouragement

You've survived more in one shift than most people face in a year. Preparing for legal exposure isn't about living in fear. It's about being as tactical with your money as you are with your gear.

Reminder

You don't control who sues you. But you *do* control how ready you are.

Takeaway

Smart first responders don't just carry the right tools on the job. They carry the right protection *off the job,* too.

Prompt to Revisit

Update your legal and financial protection checklist every year—or after a use-of-force, injury, accident, or civil incident.

Final Note

This job makes you vulnerable in ways most civilians will never understand.

But you can plan for that. Prepare for that.

Protect your family and your future—because you've already risked enough.

Don't just run toward danger. Run *smartly* toward protection.

Your legacy deserves it. Your peace of mind depends on it.

Chapter 43: "Workplace Injury and Workers' Compensation: Your Rights and Benefits"

Introduction – What Happens When the Rescuer Gets Hurt?

You don't show up to work thinking today will be the day you get injured.

But the truth is, whether you're crawling into a burning structure, trying to stop a suspect who's resisting arrest, or lifting a 250-pound unconscious patient down a narrow staircase, your body—and your mind—are constantly on the line.

This chapter isn't here to scare you. It's here to **prepare you**.

Because as much as we train for worst-case scenarios for the people we serve, too many first responders haven't been trained for their own worst-case scenario—**getting hurt on the job and trying to figure out what happens next.**

What benefits are you entitled to?

How do you get them?

What if they deny your claim?

What about long-term injuries like PTSD?

Will you still get paid?

How do you protect your finances while you heal?

Let's break it all down—honestly, clearly, and in plain language. Because this isn't a lecture from an HR office. This is a financial survival guide for people who put their lives on the line and need systems that have their back when things go sideways.

Section 1: The Foundation – What Is Workers' Compensation?

Workers' compensation is a state-regulated insurance system that provides benefits to employees who suffer job-related injuries or illnesses. Every state has its own laws, but the core principles are generally the same:

- If you get hurt or sick while performing your job duties, you may be entitled to:
- Medical treatment
- Partial wage replacement while you're unable to work
- Disability compensation if the injury results in long-term impairment
- Death benefits to your family if you die in the line of duty

It sounds straightforward, but when you're a first responder, things get complicated—fast.

Why?

Because your job is inherently dangerous, your work environment is unpredictable, and **some of the most common injuries—like PTSD or repetitive-use damage—aren't always visible.**

That's why it's critical to understand not just how workers' comp works, but how to **work the system** in a way that protects your health, your income, and your family.

Section 2: Real-World First Responder Injuries (And Why Claims Get Denied)

Let's get real for a second.

Not every injury happens in some big, dramatic moment. Sure, there are explosions, crashes, gunshots, and smoke-filled rescues—but more often, it's:

- That fourth lift assist call of the night where you blew out your back.
- The screaming domestic that left your wrist twisted from subduing the suspect.
- The year-long build-up of trauma that finally broke something in your brain.

And too often, the system doesn't understand that.

Here are **common first responder injuries** and how workers' comp might view them:

1. Musculoskeletal Injuries

Backs, knees, shoulders, and necks take a beating in this job.

- **How the system may react**: Often accepted—if documented properly and reported immediately.
- **Pitfall**: If you don't report the incident the same day, the insurer may claim the injury happened off-duty.

2. Hearing Loss

Gunfire, sirens, explosions—over time, your hearing degrades.

- **How the system may react**: Harder to prove unless regularly tested and tracked.

- **Pitfall**: Claims often denied without baseline testing or if you've passed on wearing PPE.

3. PTSD and Mental Health Conditions

Repeated exposure to trauma can cause serious mental injuries.

- **How the system may react**: Historically denied. Some states now allow PTSD claims, especially for first responders.
- **Pitfall**: If you don't seek treatment or wait too long to report symptoms, your claim may be denied.

4. Heart Attacks and Strokes on Duty

Cardiac events are one of the leading causes of death for firefighters and police.

- **How the system may react**: Some states have "**presumptive laws**" that assume heart attacks are job-related for first responders.
- **Pitfall**: Without a presumptive law, it may be treated as a pre-existing condition.

Section 3: Your Rights—Know Them Before You Need Them

When you get injured on duty, you're not asking for charity. You're requesting a benefit that **you and your department have paid into** on your behalf.

But the process is full of red tape. If you don't know your rights, you could:

- Miss deadlines
- Get shortchanged
- Get forced back to duty too soon

- Or be denied altogether

Here's what you're typically entitled to under state workers' comp laws (check your state for exact details):

1. Medical Coverage

All necessary medical treatment related to the injury should be **100% covered**. That includes:

- Doctor visits
- Surgeries
- Physical therapy
- Prescription medications
- Mental health treatment
- Medical equipment (braces, crutches, wheelchairs)

2. Temporary Disability Benefits

If you're out of work, you should receive **partial wage replacement**, often 66–70% of your gross pay, **tax-free**.

- **Tip**: This may not include overtime, specialty pay, or shift differential—unless state law or your union contract says so.

3. Permanent Disability

If the injury results in permanent impairment, you may be entitled to a lump sum or structured settlement based on:

- % of impairment
- Body part affected
- Age and job classification

4. Vocational Rehabilitation

If you can't return to your original role, some states offer retraining or placement services.

5. Death Benefits

If a first responder dies from a job-related injury or illness, the family may receive:

- A burial allowance
- A lump sum
- Ongoing benefits to surviving dependents

Section 4: Filing a Claim—Step-by-Step, No Nonsense

You'd think this process would be streamlined for people in dangerous jobs. It's not.

Here's the process most first responders face when filing a claim—and how to avoid common mistakes:

Step 1: Report the Injury Immediately

Don't wait. Even if you're "fine" or "just sore," document it. If symptoms show up later, you'll have a paper trail.

- **Tip**: Use your department's internal injury report **and** tell a supervisor in writing.

Step 2: Get Medical Care

Ask if there's a department-approved provider. If not, go to urgent care or the ER.

- Be honest about how the injury happened. Use the words: **"This occurred while I was on duty."**

Step 3: File the Official Workers' Comp Claim

This is different from your department's injury report. It's usually filed through your HR or risk management office.

- Include **everything**—not just the most obvious injury. A bad ankle sprain can cause a bad back from limping.

Step 4: Follow Up Religiously

Track your paperwork. Keep notes. Save receipts. Go to every appointment.

- **Tip**: If you're denied, you typically have 30–90 days to appeal.

Section 5: When the System Fights Back – Denials, Delays, and Dirty Tactics

This part sucks—but it's real.

Sometimes, you'll get denied. Or lowballed. Or pressured to return before you're ready.

Know this: **It doesn't mean you don't deserve the benefit. It means you're dealing with a bureaucracy.**

Common reasons claims are denied:

- "Pre-existing condition"
- "Injury occurred off-duty"
- "Inadequate documentation"
- "Missed deadline"
- "No witness to injury"

If you're denied, here's what to do:

1. **Appeal it immediately.** You have a right to a hearing.
2. **Hire a workers' comp attorney.** Many work on contingency—no win, no fee.
3. **Lean on your union rep.** They've seen it all and can be your advocate.
4. **Document everything.** Keep a journal of symptoms, phone calls, and delays.
5. **Don't give up.** The system counts on people getting frustrated and quitting.

Section 6: Special Considerations for PTSD and Mental Health Claims

This deserves its own spotlight.

If you've been in this job long enough, you've seen things that changed you.

PTSD isn't weakness. It's an injury. But proving it in the comp system is hard.

Here's how to approach it:

- See a licensed mental health provider as soon as symptoms arise.
- Get it documented as job-related.
- Know your state's rules—some allow PTSD claims only after specific events.
- Gather peer support. Get letters from coworkers who witnessed the call or saw your symptoms.

- Don't wait until you're in crisis. Filing early builds your case and gets you support faster.

Section 7: Your Financial Survival Plan While Injured

Being out on comp is stressful—not just physically, but financially. Here's how to stabilize your money while you heal:

1. Build an Emergency Fund (If You're Not Injured Yet)

You need 3–6 months of expenses saved if possible. Overtime-dependent jobs need even more.

2. Understand What's Covered—and What's Not

Your comp check might be tax-free, but it might not cover:

- Overtime
- Hazard pay
- Side jobs
- Pension contributions
- Health insurance premiums (if not negotiated)

Make a new budget. Cut non-essentials temporarily. Communicate with your family.

3. Know How Your Injury Affects Your Retirement

Injury time may or may not count toward service years. Make sure you:

- Check pension rules
- Buy back time if needed
- Contribute to retirement if possible

4. Explore Supplemental Coverage

Some first responders carry **accident, disability, or critical illness policies** that pay cash in addition to comp.

Check your union or professional association for group plans.

Section 8: When It's Time to Lawyer Up

Not every claim needs a lawyer—but if you're hitting walls, it's time.

Get an attorney if:

- Your claim is denied
- You're being pushed back to work too early
- You've been retaliated against for filing
- You're dealing with long-term disability or settlement negotiations

Don't let pride keep you from getting help. A good comp lawyer understands the system better than you ever will—and they can save you months or years of stress.

Section 9: Action Checklist

Here's your no-fluff, grab-and-go checklist:

- Report the injury immediately—in writing
- Get medical care and say, "This happened at work"
- File the formal workers' comp claim
- Track every appointment, document, and call
- Budget for reduced income
- Know what benefits you're entitled to
- Hire a lawyer if denied or delayed
- Push for PTSD claims to be taken seriously
- Know your pension, insurance, and long-term impact

- Talk to your family—they need to be informed too

Encouragement: You've Fought for Others. Now Fight for Yourself.

You've been the one running toward danger. You've carried others through fire, chaos, and heartbreak. But when you're injured, the hardest part is slowing down—and asking for help.

There is no shame in using the system you've paid into. There is no weakness in taking time to heal. There is only wisdom in protecting what you've earned and worked so hard to build.

Reminder: The Workers' Comp System Wasn't Built for You—But You Can Still Win

The system is slow, confusing, and often unfair. But it can still work for you—if you know how to work it. Be organized. Be assertive. Be persistent.

Takeaway: Smart First Responders Don't Guess with Their Recovery

They plan for it. They know their rights. They build safety nets. And when life knocks them down, they don't stay down. They **heal, fight back, and come out stronger.**

Prompt to Revisit: Review Your Workers' Comp Coverage and Policies Every Year

Talk to your HR rep, your union, and your family. Make sure your insurance, savings, and knowledge are where they need to be—before you need them.

Final Note

This chapter isn't about fear—it's about readiness.

Because if you're prepared financially and mentally for a job-related injury, you'll bounce back faster. You'll protect your family. You'll guard your pension. And you'll reclaim your strength with confidence, not confusion.

You've trained for everything else.

Now it's time to train for *this*, too.

You've got this.

Chapter 44: Public Service Loan Forgiveness: Are You Eligible, and Is It Worth It?

Imagine sitting at the station kitchen table after a long shift, the aroma of coffee lingering in the air. You're surrounded by fellow first responders, each with their own stories of sacrifice, resilience, and dedication. Among the shared experiences, one topic often surfaces: student debt. For many in public service—firefighters, police officers, paramedics—the burden of student loans is a heavy one. Balancing the demands of the job with financial obligations can feel overwhelming. But there's a program designed to alleviate this burden: Public Service Loan Forgiveness (PSLF).

PSLF promises to forgive the remaining balance on your federal student loans after 120 qualifying monthly payments under a qualifying repayment plan while working full-time for a qualifying employer. It's a beacon of hope for many, but it's also a path fraught with complexities and challenges. This chapter aims to demystify PSLF, helping you understand if you're eligible and whether it's the right path for you.

Understanding Public Service Loan Forgiveness

PSLF was established in 2007 to encourage individuals to enter and continue in full-time public service employment. The program forgives the remaining balance on Direct Loans after 120 qualifying monthly payments are made under a qualifying repayment plan while working full-time for a qualifying employer.

Key Eligibility Criteria:

1. **Employment:** You must be employed full-time by a qualifying employer, which includes government organizations (federal, state, local, or tribal) and non-profit organizations that are tax-exempt under Section 501(c)(3) of the Internal Revenue Code.
2. **Loan Type:** Only Direct Loans are eligible for PSLF. If you have other types of federal loans, such as FFEL or Perkins Loans, you must consolidate them into a Direct Consolidation Loan to qualify.Student Loan Borrowers Assistance
3. **Repayment Plan:** You must be on an income-driven repayment plan, such as Income-Based Repayment (IBR), Pay As You Earn (PAYE), or Revised Pay As You Earn (REPAYE).
4. **Payments:** You must make 120 qualifying monthly payments. These payments must be made on time, for the full amount due, and while employed full-time by a qualifying employer.AmeriCorps

The Appeal of PSLF for First Responders

As a first responder, you're no stranger to commitment and service. PSLF aligns with these values, offering a tangible benefit for your dedication. The program can provide significant financial relief, allowing you to focus on your mission without the constant weight of student debt.

Benefits:

- **Debt Relief:** After 10 years of qualifying payments, the remaining balance on your Direct Loans is forgiven.AP News
- **Tax-Free Forgiveness:** Unlike some other forgiveness programs, the forgiven amount under PSLF is not considered taxable income.
- **Career Flexibility:** PSLF allows you to pursue a career in public service without being deterred by the potential for lower salaries compared to the private sector.

Navigating the Challenges of PSLF

While the benefits are compelling, PSLF is not without its challenges. Understanding and navigating the program's requirements is crucial to avoid pitfalls.

Common Challenges:

- **Complex Requirements:** The program's criteria are specific, and missing a single requirement can disqualify you.
- **Loan Servicer Miscommunication:** There have been instances where loan servicers provided incorrect information, leading borrowers astray.
- **Administrative Errors:** Errors in payment counting or employment certification can delay or derail forgiveness.

Mitigation Strategies:

- **Regular Employment Certification:** Submit the Employment Certification Form annually or whenever you change employers to ensure your employment qualifies.
- **Maintain Detailed Records:** Keep copies of all forms, payments, and communications with your loan servicer.
- **Stay Informed:** Regularly check for updates on PSLF requirements and policies through official sources.

Is PSLF Worth It? A Personal Assessment

Determining whether PSLF is the right path depends on your individual circumstances. Consider the following factors:en.wikipedia.org

- **Loan Balance:** If you have a significant loan balance, PSLF can offer substantial relief.
- **Career Plans:** If you plan to remain in public service for at least 10 years, PSLF aligns well with your career trajectory.
- **Financial Goals:** Assess how PSLF fits into your broader financial goals, including homeownership, retirement, and family planning.

Action Steps:

1. **Review Your Loans:** Determine if your loans are Direct Loans or if consolidation is necessary.
2. **Choose the Right Repayment Plan:** Ensure you're on an income-driven repayment plan that qualifies for PSLF.
3. **Certify Employment:** Submit the Employment Certification Form annually and whenever you change employers.
4. **Track Payments:** Keep a detailed record of your payments and ensure they are counted correctly.
5. **Stay Engaged:** Regularly communicate with your loan servicer and stay updated on any changes to the PSLF program.

Conclusion: Empowering Your Financial Future

As a first responder, you've dedicated your life to serving others. PSLF is one way the system acknowledges that service, offering a path to financial freedom. While the journey requires diligence and attention to detail, the reward—a life unburdened by student debt—is well worth the effort.

Remember, financial planning isn't about perfection; it's about preparation. By understanding and leveraging programs like PSLF, you're taking proactive steps to secure your financial future. Revisit this topic every six months to ensure your plan evolves with your career and life changes.

You've faced challenges more daunting than navigating student loan forgiveness. You've got this.

Chapter 45: Survivor Benefits, Line-of-Duty Death Payouts, and Financial Protection for Families

As first responders—firefighters, police officers, paramedics—you face dangers that most people can't fathom. Every shift carries the risk of injury or worse. While you focus on protecting your community, it's crucial to ensure that your family is protected as well. This chapter delves into the financial safeguards available to your loved ones in the event of a line-of-duty death, helping you understand and plan for the unthinkable.

Understanding Survivor Benefits

Survivor benefits are financial compensations provided to the families of first responders who lose their lives in the line of duty. These benefits come from various sources, including federal programs, state and local governments, and private organizations.

Federal Programs: Public Safety Officers' Benefits (PSOB) Program

The PSOB Program, administered by the U.S. Department of Justice, offers a one-time death benefit to eligible survivors of public safety officers who die as a direct result of an injury sustained in the line of duty. As of October 1, 2024, the benefit amount is $448,575.00.

Eligibility Criteria:

- The officer's death must be the direct result of a line-of-duty injury.
- The officer must have been serving in a public safety capacity, such as

law enforcement, firefighting, or emergency medical services.
- Survivors eligible for the benefit include spouses, children, and designated beneficiaries.

Additional PSOB Benefits:

- **Disability Benefits:** For officers who suffer catastrophic injuries in the line of duty, rendering them permanently unable to perform any gainful work.
- **Educational Assistance:** Available to spouses and children of fallen or catastrophically disabled officers to pursue higher education.

State and Local Benefits

Many states and municipalities offer additional benefits to the families of fallen first responders. These can include:

- **Pension Continuation:** Some jurisdictions allow the surviving spouse to continue receiving the officer's pension benefits.
- **Health Insurance:** Extended health coverage for the surviving family members.
- **Tuition Waivers:** Free or reduced tuition for the children of fallen officers at state colleges and universities.

It's essential to consult your department's human resources or benefits coordinator to understand the specific benefits available in your area.

Private and Non-Profit Organizations

Several organizations provide financial assistance and support services to the families of fallen first responders:

- **BackStoppers:** Offers financial assistance to the families of fallen public safety officers, including debt elimination, insurance coverage, and educational support.
- **Concerns of Police Survivors (C.O.P.S.):** Provides resources such as

counseling, scholarships, and peer support to the families of fallen law enforcement officers.

- **National Fallen Firefighters Foundation:** Offers support programs and scholarships to the families of firefighters who have died in the line of duty.

Mortgage Protection Programs

Some financial institutions offer mortgage protection programs for first responders:

- **CrossCountry Mortgage (CCM):** Provides a Line of Duty Death Benefit that forgives the remaining home loan balance, up to $525,000, for first responders who die in the line of duty.

Workers' Compensation Death Benefits

In addition to the above, workers' compensation programs may provide death benefits to the families of first responders who die due to work-related injuries or illnesses. These benefits typically include:

- **Weekly Wage Replacement:** A percentage of the deceased's average weekly wage paid to the surviving spouse and dependents.
- **Funeral Expenses:** Coverage for funeral and burial costs.

Eligibility and benefit amounts vary by state, so it's important to consult your local workers' compensation board or legal advisor for specific information.

Life Insurance Considerations

While employer-provided benefits are valuable, they may not be sufficient to cover all of your family's financial needs. Supplementing with personal life insurance policies can provide additional security.

Types of Life Insurance:

- **Term Life Insurance:** Provides coverage for a specific period (e.g., 20

or 30 years) and is generally more affordable.
- **Whole Life Insurance:** Offers lifelong coverage and includes a savings component, but comes with higher premiums.

When selecting a policy, consider factors such as your family's financial obligations, your income, and future expenses like college tuition.

Action Steps:

1. **Review Your Current Benefits:** Understand what survivor benefits are provided by your employer, state, and any affiliated organizations.
2. **Consult with HR:** Speak with your department's human resources representative to clarify available benefits and necessary documentation.
3. **Update Beneficiary Information:** Ensure all beneficiary designations are current on your life insurance policies and retirement accounts.
4. **Consider Additional Life Insurance:** Evaluate whether supplemental life insurance is appropriate for your family's needs.
5. **Create a Financial Plan:** Work with a financial advisor to develop a comprehensive plan that includes estate planning, savings, and investment strategies.

Conclusion: Protecting Those Who Matter Most

Your commitment to serving and protecting your community is unwavering. Ensuring that your family is financially secure in the event of a tragedy is an extension of that commitment. By understanding and proactively managing survivor benefits and financial protections, you provide your loved ones with stability and peace of mind.

Encouragement: You've faced challenges more daunting than navigating survivor benefits. You've got this.

Reminder: Financial planning isn't about being perfect. It's about staying prepared.

Takeaway: Smart first responders don't guess with money—they train for it, just like anything else.

Prompt to Revisit: Revisit this topic every 6 months. Your job evolves. So should your financial plan.

Chapter 46: Leveraging Union Resources and Credit Unions for Financial Empowerment

As a first responder—be it a firefighter, police officer, or paramedic—you operate in high-stress environments, often putting others' needs before your own. While the nature of your work demands resilience and dedication, it's equally important to ensure that your financial well-being is not overlooked. Unions and credit unions are two pillars that can provide substantial support in this regard. This chapter delves into how you can effectively utilize these resources to enhance your financial stability and plan for a secure future.

Understanding Union Resources

Unions are established to protect and advocate for the rights and interests of their members. For first responders, unions offer a range of services that extend beyond collective bargaining.

Benefits of Union Membership:

- **Collective Bargaining:** Unions negotiate on behalf of their members for better wages, benefits, and working conditions.
- **Legal Representation:** In cases of disputes or disciplinary actions, unions provide legal assistance to ensure fair treatment.
- **Educational Opportunities:** Many unions offer training programs, workshops, and seminars to help members advance their skills and careers.

- **Health and Wellness Programs:** Access to mental health resources, counseling services, and wellness initiatives are often facilitated through union partnerships.

Action Steps:

1. **Engage with Your Union:** Attend meetings, participate in discussions, and stay informed about the initiatives your union is undertaking.
2. **Utilize Available Resources:** Take advantage of the educational and wellness programs offered.
3. **Seek Guidance:** If facing workplace challenges, consult with your union representatives for support and advice.

Exploring Credit Unions

Credit unions are member-owned financial institutions that prioritize serving their members over generating profits. For first responders, certain credit unions offer tailored services that align with the unique demands of your profession.

Advantages of Joining a Credit Union:

- **Lower Fees and Better Rates:** Credit unions often provide lower interest rates on loans and higher yields on savings accounts compared to traditional banks.
- **Personalized Services:** Being member-focused, credit unions offer more personalized customer service.
- **Community Focus:** Profits are reinvested into the community or returned to members in the form of dividends.

Notable Credit Unions for First Responders:

- **Public Safety Credit Union:** Serving first responders in Kansas and Missouri, offering specialized financial products and community support initiatives.

- **Firefighters First Credit Union:** Founded by firefighters, it provides comprehensive financial services tailored to the firefighting community.
- **PremierOne Credit Union:** Offers a First Responder Program with benefits like loan discounts and educational resources. PremierOne Credit Union

Action Steps:

1. **Research Eligibility:** Determine which credit unions you qualify for based on your profession and location.
2. **Compare Services:** Evaluate the financial products and services offered to find the best fit for your needs.
3. **Engage with the Community:** Participate in credit union events and programs to maximize your membership benefits.

Integrating Union and Credit Union Resources

By leveraging both union and credit union resources, you can create a robust support system for your financial and professional life.

Strategies for Integration:

- **Financial Planning:** Utilize credit union financial advisors in conjunction with union-provided resources to develop comprehensive financial plans.
- **Emergency Funds:** Take advantage of credit union savings programs to build an emergency fund, ensuring financial stability during unforeseen circumstances.
- **Retirement Planning:** Combine union pension plans with credit union retirement accounts to diversify and strengthen your retirement portfolio.

Action Steps:

1. **Set Financial Goals:** Define short-term and long-term financial objectives.
2. **Develop a Plan:** Collaborate with union and credit union advisors to create a tailored financial strategy.
3. **Monitor Progress:** Regularly review and adjust your plan to stay aligned with your goals.

Conclusion: Empowering Your Financial Future

As a first responder, your dedication to serving others is unparalleled. By effectively utilizing the resources provided by unions and credit unions, you can ensure that your financial well-being is equally prioritized. Engage actively with these institutions, take advantage of the services offered, and build a secure foundation for your future and that of your family.

Encouragement: You've faced challenges more daunting than financial planning. With the right resources, you can navigate this path successfully.

Reminder: Financial planning isn't about being perfect; it's about being prepared.

Takeaway: Smart first responders don't guess with money—they strategize and plan, just like in the field.

Prompt to Revisit: Reassess your financial plan every six months to adapt to any changes in your personal or professional life.

Chapter 47: How Promotions and Rank Impact Your Retirement and Financial Plan

You're off shift. Maybe it's early morning, and you're decompressing after another 24 on, 48 off. You're sipping coffee with a fellow officer, firefighter, or paramedic. The station's quiet. You're not talking about call volume or who's buying breakfast today. You're talking about what all this hard work really leads to. You're thinking ahead—retirement, pension, family, freedom. And somewhere in that conversation, a question drops that's heavier than your turnout gear:

"Should I go for that promotion?"

Sounds like a simple question, right? But if you've worn the uniform long enough, you know it isn't. Because rising in rank doesn't just affect your schedule or your brass. It changes your income, your pension calculation, your benefits, your tax situation, your workload, your risk, and your exit timeline. And if you don't understand the full financial picture—what that promotion will actually do for your money and your future—you might make a decision you regret.

This chapter is about the money behind the rank. Whether you're a patrol officer considering sergeant, a firefighter aiming for captain, or a paramedic asked to take on a supervisory role, we're going to unpack it all. What the pay raise really means. How your pension formula is calculated. The impact on overtime. Whether jumping ranks delays or accelerates your retirement readiness. And what questions you should ask before saying yes to those new stripes.

Because in the world of first responders, every promotion isn't just a title—it's a financial event. And the more informed you are, the more power you have to make the right call.

I. WHY RANK MATTERS FINANCIALLY

A. Your Paycheck Changes—But So Does the Structure of It

Promotions usually come with higher base pay. But base pay is only one part of the compensation package. Overtime opportunities, hazard pay, shift differentials, and incentive bonuses may change—or disappear entirely—when you promote. In some departments, captains don't get as much OT because they're on salary. In others, sergeants are expected to do more for the same hourly pay spread over different responsibilities.

So before you chase the raise, run the numbers. Ask:

- How much base pay increase does the promotion come with?
- Will you still be eligible for overtime?
- Are there stipends, car allowances, or bonuses included in the new role?
- Will your schedule change in a way that affects your ability to earn extra income elsewhere?

B. Pension Formulas Favor the Last Few Years—So Timing Is Critical

Most first responder pensions are based on a formula:

(Years of service) x (Multiplier) x (Final average salary) = Annual pension benefit

Here's the trick: that "final average salary" is often calculated from your highest-earning 3–5 years. So if a promotion bumps you into a higher pay bracket, even for just a few years before retirement, it can substantially increase your pension.

Let's say you're earning $85,000 as a firefighter and considering a move to captain at $100,000. If your pension multiplier is 2.5% and you retire after 30 years, that $15,000 boost in final average salary translates to an extra $11,250 per year in retirement.

But there's a catch: You usually have to hold that rank long enough for it to affect your average. If you're five years from retirement, great. If you're one year away? It may not move the needle.

C. Promotional Exams, Testing Cycles, and Political Capital

It's not just about money. Promotions often require time, preparation, and political navigation. You may need to spend months studying for a promotional exam, building relationships, or taking specialty assignments to become eligible. That's time you might otherwise spend working OT, spending time with family, or working a side hustle.

Make sure the cost—time, energy, stress—aligns with the return. That includes:

- Exam prep courses
- Study materials
- Lost OT while prepping
- Union dues or association fees that increase with rank
- Expectations of leadership beyond the job description

II. RANK AND RETIREMENT TIMING

A. Some Promotions Extend Your Timeline

Let's say you hit lieutenant. You love the title, the responsibility, and the extra money. But now you're in a spot where people expect you to stay for a certain number of years. Your department may require minimum time in rank before you retire with that title (and pension rate).

Ask HR or your benefits coordinator:

- Will I need to serve X years at this rank for it to be used in my pension calculation?
- If I leave early, is my pension calculated off my prior rank?
- Will I lose accumulated benefits if I exit within 2 years?

If you're 5–10 years out, a promotion could be a brilliant move. If you're within 1–3 years, it might not be worth it unless it's guaranteed to be included in your pension formula.

B. Deferred Retirement Incentives for Senior Ranks

Some departments offer **DROP programs**—Deferred Retirement Option Plans—which allow senior staff to lock in their pension benefit while continuing to work and collect both their salary and pension (usually paid into a separate account). These are often only available to higher ranks. So if you're looking at a DROP or extended payout program, promoting at the right time can amplify those benefits.

III. TAX PLANNING AND PROMOTIONAL PAY

A. Higher Income = Higher Taxes (Sometimes)

Promotion bumps can push you into a higher tax bracket, especially if combined with overtime. While this isn't always a bad thing (it means you're making more), it can reduce the take-home benefit of that raise.

You may also become ineligible for certain tax credits or deductions, such as:

- Child tax credits
- Roth IRA contribution eligibility
- Education deductions (if you or a child are in school)

Be proactive. If you're considering a promotion that will raise your income significantly, talk to a tax pro. And adjust your withholding to avoid surprises come April.

B. Retirement Account Opportunities

The more you earn, the more you can (and should) save. A promotion might allow you to increase contributions to:

- Your 457(b)
- Roth IRA or backdoor Roth

- Health Savings Accounts (HSAs)

Take advantage. Promotions should build wealth—not just inflate lifestyle.

IV. WORK-LIFE IMPACT: THE HIDDEN COST OF HIGHER RANKS

A. Time Away from Family

Higher ranks often come with more meetings, more on-call shifts, and more admin work. That might mean less time at home—even if your shift schedule technically improves.

Will your kids be okay with more missed events? Will your spouse feel like a single parent?

This matters, because **burnout at the top can cost more than burnout at the bottom**. When you've spent 25+ years grinding, a stressful promotion can push you to the edge. That's a financial risk. Burnout = early retirement = reduced benefits.

B. Legal and Professional Liability

With more rank comes more responsibility—and sometimes more legal exposure. If something goes wrong on your shift, the buck may stop with you. That could mean:

- Internal affairs investigations
- Suspension
- Being named in lawsuits

Consider whether your department or union provides liability insurance for supervisors. If not, purchase your own.

V. QUESTIONS TO ASK BEFORE ACCEPTING A PROMOTION

1. How does this affect my pension calculation?

Is it worth the effort and potential stress based on where I am in my career?

2. Will I lose overtime?

Is the bump in base pay enough to make up for lost OT or stipends?

3. Will this promotion help or delay my retirement timeline?

Does it create new expectations around minimum time in rank?

4. How will my lifestyle change?

New shift? More phone calls after hours? Political headaches?

5. What's the impact on my taxes and benefits?

Should I be setting aside more for retirement or adjusting my tax strategy?

6. What happens if I change my mind in 12 months?

Can I go back? Will I be stuck? Will it affect my pension?

VI. STRATEGIC TIPS FOR PROMOTING SMARTLY

- **Time promotions carefully**: Aim to be in your higher rank during your highest-earning years to maximize pension calculations.
- **Document everything**: Keep track of when you promote, what the salary changes are, and how it's affecting your pension.
- **Talk to someone who's done it**: Don't just ask about the money—ask how it changed their stress, health, and family life.
- **Don't chase titles for ego**: Promotions should serve your goals, not just your resume.
- **Include your family in the decision**: They're the ones who will feel the changes the most.

VII. REAL-LIFE EXAMPLES

Case 1: The Wise Captain

A 50-year-old firefighter promotes to captain five years before retirement. His pay jumps by $15K, and he's able to work three high-income years. His pension increases by nearly $13,000 per year because of the new average salary. He planned it well and retired exactly when it made sense—on his terms.

Case 2: The Burned-Out Sergeant

A 38-year-old patrol officer promotes to sergeant. He loses OT, picks up stress, and spends more time doing admin than patrol. His base pay increased, but overall income dropped. Within two years, he's exhausted, misses being on the street, and regrets the move. He later lateral transfers to another department at a lower rank.

VIII. TAKEAWAYS

Promotions are not just about money. They're about quality of life, timing, pension strategy, and long-term career fulfillment. The best decisions come from a place of clarity—not pressure, politics, or pride.

Before you pin on the new badge, ask yourself:

- Will this rank help me build wealth?
- Will it give me more time—or take more of it?
- Am I doing it for my family—or in spite of them?
- Is the trade-off worth it, financially and personally?

You've trained for everything else. Train for your money future, too.

Encouragement:

"You've led teams into danger. You can lead yourself into a strong retirement."

Reminder:

"Rank isn't just a title—it's a tool. Use it wisely."

Takeaway:

"Smart first responders plan promotions like missions—with strategy, awareness, and backup."

Prompt to Revisit:

"Every 6–12 months, reassess your position, pension path, and promotion opportunities. Life changes. Plans should, too."

Chapter 48: Investing Through Volatility and Trauma: Staying Focused During Crisis

You're off shift, maybe sipping coffee in the station kitchen, decompressing after a long night. The conversation drifts from the latest call to something more personal—your financial future. You've been thinking about your investments, especially with the market's recent ups and downs. It's unsettling, and you're not alone in feeling that way.

As a first responder, you're no stranger to crisis. You run toward danger, not away from it. But when it comes to your finances, especially investing during volatile times, it's natural to feel apprehensive. This chapter aims to provide you with a grounded, practical approach to investing through market volatility and personal trauma, helping you stay focused on your long-term financial goals.

Understanding Market Volatility

Market volatility refers to the fluctuations in the price of assets, such as stocks, bonds, and mutual funds. These fluctuations can be triggered by various factors, including economic indicators, geopolitical events, and changes in investor sentiment. While volatility is a normal part of investing, it can be particularly challenging during times of personal or collective crisis.

As a first responder, you might find market volatility especially stressful when coupled with the demands of your profession. The key is to understand that volatility is temporary, but your financial goals are long-term. Maintaining perspective is crucial.

The Importance of a Long-Term Perspective

Investing is a marathon, not a sprint. Short-term market fluctuations should not derail your long-term investment strategy. Historical data shows that markets tend to recover over time, even after significant downturns. For example, after the 2008 financial crisis, the market eventually rebounded and reached new highs.

By focusing on your long-term goals, such as retirement or your children's education, you can better withstand short-term volatility. It's essential to avoid making impulsive decisions based on market swings, as these can negatively impact your investment returns.

Building a Resilient Investment Strategy

1. **Diversify Your Portfolio**: Diversification involves spreading your investments across various asset classes, such as stocks, bonds, and real estate. This strategy can help reduce risk, as different assets often perform differently under the same market conditions.
2. **Asset Allocation**: Determine the right mix of assets based on your risk tolerance, time horizon, and financial goals. For instance, younger investors might allocate more to stocks for growth, while those nearing retirement might prefer bonds for stability.
3. **Dollar-Cost Averaging**: This strategy involves investing a fixed amount of money at regular intervals, regardless of market conditions. It can reduce the impact of volatility by averaging out the purchase price of investments over time.
4. **Emergency Fund**: Maintain an emergency fund with three to six months' worth of living expenses. This fund can provide a financial cushion during unexpected events, reducing the need to liquidate investments during market downturns.

Managing Emotional Responses

Investing during volatile times can evoke strong emotions, such as fear and anxiety. It's crucial to recognize these emotions and prevent them from influencing your investment decisions.

- **Avoid Panic Selling**: Selling investments during a market downturn can lock in losses and hinder your long-term financial goals. Remember that markets have historically recovered over time.
- **Stay Informed, Not Overwhelmed**: Keep yourself informed about market trends, but avoid obsessively checking your investment accounts. Constant monitoring can increase anxiety and lead to impulsive decisions.
- **Seek Professional Advice**: Consider consulting a financial advisor who understands the unique challenges faced by first responders. They can provide personalized guidance and help you stay on track.

Investing During Personal Trauma

Personal crises, such as injury, illness, or the loss of a loved one, can significantly impact your financial situation and investment strategy.

- **Reassess Your Financial Plan**: During times of personal trauma, it's essential to review and adjust your financial plan as needed. This might involve re-evaluating your risk tolerance or modifying your investment contributions.
- **Utilize Support Resources**: Many departments offer Employee Assistance Programs (EAPs) that provide financial counseling and support services. Take advantage of these resources to help navigate financial challenges during difficult times.
- **Communicate with Your Family**: Keep open lines of communication with your family about your financial situation and investment plans. This transparency can foster mutual understanding and support.

Case Study: Navigating Market Volatility

Consider the story of Alex, a 35-year-old paramedic who had been diligently investing in a diversified portfolio for several years. During a market downturn, Alex noticed a significant drop in his investment account balance. Feeling anxious, he considered pulling out of the market to prevent further losses.

However, after consulting with a financial advisor and reviewing his long-term goals, Alex decided to stay the course. Over time, the market recovered, and his portfolio regained its value, even surpassing previous levels. Alex's decision to remain invested during volatility ultimately benefited his financial future.

Action Steps

1. **Review Your Investment Portfolio**: Assess your current asset allocation and ensure it aligns with your risk tolerance and financial goals.
2. **Establish or Replenish Your Emergency Fund**: Aim to have three to six months' worth of living expenses saved in a readily accessible account.
3. **Implement Dollar-Cost Averaging**: Set up automatic contributions to your investment accounts to maintain consistency and reduce the impact of market volatility.
4. **Consult a Financial Advisor**: Seek professional guidance to develop a personalized investment strategy that accounts for your unique circumstances as a first responder.
5. **Stay Educated**: Continuously educate yourself about investing principles and market trends to make informed decisions.

Encouragement

You've faced challenges that most people can't imagine, showing resilience and courage in the face of adversity. Applying that same strength to your financial journey can help you navigate market volatility and personal trauma with confidence.

Reminder

Financial planning isn't about being perfect; it's about being prepared.

Markets will fluctuate, and life will throw curveballs, but a solid investment strategy can help you stay on course.

Takeaway

Smart first responders don't guess with money—they plan, prepare, and persevere. By maintaining a long-term perspective and a disciplined approach, you can build a secure financial future.

Prompt to Revisit

Revisit your investment strategy every six months or after significant life events. Your goals and circumstances may evolve, and your financial plan should adapt accordingly.

Final Note

This chapter isn't just about money; it's about peace of mind in a profession full of uncertainty. It's about protecting your family, even when you're the one always protecting others. It's about freedom—today, and after the badge comes off. Whether you're fresh out of the academy, working 24s with three kids at home, or planning your final shift after 30 years of service—this is your financial blueprint. Let's help you run toward wealth, too.

Chapter 49: Should You Hire a Financial Advisor? What to Ask and How to Vet One

Imagine sitting in the station kitchen after a long shift, sipping coffee with a fellow first responder. The conversation drifts from the day's calls to more personal matters—family, future plans, and finances. One topic that often surfaces is the question: "Should I hire a financial advisor?" It's a valid query, especially when considering the complexities of managing finances amidst the demands of a first responder's life.

Understanding the Role of a Financial Advisor

A financial advisor is more than just someone who suggests where to invest your money. They can help you:

- Develop a comprehensive financial plan tailored to your goals.
- Navigate complex financial decisions, such as retirement planning, tax strategies, and estate planning.
- Provide guidance during significant life events like marriage, divorce, or the birth of a child.
- Offer objective advice to help you stay on track with your financial goals.

However, it's essential to recognize that not all financial advisors are created equal. Their qualifications, compensation structures, and areas of expertise can vary significantly.

When Might You Need a Financial Advisor?

Consider hiring a financial advisor if:

- You're approaching retirement and need a clear plan for your savings.
- You've received a substantial inheritance or settlement and want to manage it wisely.
- You're experiencing significant life changes that impact your financial situation.
- You feel overwhelmed by financial decisions and need expert guidance.

Key Questions to Ask Potential Advisors

Before committing to a financial advisor, it's crucial to vet them thoroughly. Here are some questions to guide your evaluation:

1. **Are You a Fiduciary?**

- A fiduciary is legally obligated to act in your best interest. This designation can provide peace of mind that the advice you're receiving is unbiased and prioritizes your needs.

1. **How Are You Compensated?**

- Advisors can be fee-only, commission-based, or a combination of both. Understanding their compensation structure helps identify potential conflicts of interest.

1. **What Are Your Qualifications?**

- Look for certifications like Certified Financial Planner (CFP) or Chartered Financial Analyst (CFA), which indicate a high level of expertise and ethical standards.

1. **What Services Do You Offer?**

- Ensure their services align with your needs, whether it's investment management, retirement planning, tax advice, or estate planning.

1. **Who Is Your Typical Client?**

- An advisor experienced with clients in similar professions or financial situations may better understand your unique needs.

1. **How Will We Work Together?**

- Discuss the frequency of meetings, communication methods, and how they will keep you informed about your financial progress.

1. **Can You Provide References?**

- Speaking with current or past clients can offer insights into the advisor's effectiveness and reliability.

Evaluating the Pros and Cons

Pros:

- **Expertise:** Advisors bring specialized knowledge to help you make informed decisions.
- **Time-Saving:** They handle complex financial tasks, freeing you to focus on your career and family.
- **Accountability:** Regular check-ins can keep you disciplined in following your financial plan.

Cons:

- **Cost:** Advisor fees can add up, potentially impacting your investment returns.
- **Potential Conflicts of Interest:** Advisors earning commissions might

be incentivized to recommend certain products.
- **Quality Variance:** Not all advisors provide the same level of service; thorough vetting is essential.

Red Flags to Watch For

- **Lack of Transparency:** If an advisor is vague about fees or investment strategies, proceed with caution.
- **Pressure Tactics:** Be wary of advisors who push products aggressively or urge quick decisions.
- **Limited Communication:** An advisor should be accessible and willing to maintain regular contact.

Making the Decision

Deciding whether to hire a financial advisor depends on your comfort level with managing finances, the complexity of your financial situation, and your long-term goals. If you choose to proceed, take the time to research and interview multiple advisors to find the right fit.

Final Thoughts

Financial planning is a journey, not a destination. As a first responder, you've dedicated your life to serving others. Ensuring your financial well-being is a way to honor that commitment and provide security for yourself and your loved ones.

Encouragement:

You've faced challenges head-on in your career; managing your finances is another area where your resilience and determination can shine.

Reminder:

Financial planning isn't about perfection; it's about preparation and adaptability.

Takeaway:

Empower yourself with knowledge and seek guidance when needed. Your financial future is worth the investment.

Prompt to Revisit:

Reevaluate your financial plan every six months. Life evolves, and your financial strategies should adapt accordingly.

Chapter 50: Teaching Your Kids About Money (When You Didn't Grow Up With It Yourself)

In the world of first responders, where courage and resilience are daily necessities, there's an unspoken challenge many face when the uniform comes off: managing personal finances. For those who grew up without financial guidance, the task of teaching their children about money can seem daunting. Yet, the same determination that drives you to protect and serve can empower you to break the cycle and equip your children with the financial literacy they need.

Understanding the Importance of Financial Literacy

Financial literacy is more than balancing a checkbook or understanding interest rates; it's about making informed decisions that lead to financial stability and freedom. By instilling these values in your children, you're not only preparing them for a secure future but also fostering confidence and independence.

Starting the Conversation

Begin by integrating money talks into everyday life. Discuss budgeting during grocery shopping or explain the importance of saving when planning a family vacation. These real-life scenarios make financial concepts relatable and understandable for children.

Age-Appropriate Lessons

Young Children (Ages 3-7):

- Introduce basic concepts like identifying coins and understanding that money is used to buy things.
- Use play-based learning, such as pretend stores, to make it engaging. WOD Firefighter Fund+12NVFC Learning+12NPR+12

School-Age Children (Ages 8-12):

- Teach them about earning money through chores, the importance of saving, and distinguishing between needs and wants.Consumer Financial Protection Bureau+5AP News+5SlideServe+5
- Encourage them to set savings goals for items they desire.

Teenagers (Ages 13-18):

- Delve into more complex topics like budgeting, credit, and investing.
- Discuss the implications of student loans and the importance of building credit responsibly.

Practical Strategies for Teaching Money Management

1. **Use the Three Jar Method:**
2. Allocate jars for saving, spending, and sharing. This visual tool helps children understand money allocation and the importance of each category.
3. **Set Savings Goals:**
4. Encourage your child to save for a specific item, teaching patience and the value of delayed gratification.
5. **Involve Them in Budgeting:**
6. Let them participate in planning a family outing budget, fostering a sense of responsibility and understanding of financial planning.
7. **Discuss Mistakes Openly:**
8. Share your financial missteps and the lessons learned. This transparency builds trust and provides valuable learning opportunities.

Leveraging Resources

Utilize available resources to aid in teaching financial literacy:

- **Books:** Titles like The Berenstain Bears' Trouble with Money or Money Ninja can introduce financial concepts in a fun way.
- **Apps:** Tools like Greenlight or GoHenry offer interactive platforms for kids to manage their money digitally.
- **Community Programs:** Many local organizations offer workshops or seminars focused on financial education for families.

Modeling Financial Responsibility

Children learn by example. Demonstrate good financial habits, such as budgeting, saving, and responsible spending. Your actions will reinforce the lessons you teach.

Encouragement

Remember, it's never too late to start. Every step you take towards financial literacy benefits not only you but sets a foundation for your children's future.

Reminder

Financial education is a journey. Celebrate small victories along the way and continue to build upon them.

Takeaway

By proactively teaching your children about money, you're empowering them with the knowledge and skills to make sound financial decisions throughout their lives.

Prompt to Revisit

Reassess your family's financial education plan every six months. As your children grow, their understanding and needs will evolve, requiring adjustments to your approach.

Chapter 51: "Your Financial Victory Lap: Rewriting the Narrative of First Responders and Wealth"

Part 1: Breaking the Myth of "Just Getting By"

You hear it in the break room. You hear it at retirement parties. You hear it in the way people laugh when someone mentions a luxury car or a beach house and then follows it with, "Yeah, but I'm just a firefighter." Or, "Right—on a cop's salary?"

There's an unspoken assumption in the world of first responders: that you signed up to serve, not to get rich. That you're here for the mission, not the money. And while the mission is sacred—make no mistake—it's time we rewrite the second half of that sentence.

You don't have to choose between meaning and money.

You don't have to settle for financial stress as the price of public service.

You don't have to retire hoping your pension is "enough" and praying Social Security doesn't change the rules on you.

You can serve with honor **and** build wealth.

This chapter is your permission slip to stop apologizing for wanting more. To stop believing that just because you chose a uniform, you're stuck in a financial box.

It's not about greed. It's not about chasing status. It's about giving yourself a *financial victory lap*—a life where the discipline you bring to the job shows up in your money, too.

It's about rewriting the script—so your kids, your colleagues, your community see that building wealth is *not* a betrayal of your service. It's an extension of it.

This Isn't the Hollywood Version of Money

When people think about wealth, their minds often jump to movie stars or Wall Street sharks. Penthouses, private jets, champagne. That's noise. That's marketing.

That's not what we're talking about here.

The financial victory lap isn't about showing off. It's about showing up—for your future, for your family, and for your peace of mind.

It's about being able to retire when *you* want to—not when the system says you're "done."

It's about buying back time.

It's about breathing room when a transmission goes out, or your kid needs braces, or your spouse wants to change careers.

It's about *not* living in quiet fear of every overtime cut or policy change.

It's about *freedom.*

The Blueprint We Were Never Given

Let's be honest. Most first responders didn't grow up talking about Roth IRAs at the dinner table.

You were taught how to work. You were taught how to serve.

But very few of us were taught how to turn a paycheck into a portfolio.

So we learned through trial and error.

We picked up habits from our academy buddies, our senior officers, our station captains.

And while some of that advice was gold—some of it was garbage dressed in tradition.

We were told:

"Live within your means." True.

But we weren't told:

"Invest the gap between your income and your spending so future-you has choices."

We were told:

"Get the pension and you'll be fine."

But we weren't told:

"What happens if the pension isn't enough?"

We were told:

"Don't trust the stock market—it's a scam."

But we weren't told:

"How to use low-cost index funds to grow real wealth with low risk over time."

Nobody gave us a playbook for building wealth on a first responder's salary. So we hustled. We picked up extra shifts. We got smart with coupons and cash-back cards.

But now? Now it's time to level up.

This Chapter Is Not About Theory. It's About Ownership.

If you're reading this chapter, you've already done the hard part: you've shown up for years. You've braved smoke, blood, confrontation, trauma.

You've poured into a profession that demands everything of you—and asks you to leave the ego at the door.

Now it's time to bring that same courage to your money.

Not because you want to be a millionaire for its own sake—but because wealth means **options**.

Wealth means:

- Retiring with dignity—not dread
- Helping your kids without enabling them
- Saying yes to what excites you—and no to what drains you
- Taking the vacation without guilt
- Handling emergencies without derailing your entire plan
- Leaving a legacy—not just a folded flag and a pension

Your Financial Victory Lap Starts Now

This isn't about where you've been—it's about where you're going.

It doesn't matter if you're 25 or 55. It doesn't matter if you've got six figures in debt or six figures in savings.

You're still in the fight. And this is your next gear.

You've trained for chaos. You've learned to lead under pressure.

You know how to compartmentalize, execute, and stay calm when the world's on fire.

All those traits? They translate to your money.

You just haven't been told that yet.

But by the end of this chapter, you'll have something no one can take away:

A clear vision for your financial future—and the tools to start walking it out.

Part 2: Reframing Your Identity – Wealth and the Warrior Mindset

There's a reason why most people don't associate first responders with wealth. It's not because you don't work hard enough. It's not because you don't deserve it. It's because the **culture of service** often clashes with the **culture of money.**

Let's break this down.

You were trained to protect others.

To stay humble.

To follow orders.

To not make it about you.

But here's the problem: that same humility that makes you an incredible firefighter, EMT, or officer can quietly train you to think that wealth isn't for people like you.

That planning for more is selfish.

That talking about money is arrogant.

That dreaming of financial freedom somehow makes you soft.

Let's challenge that head-on.

What If Building Wealth Is an Extension of Your Service?

Imagine this: You're still in uniform, still serving—but now you're mentoring rookies because you *want* to, not because you *have* to.

You're showing younger teammates how to buy a home, how to invest, how to avoid payday loans and predatory debt traps.

You're giving generously to the families of fallen officers or to burned-out coworkers who just need a break—because your own financial life is *solid.*

Does that sound selfish? Or does that sound like *the next level of service?*

Wealth allows you to show up for your community in ways that extend beyond your shift.

Wealth is a *multiplier* for your values.

You're Already Mentally Tough—Now Let's Make It Financial

First responders are some of the most mentally resilient people on the planet.

You've seen tragedy.

You've walked into burning buildings, crashed vehicles, domestic violence scenes, overdoses, high-speed pursuits—and still showed up the next day.

But when it comes to money?

Many of you feel *exposed.*

Here's why:

Nobody ever taught you how to apply your *resilience* to your *resources.*

You were told to suck it up emotionally.

Not to plan ahead financially.

So when the market dips or inflation hits or a major home repair comes due, it feels like the world's closing in.

But it's not because you're weak with money. It's because you haven't learned how to take your **mental toughness** and **apply it to long-term wealth building.**

Let's fix that.

Rewriting the Script: From "I'm Just a Cop" to "I'm a Financial Leader"

Let's talk about identity.

For too long, the financial world has looked at first responders as paycheck-to-paycheck workers.

Not wealth-builders.

Not investors.

Not decision-makers.

That stops here.

You are the CEO of your family's finances.

You are the lead strategist for your household wealth.

You are the legacy architect for your children, your spouse, your future.

It doesn't matter if you've made mistakes.

It doesn't matter if you've had debt, got divorced, missed some years of saving.

What matters is **who you become from this day forward.**

From this point on, you think like someone who's **training for their financial future.**

Not reacting.

Not hoping.

But training.

You've Trained for the Fire—Now Train for Financial Firestorms

When you show up on scene, you don't hope the fire behaves.

You're ready for the worst.

You've got protocols.

You've got layers of backup.

You've drilled for chaos.

Your money life should be the same.

You don't hope the economy plays nice.

You plan for recessions.

You build cash reserves.

You diversify your investments.

You protect your income with insurance.

You keep your estate plan updated.

That's not paranoia. That's **command thinking.**

And guess what?

That mindset is already inside you.

We're just redirecting it—from the street to your savings.

From the radio to your Roth IRA.

From trauma triage to wealth planning.

Identity Shift = Behavior Shift

Once you start seeing yourself as a wealth builder—not just a wage earner—your behavior starts to change.

You start asking:

- "How can I put this overtime check to work for future me?"
- "Does this spending reflect my values—or my stress?"
- "What would a financially free version of me do right now?"

And that's when the breakthrough happens.

That's when you stop living month-to-month.

That's when you stop letting burnout dictate your spending.

That's when you start moving with *confidence*—not just courage.

A Wealth Mindset for the Badge-Wearing Warrior

Let's get real:

You didn't become a first responder for the money.

But let's also get honest:

You don't have to die broke just because you lived to serve.

Wealth isn't about ego.

It's about **options**.

And you, more than anyone, have earned those options.

Coming Up in Part 3: How to Take the Victory Lap—Step-by-Step Systems for First Responder Wealth

In the next part of this chapter, we'll shift from mindset to **method.**

We'll lay out what the "Victory Lap" actually looks like in dollars and sense:

- How much to save, where to invest, and how to make it automatic
- What "retiring early" means when you've got a pension—*and* what to watch out for
- How to talk to your spouse about wealth, even if you weren't raised talking money
- How to protect your legacy from lawsuits, taxes, and bad decisions

Part 3: Step-by-Step Systems for Your Victory Lap

You've earned every stripe, every pin, every scar. Now it's time to earn peace of mind.

This section isn't about dreaming—it's about doing. Let's break your financial victory lap into real, repeatable steps. Simple systems. No fluff. Just straight-line strategy for real people with shift work, unpredictable schedules, and serious responsibilities.

Step 1: Clarify What Winning Looks Like to You

Let's start here because too many people chase money without ever asking: *"Why?"*

Your Victory Lap has to mean something.

Is it...

- Retiring at 55 and volunteering full-time?
- Moving to a lake town and fishing with your grandkids?
- Paying off your house and becoming the first person in your family to die without debt?
- Funding your kids' college so they don't start adulthood buried in loans?
- Traveling twice a year and finally relaxing without checking your phone every 10 minutes?

There is no wrong answer—except not answering at all.

Write it down. Make it visual. Talk about it with your spouse. The clearer the vision, the stronger the follow-through.

Step 2: Know What You Actually Make—and Keep

You'd be shocked how many high-ranking first responders still don't know what their *net pay* is each month.

Here's your drill:

- Look at your last 2–3 pay stubs.
- Add up all sources of income: base salary, shift differential, overtime, bonuses, special unit pay.

- Subtract what goes to taxes, retirement contributions, union dues, insurance premiums, etc.
- What you're left with is your **net take-home pay**.

Now calculate your monthly expenses—*honestly*:

- Mortgage/rent
- Groceries
- Gas
- Childcare
- Cell phones
- Streaming services
- Credit cards
- Loans
- Eating out
- Gym membership
- Coffee runs

Now compare income vs. outgo.

Are you positive, breaking even, or sinking a little each month?

You can't run a victory lap if your financial treadmill is stuck.

Step 3: Automate Wealth Like It's a Backup System

You don't trust a building will stay standing without structural integrity.

Don't trust your future to willpower alone.

Automate:

- Contributions to your **457(b)** plan
- Deposits into a **Roth IRA**
- Transfers to an **emergency fund**
- Monthly **debt payments**
- Contributions to a **kids' education account**

Make it boring. Make it brainless. Make it automatic.

Why? Because life will get crazy. Calls will come in. Schedules will flip. But if your systems run in the background, wealth builds itself while you serve the public.

Step 4: Know Your Pension—Inside and Out

Far too many first responders don't understand the most valuable asset they'll ever own: their pension.

Don't just assume you'll "get a check." Ask:

- When am I vested?
- What percentage of my final salary will I get—and is it averaged over 3 years, 5, or just final pay?
- How is overtime calculated into pension (or is it)?
- What happens if I retire early?
- What are survivor benefits for my spouse?
- Is my pension COLA-adjusted (Cost of Living Adjustment)?
- What happens if I move states?

Pensions are great—*until they're not understood.*

Talk to your HR rep. Meet with a retirement specialist. Don't wing it.

Step 5: Get Insurance That Protects Your Mission

Life insurance, disability insurance, long-term care—these aren't extras. They're your perimeter security.

You insure your cruiser or fire truck.

You insure your radio.

You insure your boots.

Insure your **income** and your **legacy.**

- Term life insurance (20–30 years) is cheap and effective for most families.
- Disability insurance replaces your income if you get hurt off the clock.
- Umbrella liability insurance protects your assets from lawsuits.
- Long-term care planning keeps your kids from going broke if you ever need extended care.

First responders are high-risk, high-responsibility professionals. Don't leave your family one accident away from financial ruin.

Step 6: Build "Freedom Funds" Outside the System

Your pension might be your backbone—but you still need flexibility. That means:

- A **Roth IRA** for tax-free retirement money
- A **brokerage account** for midlife goals like travel, renovations, or leaving the job early
- A **Health Savings Account (HSA)** if your plan qualifies (triple tax-advantaged!)
- A **side business fund** if you want to build something after the badge

These are your *Victory Lap accelerators.*

They give you leverage. Options. Freedom to say "yes" to opportunities and "no" to burnout.

Step 7: Eliminate Debt Like a Fire Hazard

Debt is an emergency you can *prevent.*

If you've got:

- Credit card balances
- Personal loans
- Car loans
- Payday loans
- High-interest debt

Then make it a mission to knock it out. One by one. Smallest to largest or highest interest rate first. Just get it *gone.*

Each dollar of interest you pay is a dollar stolen from your future freedom.

Step 8: Talk Money With Your Crew—and Your Family

Money isn't just a math problem. It's a conversation problem.

Your partner can't support your goals if they don't know them. Your kids won't grow up financially literate if they never hear about savings or investing. Your coworkers won't learn if nobody breaks the silence.

Be the one to bring it up.

"I just increased my 457(b). Anyone else using theirs?"

"We started doing monthly budget check-ins at home. Game-changer."

"I'm working OT this month to knock out the last of our car loan."

Normalize *winning.*

Step 9: Build a Post-Retirement Life Worth Living

You didn't go through all this just to sit on a couch at 58 wondering what's next.

Start planning your life *after the job.*

- Will you teach, mentor, consult?
- Will you travel, volunteer, or coach youth sports?
- Will you move, downsize, or upgrade?
- Will you start a business or write a book?

Your Victory Lap isn't just financial—it's personal.

Don't wait for life to happen to you after you hang up the uniform. Create it now.

Step 10: Revisit, Rework, Recommit—Every 6 Months

Financial planning is like tactical readiness: it's never a "one-and-done."

Set a calendar reminder every 6 months:

- Review your budget
- Update your beneficiaries
- Check your pension status
- Rebalance your investments
- Talk with your spouse about goals

You don't stay fit for the job by skipping training.

Same with wealth. You **stay sharp** by staying engaged.

The Final Word of Part 3

Wealth doesn't make you better than anyone else.

It just makes you **better able**—to respond, to rest, to give, to grow.

You are not "just" a firefighter, paramedic, or officer.

You are a *builder.*

A *protector.*

A *legacy maker.*

And this? This is your Victory Lap.

Chapter 52: The Last Call: Financial Strength That Lasts Beyond the Badge

You've spent your career answering calls—some in the middle of the night, some in chaos, some with no guarantee of coming home the same way you left. You've carried the burden, the radio, the trauma, the pride. You've worn the uniform not just on your chest, but deep in your identity.

This book wasn't written to teach you how to clip coupons or chase the next hot stock tip. This wasn't about theory. It was about *freedom*. About resilience. About finally putting your own financial oxygen mask on first.

It was about giving you tools to build the life you've earned—and protect the people you love, even when you're no longer the one standing between them and danger.

Because here's the truth we don't say out loud often enough:

Your job is heroic. But your paycheck won't be your rescue.

And if you want to retire on your terms—not the city's, not the pension board's, not the system's—you have to play this game like your life depends on it. Because your future life *does.*

You're Not Behind. You're Just Not Done Yet.

Maybe reading this book stirred up some regret.

Maybe you thought: *"Damn, I should've started this 10 years ago."*

But listen to me clearly:

You are not behind.

You are not disqualified because you grew up without money.

You are not less-than because you're still carrying debt.

You are not too late if you've got breath left in your lungs and a shift still to serve.

Financial progress doesn't require perfection. It requires action.

And now, you've got a blueprint.

No One Teaches This at the Academy

Let's be real: no one taught you how to open a Roth IRA during defensive tactics class.

You didn't learn how compound interest works while running ladder drills.

Nobody covered estate planning when you were being taught CPR compressions.

And yet—this is the knowledge that protects your family, just as surely as your vest, your turnout gear, or your trauma bag. It's the backup plan that never makes the news but changes lives.

This book was written because someone needed to say out loud what too many of us have whispered in silence:

"We give everything to this job. But we still deserve to win when it's over."

You Don't Have to Go It Alone

You've probably noticed by now: much of this book wasn't about spreadsheets or calculators. It was about **decisions**. **Boundaries**. **Legacy**. **Relationships**.

It was about how to have real conversations with your spouse, your kids, your union, your crew.

It was about knowing when to call in professional help—a financial advisor, a tax pro, an estate attorney—because the mission is too big to tackle solo.

You've worked in teams your whole life. Your finances deserve the same approach.

Just like no one runs into a burning building alone, you don't have to figure this out by yourself either.

Money is a Tool, Not a Trophy

You've been measured your whole career—by response times, by reports written, by clearances and saves and arrests and calls per shift.

But wealth? Wealth isn't about impressing anyone. It's not about fancy cars or who has the biggest house in the county.

It's about **peace of mind**.

It's about **options**.

It's about **control**.

The ability to say:

- "I can walk away from this job if it ever compromises my soul."
- "I can send my kid to college without breaking our budget."
- "I can take care of my spouse if something happens to me."
- "I can retire and finally rest."

Money doesn't define your worth. But it absolutely affects your **freedom.**

Write a New Story

This book exists to rewrite the narrative.

The old story says first responders are heroes—but always broke.

The old story says you'll burn yourself out to serve others, but never get ahead.

The old story says you don't deserve wealth because you didn't come from it.

That story is garbage. And it ends with you.

You are the one who:

- Starts saving in a Roth even if no one else in your family ever did.
- Buys insurance to protect your spouse while your friends say "it'll be fine."
- Builds a trust so your kids inherit structure, not confusion.
- Creates a plan that doesn't rely on overtime forever.
- Has real money conversations at the kitchen table—not just the station one.

You are the proof that first responders can build *generational wealth.*

This Is Your Financial Victory Lap

You've given the job everything you had. But you don't have to give it your future too.

This chapter is your permission slip to:

- **Slow down** and enjoy what you've built.
- **Plan ahead** with intention and wisdom.
- **Teach others** what you've learned.
- **Take pride** in financial strength—not just physical toughness.
- **Rest**—because you've earned it.

You're not a statistic.

You're not "just getting by."

You're not another overworked civil servant waiting on a broken system.

You are a builder of wealth.

You are a protector of your family.

You are a leader—at home, in the station, and in your legacy.

Let this book be the end of excuses and the beginning of ownership.

Let your next chapter be the best one yet.

Because You've Run Toward Danger Your Whole Life—

Now it's time to run toward wealth.

And never look back.

Disclaimer and Purpose of This Book

Financial Literacy For First Responders was written to **educate**, **empower**, and **encourage** those who serve on the front lines—firefighters, paramedics, law enforcement officers, dispatchers, corrections personnel, and all public safety professionals—to take control of their financial lives with clarity, confidence, and purpose.

The lessons throughout this book reflect the author's experience as a financial educator, advisor, and advocate with over two decades in financial services, healthcare planning, and public sector benefit education. The content also draws deeply from personal relationships with family and friends who have served in uniform, and from the author's sincere respect for those who run toward danger when others run away.

That said, this book is not a substitute for personalized advice. You deserve a financial plan as thoughtful and tailored as the work you do. This book is a starting point—a compass, not a GPS.

Educational Use Only

This book is intended for **general educational purposes**. It provides foundational financial concepts, insights, and guidance to help first responders build stronger, more informed financial lives. From pensions and 457(b) plans to insurance, estate planning, investing, and lifestyle decisions, the content is designed to build awareness—not make specific recommendations.

It is not tailored financial advice.

What works for one lieutenant might not work for a rookie firefighter. What's right for a paramedic with three kids may not be ideal for a single corrections officer nearing retirement. The numbers, goals, timelines, and emotional stakes vary.

Before making financial decisions—especially those involving retirement, investments, taxes, real estate, or estate documents—**consult a licensed professional** such as a Certified Financial Planner™, CPA, fiduciary advisor, or estate attorney.

No Legal Advice Provided

This book does **not provide legal advice**. It does not replace the role of a qualified attorney. If you are considering forming a business entity, creating a will or trust, navigating survivor benefits, reviewing a public employee contract, or understanding liability protections as a first responder, you should seek legal counsel specific to your state and role.

No Personalized Financial or Investment Advice

Although this book covers vital financial topics—investing, retirement savings, insurance, credit, debt reduction, and income protection—it does so from a general, educational lens. It is not a financial plan. It does not recommend specific stocks, funds, strategies, or account providers.

Do not make investment decisions based solely on this book. Always seek personalized guidance from a fiduciary financial advisor who understands public sector compensation, pensions, DROP plans, and benefits unique to your profession.

No Tax or Accounting Advice

While this book may reference tax-advantaged accounts (such as HSAs, IRAs, 457(b)s, and pensions), or general rules about deductions, income, or retirement distributions, it does **not** constitute tax advice.

Tax laws are complex and subject to change. Your filing status, income, overtime, state pension rules, and even hazard pay can all affect your tax strategy. For decisions involving tax planning, side gigs, pre-tax benefits, or estate transfers, consult a licensed tax professional, enrolled agent, or CPA.

No Guarantees or Promises

This book is not a promise of wealth, early retirement, or financial perfection. Real financial success depends on a number of factors: your habits, income, spending, timing, discipline, market conditions, and sometimes—just like in the field—plain luck.

This book provides structure and strategy—not guarantees. Any examples, stories, or scenarios are illustrative only.

Limitation of Liability

By reading this book, you agree that the author, Pat Brown, MBA, and affiliated platforms (including *FinancialLiteracyForFirstResponders.com*, *FinancialLiteracyForDoctors.com*, and others) are **not liable** for the results of any financial, legal, or tax decisions made from this book's content.

Neither the author nor any affiliated resource shall be held responsible for losses, penalties, or outcomes resulting from the application or misapplication of any ideas presented here.

Build Your Team—Don't Go It Alone

A core principle in this book is **you don't have to figure this out alone**. Just like you don't go into a burning building solo, you shouldn't try to handle all your finances by yourself either.

If you don't yet have a financial advisor, estate planning attorney, insurance broker, or tax professional you trust—start looking. Interview them. Ask questions. Make sure they understand **your world**—your pension, your union, your risk, your benefits.

You've trained for the job. They should be trained for you.

You Deserve a Financial Plan That Honors Your Service

First responders are some of the most disciplined, courageous, and selfless people in our society. You take care of your neighbors, your cities, your teams—often at the expense of yourself.

This book was written to help **put you back on your own priority list**—without guilt, shame, or overwhelm.

It's not about chasing wealth for the sake of money. It's about making smart decisions that protect your family, reduce your stress, and give you options in a profession where you don't always have them.

Use this book to ask better questions.

Use it to start the conversations you've been putting off.

Use it to finally take your future seriously—not because you're scared, but because you're ready.

Because when you plan with clarity, you live with freedom.

And you've earned that freedom—on the clock and off.

A Month-by-Month Guide to Staying Ahead Financially

This isn't just a tax calendar. It's a command post for your money.

Whether you're a rookie firefighter figuring out your first pension contribution, a mid-career patrol officer juggling overtime and college tuition for your kids, or a paramedic moonlighting on the weekends, knowing **when** to make financial moves is just as important as knowing **what** to do.

Time your steps right, and you'll gain momentum all year long.

JANUARY – Set the Tone

- **New Tax Year Begins**
- Reset your tracking systems—log your income, expenses, deductions, mileage, and receipts.
- **Refresh Your Budget**
- Review your monthly budget with new numbers—health insurance premiums, property taxes, payroll deductions. Adjust your savings targets based on last year's results.
- **Check Your W-4**
- Did your marital status, number of dependents, or income streams change? Make sure your paycheck withholding still fits your life.
- **Deadline: Jan 15 – 4th Quarter Estimated Tax Payment Due**
- If you made side income (off-duty details, teaching, contracting, consulting), you might owe now.
- **Rule of Thumb**: Save 25%–30% of any 1099 or freelance income for

taxes.

FEBRUARY – Get Organized

- **Collect and Sort Tax Documents**
- W-2s, 1099s, pension forms, mortgage interest, charitable contributions, tuition credits, etc.
- **Self-Employed?**
- If you worked a second job, trained new recruits for pay, or taught safety classes, track your business mileage and expenses.
- **Know Your Schedules**:
- Schedule C – Self-employment
- Schedule E – Rental income
- Schedule SE – Self-employment tax

MARCH – Business Filers, Be Ready

- **March 15 – S-Corp/Partnership Tax Deadline**
- If you've structured your side business or LLC as a pass-through entity, this is your deadline. Don't wait until April.
- **Check Your Quarterly Strategy**
- How are you allocating your savings? Are you over-relying on OT or bonuses to "catch up"? Tighten the ship.

APRIL – The Big One

- **April 15 – Federal Tax Day**
- File your return (or extension) and pay what you owe. Submit 1st quarter estimated taxes if self-employed.
- **Last Chance Contributions**
- Fund your Traditional IRA, Roth IRA, or HSA for the prior year.
- **Forms to Know**:
- Form 1040 – Tax return

- Form 4868 – To request an extension
- **Tax Tip**: Can't pay? File anyway. The IRS fine for not filing is worse than not paying.

MAY – Mid-Year Reality Check

- **Review Your Spending**
- Are you hitting your financial goals—or just getting by? Compare your actual numbers with your January plan.
- **Revisit Debt and Savings Targets**
- Check your emergency fund, retirement contributions, and credit card balances.
- **Book a Meeting With Your Advisor or Union Rep**
- Look at benefit elections, pension contributions, or investment allocations. It's easier to make adjustments now than to play catch-up in December.

JUNE – Quarter-End Assessment

- **June 15 – 2nd Quarter Estimated Taxes Due**
- For those with side gigs, businesses, or 1099 income—pay now or face penalties later.
- **Check Your Withholding Again**
- Are you having enough withheld from your primary job to cover OT, bonuses, or secondary income? Don't let the IRS catch you off guard.

JULY – Mid-Year Reset

- **Are You on Track?**
- Half the year is gone. Are you halfway toward your savings, investment, or debt goals?
- **Review Insurance Coverage**
- Look at:

- Disability coverage
- Malpractice or liability protection (especially for paramedics or officers)
- Life insurance (term vs. permanent)
- Auto, home, and umbrella policies
- **Update Your Estate Plan**
- Did you get married, divorced, or have kids? Revisit your will, beneficiaries, and powers of attorney.

AUGUST – Back-to-School, Back to Basics

- **Loan Check-In**
- Reassess student loan repayment plans. Consider income-driven repayment if your hours have changed.
- **Credit Health**
- Pull your free credit report (AnnualCreditReport.com). Check for errors and improve your utilization ratio.
- **Family Financial Planning**
- If your kids are nearing college, it's time to talk FAFSA, custodial accounts, or 529 plans.

SEPTEMBER – Quarter-End Prep

- **September 15 – 3rd Quarter Estimated Tax Payment Due**
- If you've earned any unreported income from contract work, don't miss this payment.
- **Start Year-End Planning Early**
- Think about upcoming expenses, possible Roth conversions, or retirement contribution boosts.

OCTOBER – Planning and Paperwork

- **October 1 – FAFSA Opens**
- If you have college-bound dependents, complete early for best aid consideration.
- **October 15 – Final Tax Filing Deadline**
- If you filed for an extension in April, now's the moment.
- **Health Benefits Season**
- Most employers begin Open Enrollment this month or next. Review options for HSA, FSA, dental, vision, and supplemental insurance.

NOVEMBER – Year-End Game Plan

- **Meet With Your Financial Team**
- Have a CPA? A fiduciary advisor? This is the time to sit down and:
- Maximize tax deductions
- Plan for charitable giving
- Adjust retirement savings
- Evaluate business write-offs
- **Bonus Tip**: If you bought equipment, gear, or uniforms for a side gig, see if you qualify for Section 179 deductions.

DECEMBER – Final Stretch

- **December 31 – Final Day for Many Moves**
- Contribute to your Solo 401(k) or SEP IRA if self-employed
- Complete any Roth conversions
- Execute charitable donations
- Finalize business expenses or investments
- **Tax Tip**: Make sure your federal withholding or estimated payments cover 100% of last year's liability (or 110% if you made over $150,000) to avoid penalties.

Bonus: First Responder Financial Best Practices

- **Save 25%–30% of All Side Hustle or OT Pay for Taxes**
- **Separate Your Accounts**
- Business expenses, mileage, gear, and training should be tracked separately.
- **Use Free Tools to Stay Organized**
- Apps like MileIQ, Keeper, QuickBooks Self-Employed, and Google Sheets can simplify your money life.
- **Review Benefits Annually**
- Take full advantage of your employer's benefits: HSA, FSA, pension match, union perks, tuition reimbursement.
- **Build Your Financial Crew**
- A great CPA, fiduciary financial advisor, and estate planning attorney are just as important as a solid squad at work.

Final Note

Just like incident command, financial success is about timing, structure, and teamwork. This calendar isn't a to-do list—it's a guidepost. Revisit it often. Mark your wins. Course correct where needed.

You've trained to respond under pressure. Use this calendar to lead your money with the same courage and control you bring to the job every day.

Let your financial discipline match your professional discipline. Because the badge doesn't last forever—but your wealth, legacy, and peace of mind can.

Terms & Definitions

Financial Terms

Asset

Anything valuable that you own, such as cash, stocks, real estate, or equipment.

Liability

Any debt or financial obligation you owe, like loans, credit card balances, or mortgages.

Net Worth

The difference between your total assets and total liabilities. A positive net worth means you own more than you owe.

Budget

A plan that outlines your income and expenses, helping you manage your money effectively.

Emergency Fund

Savings set aside to cover unexpected expenses, such as medical bills or urgent repairs.

Compound Interest

Interest calculated on the initial principal and also on the accumulated interest from previous periods.

Diversification

An investment strategy that spreads your investments across various assets to reduce risk.

Roth IRA

A retirement savings account where contributions are made with after-tax dollars, and qualified withdrawals are tax-free.

Brokerage Account

An account that allows you to buy and sell investments like stocks, bonds, and mutual funds.

ETF (Exchange-Traded Fund)

A type of investment fund that holds a collection of assets and is traded on stock exchanges.

Inflation

The rate at which the general level of prices for goods and services rises, eroding purchasing power.

Credit Score

A numerical representation of your creditworthiness, influencing your ability to borrow money.

Interest Rate

The percentage charged on a loan or earned on an investment over a period of time.

Risk Tolerance

Your ability and willingness to endure market volatility in your investments.

Stock

A share representing ownership in a company, entitling you to a portion of its profits.

Bond

A fixed income instrument representing a loan made by an investor to a borrower, typically corporate or governmental.

Capital Gain

The profit realized when selling an asset for more than its purchase price.

Insurance that provides protection against claims resulting from injuries and damage to people or property.

Term Life Insurance

Life insurance that provides coverage at a fixed rate of payments for a limited period.

Financial Literacy

The ability to understand and effectively use various financial skills, including personal financial management, budgeting, and investing.

Accounting Terms

Income

Money received, especially on a regular basis, for work or through investments.

Expenses

The costs incurred in the process of earning income, such as rent, utilities, and supplies.

Profit

The financial gain when revenue exceeds expenses.

Loss

Occurs when expenses exceed revenue, resulting in a negative financial outcome.

Cash Flow

The total amount of money being transferred into and out of a business or personal account.

Invoice

A document issued to a buyer by a seller indicating items sold, prices, and payment terms.

Receipts

Documents acknowledging that payment has been received for goods or services.

Write-Off

A deduction in the value of earnings by the amount of an expense or loss.

Deduction

An amount that reduces taxable income, thereby reducing the amount of tax owed.

Depreciation

The reduction in the value of an asset over time, used for accounting and tax purposes.

Revenue

The total income generated by the sale of goods or services related to the company's primary operations.

Net Income

The amount of money remaining after all operating expenses, taxes, and costs have been subtracted from total revenue.

Gross Income

The total income earned before taxes and other deductions.

Audit

An official inspection of an individual's or organization's accounts, typically by an independent body.

Chart of Accounts

An organized listing of all the accounts used in the general ledger of an organization.

Bookkeeping

The recording of financial transactions and is part of the process of accounting in business.

Taxable Income

The portion of income that is subject to taxation, after all deductions and exemptions.

Form 1099

A tax form reporting various types of income other than wages, salaries, and tips.

Form W-9

A form used to provide a taxpayer identification number to entities that will pay income to the taxpayer.

Schedule C

A tax form used to report income or loss from a business operated or a profession practiced as a sole proprietor.

Questions to Ask Financial Professionals

Financial Advisor

- Do you have experience working with first responders?
- Are you a fiduciary, and how are you compensated?
- Can you assist with both immediate budgeting needs and long-term retirement planning?
- How do you approach tax planning, insurance, and investment strategies?
- What is your overall philosophy on wealth building?

Certified Public Accountant (CPA)

- Do you have experience with clients in public service or small business owners?
- Can you help me organize and track expenses related to my work?
- Do you offer proactive tax planning services throughout the year?
- What documentation should I maintain to prepare for tax season or potential audits?
- Do you provide representation in case of IRS audits or disputes?

Attorney

- Do you review contracts and agreements pertinent to first responders?
- Can you explain legal risks in straightforward terms before I commit to agreements?
- Can you assist in setting up an LLC or appropriate business structure for side income?
- Do I need a will or estate plan, and can you help draft these documents?
- What legal protections should I consider if I create content or offer services outside my primary employment?

Questions to Ask Potential Business Partners

- What are your long-term objectives for this venture?
- What roles and responsibilities do you expect each partner to undertake?
- How will we address disagreements or challenges that arise?
- Are you financially prepared to invest in and sustain this business?
- How will profits be distributed, and what is the process if a partner decides to exit the business?

This Book Exists for You

This book exists because financial education is one of the most powerful tools a first responder can carry. Just like your turnout gear, vest, or trauma kit—it's about protection. It's about preparation. And it's about giving you the confidence to face the unknown with clarity and control.

Whether you're a rookie firefighter just settling into your first apartment, a mid-career paramedic trying to juggle family and finances, or a police lieutenant thinking ahead to retirement, you deserve to know how money works—and how to make it work for you.

Financial literacy isn't about being perfect. It's about being prepared.

It can open doors, protect your family, give you options, and help you build something solid—something lasting. But just like in the field, success doesn't happen by accident. It requires discipline. A plan. Systems. And the wisdom to call in experts when you're outside your scope.

Use This Book Like a Tool—Not a Rulebook

This book isn't here to preach, overwhelm, or talk down to you. It's here to offer structure.

You'll find strategies, definitions, questions to ask, and examples that are grounded in your world—not some generic financial classroom. But even the best playbook can't account for every scenario. That's why this book should be a guide, not gospel. Let it motivate you to take action—but don't let it replace the value of solid, licensed, professional advice.

Stay curious. Stay informed. Ask questions. Ask again.

Before you sign a contract, change insurance policies, start a business, or shift your retirement contributions—get guidance. That's not weakness.

That's wisdom. You wouldn't enter a burning structure without a game plan. Don't enter your financial future without one either.

Need Backup? Start Here.

You don't have to go it alone. There are advisors who understand the unique risks, schedules, and decisions that first responders face. We work weird hours. We work under pressure. We carry a different kind of weight.

So find a financial team that respects that.

Contact:

Pat Brown, MBA
Financial Literacy Advocate
Advisor to First Responders and Healthcare Professionals Nationwide
info@financialliteracyforfirstresponders.com
www.financialliteracyforfirstresponders.com

Subscribe to our free newsletter for ongoing insights, money tips, and updates designed specifically for the first responder community.

Final Word: Use This. Don't Shelf It.

This book wasn't meant to sit pretty on a coffee table. It was meant to ride along in your locker, your glove box, your gym bag—ready whenever you need to revisit a chapter, answer a question, or recalibrate your plan.

Highlight it. Dog-ear the pages. Write in the margins. Share it with a colleague who just got promoted, or a buddy dealing with a divorce. Pass it to someone who just graduated from the academy.

Because your financial peace of mind isn't about hitting a magic number—it's about owning your decisions. And when you do that with purpose, the ripple effect is massive. For your family. Your team. Your future.

You've trained your entire career to run toward danger.

Now it's time to run toward wealth, too.

You've got this.

— Pat Brown, MBA

Author, Financial Literacy for First Responders

Made in the USA
Monee, IL
04 November 2026

67386753R00223